Navigating Social Exclusion and Inclusion in Contemporary India and Beyond

Navigating Social Exclusion and Inclusion in Contemporary India and Beyond

Structures, Agents, Practices

Edited by
Uwe Skoda, Kenneth Bo Nielsen and
Marianne Qvortrup Fibiger

ANTHEM PRESS
LONDON · NEW YORK · DELHI

Anthem Press India
An imprint of Wimbledon Publishing Company India Private Limited (WPCIPL)
WPCIPL is a subsidiary of Wimbledon Publishing Company Limited (UK)

This edition first published in India 2014
by ANTHEM PRESS INDIA
www.anthempress.co.in

First published in UK and USA 2013
by ANTHEM PRESS
www.anthempress.com

ISBN-13: 978 93 80601 88 5 (Hbk)
ISBN-10: 93 80601 88 3 (Hbk)

CONTENTS

Part III: Resources and Development

ACKNOWLEDGEMENTS

The editors would like to thank the Contemporary India Study Centre Aarhus (CISCA) at Aarhus University, Denmark, for hosting a workshop – funded by the European Union – bringing together several of the contributors in this volume on 16–17 June 2010. We are also grateful for the support extended by the Aarhus University Research Foundation, which proved instrumental in speeding up the editorial process. Special thanks are due to those authors who joined the process in its later phases, enabling us to secure a wider thematic coverage. We would also like to thank Janka Romero, Tej P. S. Sood and Rob Reddick at Anthem Press for their efficiency and kind encouragement along the way. The chapter by Kenneth Bo Nielsen entitled 'In Search of Development: Muslims and Electoral Politics in an Indian State' was published in *Forum for Development Studies* 38 (3): 345–70 in 2011 (© Norwegian Institute of International Affairs – NUPI). It is reprinted here with the kind permission of Taylor & Francis Ltd on behalf of NUPI.

LIST OF CONTRIBUTORS

About the Editors

Kenneth Bo Nielsen is a research fellow at the Centre for Development and the Environment, University of Oslo, Norway. An anthropologist by training, Nielsen's research has focused on rural social movements in West Bengal, India, and on the Hindu diaspora in Denmark. He has published widely on Indian politics and development in international journals and in edited book volumes. Nielsen is the coeditor of *Trysts with Democracy: Political Practice in South Asia* (Anthem Press 2011) and *Development and Environment: Practices, Theories, Policies* (Akademika Publishing 2012).

Marianne Qvortrup Fibiger is associate professor of religious studies at Aarhus University. Her work focuses on Hinduism in general (and in Denmark in particular), Shaktism, religious plurality and diversity as well as on religion in cultural encounters. She has conducted extensive field research among Srilankan Tamil Hindus in Denmark, and in Mauritius, India, Sri Lanka, Kenya and England. Her recent publications include 'When the Hindu-goddess Moves to Denmark – The Establishment of a Śaktā-tradition' in *The Bulletin for the Study of Religion* (2012); 'Wilderness as a Necessary Feature in Hindu Religion' in *Wilderness in Mythology and Religion: New Approaches to the Study of Religious Spatialities, Cosmologies, and Ideas of Wild Nature*, edited by Laura Feldt (2012); and 'Religious Diversity and Pluralism: Empirical Data and Theoretical Reflections from the Danish Pluralism Project' in *Journal of Contemporary Religion* (2012).

Uwe Skoda is associate professor of South Asian studies at Aarhus University, Denmark. He is currently working on transformations of kingship, combining an anthropological approach with historical perspectives, and focusing particularly on Odisha and Central-Eastern India. His research interests also include Hindu nationalism and politics and political anthropology more generally as well as social organization and kinship. He is the author of *The Aghria: A Peasant Caste on a Tribal Frontier* (Manohar 2005) and the coeditor of *Power Plays: Politics, Rituals and Performances in South Asia* (Weissensee 2008), *State, Power and Violence* (Harrossowitz 2010) and *Trysts with Democracy: Political Practice in South Asia* (Anthem Press 2011).

Contributors

Deepak Kumar Behera is professor and head of the Department of Anthropology, Sambalpur University, India. He has to his credit more than 100 research publications in reputed journals and edited volumes. Most of his publications are in the fields of tribal studies, social exclusion and childhood. Professor Behera has authored or edited seventeen volumes, including eight volumes of *Contemporary Society: Tribal Studies* (Concept Publishing Company), edited jointly with Professor Georg Pfeffer of the Free University of Berlin, Germany. Other publications include *Contemporary Society: Childhood and Complex Order* (Manak Publication 1996), *Children and Childhood in Contemporary Societies* (Kamla-Raj Enterprise 1998), 'Public Images of Children' (special issue of *Journal of Social Sciences* 1999) and *Childhoods in South Asia* (Pearson Education 2007). Behera is the founding chairman and member of the Permanent Council of the IUAES Commission on Children, Youth and Childhood, and a member of the International Advisory Board of the journals *Sociological Analysis*, *Boyhood Studies*, *Practicing Anthropology* and *Acta Academica.*

Sarah Byrne is a PhD student and researcher at the University of Zurich, Switzerland. Drawing on the fields of political geography, political anthropology and political ecology, her research explores the negotiation and constitution of public authority and its relation to governmental and territorial strategies, including the production of 'stateness', contestations over political and forest borders, and practices of resistance and compromise. Entitled 'Negotiating Public Authority: Local Political and Local Development in Mid-Western Nepal Between "War" and "Transition"', Byrne's PhD is funded by the Swiss National Science Foundation. Byrne previously studied at the University of Toronto and the Graduate Institute of International and Development Studies in Geneva, and worked as a governance advisor with Helvetas Swiss Intercooperation.

Jane Carter works as gender and social equity coordinator for Helvetas Swiss Intercooperation, based in Bern, Switzerland. She is responsible for the overall strategic direction and coordination of the organization's approach to promoting gender equality and social inclusiveness, both in its internal processes and in field implementation. From late 2002 to early 2006 she was based in Bangalore (Bengaluru), India, as senior advisor on natural resource management to the Intercooperation delegation office, during which time she regularly visited the Indo-Swiss Participatory Watershed Development Project (ISPWDK). Carter holds a first-class degree in agriculture and forest sciences from the University of Oxford (1982) and a doctorate from the same university (1991). She has worked widely on participatory natural resource management, particularly in South Asia. The website www.surikokura.org provides her personal perspective on the changes that have occurred over the past 25 years in the lives of the people of Suri, Nepal, the hill village in which she conducted her doctoral research.

Devanshu Chakravarti is currently working as an assistant vice president with NR Management Consultants India Private Limited, a development consulting firm, and heads their South India office in Hyderabad. Chakravarti has more than 14 years of experience in rural development and has worked in different capacities with a government agency, a field-based NGO, a bi-lateral project, an India subsidiary of a Swiss foundation and most recently a consulting firm. His experience is in the domains of natural resource management, water, decentralization, micro-finance, rural livelihoods, climate change adaptation and value chain analysis. Chakravarti has extensive experience in programme management, capacity building, programme monitoring, and evaluation and documentation. His contribution to this volume is based on his association with the Swiss Agency for Development and Cooperation (SDC)–funded ISPWDK project between 2003 to 2006 as a monitoring and evaluation specialist. Chakravarti is a graduate in agricultural engineering and holds a postgraduate degree in forest management.

Radhika Chopra is associate professor, Department of Sociology, at the University of Delhi. She is the author of *Militant and Migrant: The Politics and Social History of Punjab* (Routledge 2010) and has edited *Reframing Masculinities: Narrating the Supportive Practices of Men* (Orient Longman 2006) and *South Asian Masculinities: Contexts of Change, Sites of Continuity* (Women Unlimited 2004, with Caroline and Filippo Osella). She has been a co-chair of the UN Expert Group on the Role of Men and Boys in Achieving Gender Equality (2003); curator of the film-cum-discussion series *Making Migrants: Dialogues through Film* (2009) and curator, *School in Cinema* (2004).

Kathinka Frøystad is associate professor of social anthropology at the University of Bergen, Norway. Her previous works include *Blended Boundaries: Caste, Class and Shifting Faces of 'Hinduness' in a North Indian City* (Oxford University Press 2005) as well as various articles and book chapters on political anthropology and religious change in India.

Satendra Kumar is an assistant professor at the G. B. Pant Social Science Institute, University of Allahabad, Uttar Pradesh, India. He is a specialist on caste in India and an ethnographer of Indian democracy, elections, politics and labour. He has conducted long-term fieldwork in western Uttar Pradesh, India, focusing on caste, family, kinship, democracy and the local state. His has published articles in, for example, *Economic and Political Weekly* and *History and Sociology of South Asia: Contemporary Perspectives*, in addition to contributions to edited book volumes. He has recently started a new research project on higher education and youth in North India.

Sumeet Mhaskar is a visiting scholar at the Center for South Asia, Stanford University. Prior to Stanford, he was based at the Max Planck Institute for the Study of Religious and Ethnic Diversity, Göttingen, Germany. He obtained his doctorate from the Department of Sociology, St. Antony's College, University of Oxford, where his thesis explored Mumbai's ex-millworkers' responses to their job loss as a result of textile mill closures during the last decade and a half. His research interests include labour studies, political economy, economic sociology, discrimination and exclusion at workplaces, Indian politics, urban transformation and social movements.

Guro W. Samuelsen is a research fellow at the Department of Culture Studies and Oriental Languages at the University of Oslo, Norway. Her MA thesis focused on Dalit activism and the remaking of caste identities in contemporary India. Samuelsen also studied at Delhi University and the University of Hyderabad, and has worked as a teacher and seminar leader for *Kulturstudier* in Pondicherry.

Jens Seeberg is associate professor of anthropology in the Department of Anthropology, Archaeology and Linguistics, Aarhus University, Denmark. He has worked on South Asia for 20 years, particularly in the field of medical anthropology. Between 2004 and

2008 he headed a multidisciplinary project on private health care practitioners and urban slums in India, Thailand and Indonesia, and his contribution to this volume is based on research in Bhubaneswar that formed part of that project. Seeberg has also worked extensively with tuberculosis and TB treatment in Orissa, India, and has edited and published a number of books on research in this area. His research has also included the social dimensions of the earthquake in Yogjakarta, Indonesia, in 2006. Currently, he is developing a new research project on national and transnational migration related to the recent conflict in Nepal. Seeberg is the chair of one of four platforms under the Universities Denmark initiative Building Stronger Universities, Platform for Stability, Democracy and Rights.

Tanka B. Subba is the vice-chancellor of Sikkim University, Gangtok, India. He has authored and edited about a dozen books and over 60 articles on various issues related to the eastern Himalayas. He has been the editor of the internationally refereed biannual journal *The NEHU Journal* for the past ten years and was a member of the editorial advisory boards of several international journals including *Contributions to Indian Sociology* (Institute of Economic Growth, Delhi) and *Asian Anthropology* (Chinese University of Hong Kong). His current areas of interest are ethnicity and development, health and disease, politics of culture and identity and diaspora.

Chapter 1

INTRODUCTION: NAVIGATING EXCLUSION, ENGINEERING INCLUSION

Uwe Skoda and Kenneth Bo Nielsen

Social exclusion has in recent years received increasing attention from scholars and academics working on issues such as poverty, inequality and development. Indeed, already 15 years ago Else Øyen lamented the fact that the idea of social exclusion had made such rapid inroads into academia that scholars were now 'running all over the place arranging seminars and conferences to find a researchable content in an umbrella concept for which there is limited theoretical underpinning' (quoted in Sen 2000, 5). The present volume is the outcome of one such seminar, held in Aarhus in Denmark in the spring of 2010. The aim of the seminar was, however, not to provide further theoretical 'underpinnings' to the concept of social exclusion, but rather to examine its empirical applicability in contemporary India: How does an increasingly liberalized Indian economy contribute to processes of in- and exclusion? To what extent does the deepening of Indian democracy offer hitherto marginalized social groups new opportunities for pursuing strategies of inclusion through, or in opposition to, the state? And how does 'development' alter the social terrain on which inequalities are negotiated and played out? Finally, how are these processes intertwined? These and related questions emerged as focal points for discussion during the seminar, the spirit of which we seek to convey in this volume. The contributions contained here all seek to considerably expand the notion of social exclusion by applying it in the study of a broad range of cases. The chapters focus on issues ranging from kinship and gender, to censorship, elections, caste, labour, migration and more.

In this introduction we revisit the history of the interlinked concepts of social exclusion and inclusion, and examine how academic debates on these issues have played themselves out in the Indian context. We then adopt the metaphor of navigation to argue for an approach to social exclusion that is more sensitive to the interplay between structural changes and the agency of those social groups and actors, whose lived experience is embedded in relations of inequality. We also, following Karl Popper, introduce the notion of 'social engineering' to highlight how various strategic alliances can be formed in response to the experience of exclusion.

Social Exclusion: From Concept to Analytical Practice

Originating in the writings of René Lenoir (Borooah 2010, 31), the notion of social exclusion was initially promoted by a research project at the International Institute in the mid-1990s. Later, an Institute of Development Studies (IDS) Bulletin from 1998 focused on the subject (de Haan 2004, 4), and with the entry into the debate of Nobel laureate Amartya Sen, who authored an Asian Development Bank document on social exclusion the same year, the 'uncontrolled proliferation' (Borooah 2010, 31) of studies of exclusion was well on its way. Today, according to one observer, 'social exclusion' and its twin term 'social inclusion' are the two terms most widely used in recent years by both politicians and social scientists (Sonowal 2008, 123). If this is the case, one could reasonably ask: Why do we need yet another book on the topic? Our argument in this introduction is that there is a need to scrutinize the concept of social exclusion from an empirically grounded point of view. We feel that a large part of the scholarship on social exclusion has been too *broad* in its analytical ambition, and too *narrow* in its empirical application. In this volume we seek to address this imbalance by letting the empirical base dictate the scope of analysis. The chapters demonstrate that this opens up new avenues in the study of social exclusion and inclusion.

Amartya Sen's work on social exclusion has by now acquired an almost iconic status within the field. Sen introduced a series of distinctions that underpin his view of the social processes that either produce or mitigate social exclusion. For instance, people may be both unfavourably *excluded* and unfavourably *included*, that is, included on greatly unfavourable terms or conditions. Exclusion may similarly be either active or passive. It can be the result of deliberate attempts by social or political elites to deprive people of opportunities, or the outcome of more subtle and mundane everyday social practices embedded in local relations of power. Exclusion can be partial or complete, and its formal and informal forms may coexist (Oommen 2010, 22–3). The list of foundational distinctions is considerable and has continued to grow in the wake of the Sen's intervention. But as Sen points out, the real importance of the idea of social exclusion lies in its practical influence in emphasizing the role of relational features in deprivation (Sen 2000, 8); or, in Sukhdeo Thorat's (2011) terms, the importance of social relations in the analysis of poverty and inequality.

Yet, as more than a century of Marxist scholarship amply demonstrates, the argument that poverty and deprivation are relational and social phenomena is certainly not a recent invention. One could plausibly argue that the surge in popularity of the concept of social exclusion after the year 2000 has a lot to do with the fact that it seems to offer a Marxist-inspired approach to inequality and poverty, without the ideological baggage of a more-or-less discredited Marxism. While some see this as a dilution of the radical potential of a more conventional Marxist analysis, others appreciate the efficacy of 'social exclusion' in stressing the need to consider the social bases of economic activity in any analysis of deprivation (Hickey and du Toit 2007, 2). In any event, the fact that the idea of social exclusion has become widely accepted and even mainstreamed in both academic and policy circles is mirrored, in the context of India, in the establishment of the many new university centres across the country by the University Grants Commission (UGC), and recently, the publication of a comprehensive World Bank report titled *Poverty and Social Exclusion in India* (World Bank 2011).

In the wake of the publication of the IDS Bulletin and Sen's work, scholarship on social exclusion greatly proliferated and, unsurprisingly, interpretations of the concept have differed greatly. France, the United States and the United Kingdom (along with the rest of Northern Europe) would develop very different paradigms of social exclusion, associated with different forms of theoretical and ideological baggage. Yet, as de Haan points out, the paradigmatic forms of conceptual critique and honing that led to the diversification of definitions have tended to come at the expense of more rigorous empirical applications of the concept (de Haan 2004, 4). In this volume we therefore focus on precisely the empirical applicability of the concept of social exclusion in the Indian context. While this does not mean that we discount or dismiss conceptual discussions, as the chapters by Frøystad, Byrne, Carter and Chakravarti amply demonstrate, it does mean that our authors explicitly foreground the empirical and processual dimensions of social exclusion and its lived consequences. Below, we elaborate on how our approach to social exclusion in India differs from the available scholarship on the topic.

Indian Debates on Exclusion and Inclusion: Foregrounding Caste

It is generally recognized that social exclusion in India revolves around social relations and institutions that exclude, discriminate or deprive certain social groups on the basis of a broad range of group identities (Thorat and Louis 2003). Contributions to the debate have accordingly focused on the 'excluding' operations of tribal identity (Kjosavik and Shanmugaratnam 2004; Sonowal 2008), religious minority identity (Alam 2010), ethnicity (Das 2009) or gender (Sreekumar 2007). But generally speaking, the field of social exclusion studies has been dominated by caste and by studies of the exclusion of Dalits in particular (e.g. Jenkins 2006), although recent studies have begun to include a focus on the in-/exclusion of Other Backward Classes (OBCs) (Verma 2005).

The literature on the exclusionary principles and practices of the caste system goes back to the dharmashastric literature and the Manu smriti, through early travellers' accounts and census reports. The literature is too vast to review here (e.g. Dubois 2007; Hutton 1947), so for the present purpose we shall discuss only what two prominent scholars of the caste system in the early postcolonial era – Pocock (1957) and Dumont (1980) – have had to say.

In his article 'Inclusion and Exclusion: A Process in the Caste System of Gujerat', Pocock wrote of how a 'dialectical' formula of inclusion and exclusion formed the basis of caste hierarchies. Pocock argued that

> To speak of inclusion is to recognize at once its corollary exclusion. A caste that includes itself with a superior at the same time excludes an inferior and we shall see that this is also the case within the caste. (Pocock 1957, 28)

This double process, Pocock suggests, is structural in character and operates continuously between castes, villages, marriage circles, and even down to the family level. Each group at every level seeks to 'include' itself into higher ranked groups, who in turn seek to maintain their superior status by 'excluding' downward.

Dumont focused on the ideology – the ideas and values – of the caste system. He understood the caste hierarchy as essentially religious in nature, and conceptualized it as a series of dichotomies or inclusions which he termed 'hierarchical oppositions'. This can be exemplified by the *varna* system. In the *varna* system, Shudras are 'opposed' to all other *varnas* that are collectively considered as twice-born; yet the Shudras are included in the *varna* scheme vis-à-vis non-*varnas* or *avarna* (outcastes). The twice-born retain their higher rank but include the Shudras as *varna*, nonetheless, in a process that Dumont calls 'an encompassing of the contrary'. Dumont thus reminds us of the inherent complexity and complementarity of the caste system, which requires both Brahmins and Dalits to achieve the hierarchical coexistence of the pure and the impure at a general level.

When Pocock and Dumont wrote, the institution of caste had already assumed an authority within the anthropology and sociology of India that continues to shape discussions today. Caste in India is the classic example of a 'gate-keeping concept', or a foundational category, that implicitly informs analysis and limits theorizing and description (Mathur 2000, 97). The 'authority' of caste has thus tended, paradoxically, to partially 'exclude' studies of other forms of social exclusion from the academic field. For instance, few studies have attempted to look simultaneously or comparatively at the experience of different social groups (Hasan 2009, 11). Moreover, the conspicuous influence of caste on the scholarship of social exclusion in India may well be related to the fact that policy debates on the topic have centred on the question of reservations. And here, there has been a broad consensus on the need for special policies designed for the Scheduled Caste (SC) and Scheduled Tribe (ST) populations; as Zoya Hasan notes, it was from the outset generally agreed that SCs and STs had historically been subjected to an appalling degree of subordination and exclusion that was too stark to overlook (Hasan 2009, 5). In contrast, reservations for other excluded groups have been much more controversial. Both 'Mandal I' and 'Mandal II' generated fierce political contestation, and the recurring debates about reservations for religious minorities like Christians and Muslims continue to generate considerable heat and remain hotly contested issues among the public and policymakers. In both policymaking and academic discourse on social exclusion in India, certain identities are thus privileged while others are neglected or marginalized. This, we believe, has unnecessarily limited the scope of application of the concept of social exclusion in the context of India. The contributions to this volume seek to considerably broaden the scope of social exclusion and inclusion by focusing on a broad range of topics that have so far not been analysed under this umbrella. As stated, this includes kinship, elections, migration, censorship and much more. We propose to view the processes of in- and exclusion through the conceptual prism of navigation and engineering, which we introduce below. Though our authors do not necessarily and explicitly refer back to these terms, we use them here as a broader framework for the discussions that follow in the individual chapters. In so doing, we have found particular inspiration in the works of Appadurai (2004) and Vigh (2009).

Navigating and Engineering

Navigation is a metaphor drawn from seafaring. It does not merely refer to simple or everyday movements in time and through space. Rather, as Vigh argues:

> The concept [...] highlights motion within motion; it is the act of moving in an environment that is wavering and unsettled, and when used to illuminate social life it directs our attention to the fact that we move in social environments of actors and actants, individuals and institutions, that engage and move us as we move along [...] Where we normally look either at the way social formations move and change over time, or the way agents move within social formations, navigation allows us to see the intersection – or rather interactivity. (Vigh 2009, 420)

Thus, Vigh emphasizes a double dynamic. As actors strategically (re)position themselves within social formations, both undergo processes of change. Sometimes the ground may be shaky; at other times more stable. Moreover, both Vigh and Appadurai highlight the immediate *and* the imagined nature of social navigation, which is informed both by concerns in and for the present as well as with future dreams and aspirations (Vigh 2009, 425). It is in this sense that Appadurai speaks of 'the capacity to aspire' as a 'navigational capacity'. From the point of view of the poor and excluded, this capacity may be limited. Yet, despite all societal constraints, what marginalized groups often seek strategically is to optimize the terms of trade between recognition and redistribution in their immediate, local lives (Appadurai 2004, 65).

It is the ambition of this volume to uncover and make visible navigational efforts and techniques by excluded groups in specific but oftentimes opaque cultural contexts. A related advantage of foregrounding such efforts with a firm empirical point of departure is that it brings out the much more messy and contested nature of social experience. In a given context, a multitude of social processes combine to produce complex patterns of inclusion and exclusion that are neither stable nor fluid, but which may be made malleable by both individual and collective agency. The fact that diachronic or synchronic configurations of structure and agency close off certain avenues of influence while opening up others is a central theme in all contributions in this volume. Thus, we follow Vigh in suggesting that the idea of navigation

> [...] directs our attention both to the way people engage in the world and the way they move towards positions they perceive as being better than their current location and the possibilities within them. Yet in doing so it highlights the limits of the power embedded in our capacity to define and control our social world. (Vigh 2009, 432)

At the same time, we suggest that in the study of social in- and exclusion, it is fruitful to marry the concept of navigation to that of social engineering. We make this suggestion well aware of the fact that the concept of social engineering in the Indian context often denotes strategic manipulation and is colloquially tinged with certain negative connotations. The prime example is the strategically forged electoral alliances between formerly antagonistic communities such as the Dalits and Brahmins by the Bahujan Samaj Party (BSP) in Uttar Pradesh (UP), or the attempt to 'unite' the Most Backward Castes and the lower sections of the Dalits in Bihar – a formula recently emulated by the Congress. At the same time, however, the notion of social engineering has also been used in India to describe socioeconomic changes brought about by certain actors, schemes and tools such as self-help groups, microcredit organizations or food-for-work programmes, which aim to reduce poverty and further social inclusion.

Outside the Indian context, however, the concept has been widely used across disciplinary boundaries, and particularly in political science. Our understanding of the term is guided by Karl Popper who, in the slightly technocratic language of the 1960s, advocated 'piecemeal social engineering'. By this he implied a stepwise improvement or reform of social structures. Popper wrote that

> The politician who adopts this method may or may not have a blueprint of society before his mind, he may or may not hope that mankind will one day realize an ideal state, and achieve happiness and perfection on earth. But he will be aware that perfection, if at all attainable, is far distant, and that every generation of men, and therefore also the living, have a claim; perhaps not so much a claim to be made happy, for there are no institutional means of making a man happy, but a claim not to be made unhappy, where it can be avoided. They have a claim to be given all possible help, if they suffer. The piecemeal engineer will, accordingly, adopt the method of searching for, and fighting against, the greatest and most urgent evils of society, rather than searching for, and fighting for, its greatest ultimate good. (Popper 1966, 161–2)

'The piecemeal engineer' figures in several of the contributions here, whether in the avatar of Dalit activist, champion of minority rights or staunch defender of harmony-enhancing censorship. All draw inspiration from the desire to fight perceived evils in society, howsoever defined. Their navigation is guided by their more or less complete blueprints for improving the conditions of their communities, compatriots or constituencies who seek greater inclusion into one or several social domains.

The framing of our discussion of social in- and exclusion using the twin terms of navigation and engineering defines the agenda of this volume. We do not just seek to describe situations of deprivation and marginalization, or to categorize them as the outcome of various species of exclusion, whether active or passive, or instrumental or constitutive. Moving beyond such largely academic exercises in classification, the contributions explore how people navigate and manage the very social, political or economic processes that produce their exclusion. In doing so, a number of contributions in this volume offer a critical corrective to the large body of social exclusion literature which lacks an inherent focus on agency and which often portrays the excluded as helpless victims (Hickey and du Toit 2007, 3). Our authors thus locate a sense of agency amidst exclusion and refuse to treat people as mere objects of exclusionary processes, institutions and structures. As several of the contributions demonstrate, it is on this agency that inclusionary practices and policies can be built and strengthened. At the same time, we do not lose sight of how power relations and socially embedded inequalities condition political agency, navigational capacity and the prospects for engineering, in crucial ways. It is at the intersection of these processes that our interest in the dynamics of social exclusion is located. We now introduce the three thematic sections of the volume, and the eleven chapters contained therein, in light of the navigation–engineering nexus.

Spaces and Values

The chapters by Frøystad, Chopra and Fibiger focus on how values that simultaneously include and exclude are inscribed into social spaces. Frøystad examines how the use of censorship in the name of national integration and harmony both redraws and cements social identities and relations. Chopra analyses the workings of kinship and ideology in her study of a relatively rare 'husband out of place', namely, the *ghar jawai* who after marriage lives with his wife's family. While the *ghar jawai* may often be stigmatized and ridiculed, Chopra demonstrates that the *ghar jawai*'s spatial movements through migration may both alter and reinforce his standing as a semi-excluded family member, depending on the context. Fibiger also focuses on the significance of spatial movements as she examines how migrant Hindus who settle in Denmark go about re-engineering their religion *ex situ*. In the process, they both reproduce and reconfigure elements of religious tradition as they seek inclusion into Danish society, by excluding those elements of tradition that appear as obstacles in the Danish context.

The question that drives Kathinka Frøystad's analysis is: Does India's ban on expressions that offend religious sensibilities promote exclusion, inclusion, or both at the same time? Frøystad surveys a body of literature written by scholars who have attempted to navigate the muddy waters of harmony-promoting censorship, and identifies the two most influential perspectives: one camp sees India's censorship as a benign attempt at including religious minorities in a common national space; the other sees it as reinforcing social exclusion by adding further cement to the boundaries between communities. Whose perspective is right? Frøystad argues that there can be no clear-cut answer to a question like this. Rather, social exclusion and inclusion often go hand in hand, and what we need to examine is which of these forces gains the upper hand in which contexts and time frames. Along the way, Frøystad provides glimpses of some of India's many censorship dramas in which social, religious and political actors have sought to navigate moral or religious absolutes with more or less contextual sensitivity.

Radhika Chopra's chapter centres on the ideologies of kinship and gender and the patterns of in- and exclusion they produce. India's poor track record in terms of gender equality and the empowerment of women is indicative of the discrimination and exclusion of women from many spheres of social, economic and political activity. While this is both widely documented and acknowledged (e.g. World Bank 2011, 127–73), Chopra, in contrast, focuses on the seldom-explored topic of marginalized masculinities in her study of the *ghar jawai* and his role in the household and family. The famous Indian 'joint family' may in some places be losing out to the 'nuclear family', but in ideological terms it remains the most desirable form of family organization. It possesses, in the words of Sudhir and Katharina Kakar (2007, 9), a 'psychic reality' that is independent of its actual occurrence. Chopra maps out how, from the point of view of kinship ideology, marginality and exclusion define the status of the *ghar jawai* in his paternal family. However, when one looks at kinship as situated practices that unfold over time in spatial settings, the situation of the *ghar jawai* becomes more ambiguous and subject to negotiation. Importantly, Chopra argues that time, space and travel combine to critically reconfigure the figure of the *ghar jawai*. Migration out of India to the UK may offer the 'transnational *ghar jawai*', or 'the imported spouse', new possibilities for negotiating his standing and status within the family. The transnational *ghar jawai*, especially as a young man, continually has to navigate between dependence and autonomy. To the extent that he does so with skill and efficiency, he may engineer the recouping of his lost masculinity, if not immediately then over time, as he achieves the status of a household head.

Marianne Qvortrup Fibiger's study of Sri Lankan Tamil Hindus in Denmark brings out the ambiguity with which migrants relate to their religious values and traditions as they relocate. Religious values are often an important tool for migrant communities when they navigate the culture and politics of their new home country. In rare cases migrant communities may, intentionally or otherwise, reproduce the values of the homeland as they seek a footing in an unfamiliar context (Madsen and Nielsen 2009). Yet more generally, migrant communities reconstitute themselves with at least one eye on the sociopolitical map of the new home country, a map which defines the spaces within which minority identities can be engineered and expressed (e.g. Matthew and Prasad 2000; Gayer 2002; Madsen and Nielsen, forthcoming). Fibiger provides a compelling account of the establishment of Hindu religious practices in Denmark, and traces their transformations through generations and across global spaces. What emerges is a complex picture of how elements of religious practice are included or excluded from 'tradition' in a continuous process of negotiation and compromise.

Communities and Politics

The five contributions in this section all focus on the interplay between social structures, political mobilization and state institutions and policy in reproducing or addressing social exclusion. The authors explore how different communities have sought to navigate, with a greater or lesser degree of success, the social and political forces that exclude them. The forging of politicized community identities is the key issue addressed by Nielsen, Samuelsen and Subba. Nielsen and Subba also, along with Kumar, address the policy of reservations and the articulation of aspirations for political inclusion in the language of quotas. Kumar and Samuelsen, in addition, shed light on the intricacies, complexities and contested nature of official categories like SC and OBC and unearth the hidden patterns of exclusion that such encompassing labels may gloss over. And Nielsen and Mhaskar focus on India's largest religious minority, the Muslims, and their struggles for political and economic inclusion.

The five contributors all proceed from the observation that socioeconomic and power stratification along ethnic, caste and religious lines often effectively pushes certain minority groups to the margins of society. In India, evidence of continued glaring socioeconomic disparities between the two major religious groups, Hindus and Muslims, has recently reignited the debate about whether Muslims should also be entitled to inclusion into affirmative action programmes (Alam 2010, 44). In his chapter, Kenneth Bo Nielsen traces the emergence of this demand in the state of West Bengal and demonstrates how local political dynamics and electoral competition combined to propel the idea of reservations for Muslims to the top of the political agenda of almost all political parties. Nielsen focuses on the role of new technologies of governance and enumeration in articulating demands for social inclusion and examines how the production of the reports of, for example, the Sachar Committee and the Mishra Commission provided indispensable ammunition to those Muslims groups and organizations that pressed the demand for reservations. The mobilization of Muslim voters – or the threat of it – behind this demand was remarkably successful, as all major parties in the state came out in support of the demand, while also promising or delivering a range of other development initiatives aimed specifically at the Muslim electorate. While political commentators may well dismiss such electoral promise making aimed a particular communities as yet another instance of a parochial politics based on vote banks and patronage, Nielsen suggests that we place more emphasis on the agency of excluded groups and political opportunity structures. Under certain conditions, excluded groups may mobilize to great effect and rapidly navigate to alter the terrains of power on which relations of exclusion and inclusion can be negotiated and transformed.

Guro W. Samuelsen is in agreement with Nielsen that the mechanism of competitive electoral politics can and indeed has led to an increasing politicization of issues and identities. Drawing on Yogendra Yadav's work, she argues that this has produced new political bodies representing newly politicized groups that express new demands in a new language. The rights claims espoused by such groups have happened increasingly along caste and community lines. Samuelsen focuses on Dalit activists in Delhi to examine how demands are aggregated and articulated through the dynamic interplay between urban-based activists and, often, rural Dalit constituencies. Yet, while Nielsen at times appears to take the existence of a more or less uncontested political Muslim identity for granted, Samuelsen investigates in more detail how such politicized identities are forged, understood and applied as a political resource. Samuelsen narrates the often gruelling schedule and experience of Dalit activists as they struggle to navigate the social distance between their own educated middle-class selves and the poor and oppressed Dalit of their discourse, even as they subscribe to a unitary Dalit identity. Samuelsen's analysis centres crucially on the notion of 'Dalithood' which, she argues, is emancipatory to the extent that it provides an alternative framework for experiences of social exclusion that reflect belief in a both a common history, shared needs and a collective future destiny for Dalits at large. Yet, because the effect is to create a homogenous representation which compounds social differentiation within the Dalit category itself, new spaces may open up for status games of other kinds that threaten to articulate new but perhaps more invisible exclusionary practices. Moreover, the political efficacy of the activists' prime mobilizing notion of 'Dalithood' may well face an uncertain future if, as Surinder Singh Jodhka has recently suggested, Dalits in some parts of rural India no longer see themselves as being part of the social order of the caste system (Jodhka, cited in World Bank 2011, 16).

In Satendra Kumar's chapter we turn our attention from Dalits to OBCs. With the implementation of the recommendations of the Mandal Commission more than 20 years ago, the policy of reservations was extended to include the OBCs. In addition, Uttar Pradesh (UP), where Kumar has done extensive fieldwork, introduced a 27 per cent quota to OBCs in *panchayati raj* institutions in 1994. Kumar traces the evolution and reconfiguration of local power relations from the introduction of the OBC quota in 1994 and up to today, focusing primarily on one village panchayat in the village of Khanpur.

The politicization of certain OBCs in UP has happened rapidly and with great effect. As Lucia Michelutti (2008) has recently shown, the Yadavs of UP have become so effectively drawn into the ambit of organized politics that they now see themselves as a caste of natural politicians and leaders. At the aggregate state level Yadavs have rallied around Mulayam Singh Yadav's Samajwadi Party. Here, they compete with the SC Chamars, who have spearheaded the new forms of Dalit assertion (Pai 2002) that have propelled Mayawati and her BSP to power on several occasions. In Khanpur, too, the Chamars have experienced upward social mobility, but Kumar demonstrates how it is the Yadavs (along with the Gujjars and other land-owning OBCs) who have most efficiently moved into new positions of power and influence. By navigating the new opportunities at hand, they have successfully displaced the upper castes from their traditional position of social and political dominance. While this may be seen as 'the rise of the OBCs' in rural UP, in reality only certain 'upper' castes within the OBC category have been able to successfully avail themselves of these new opportunities for social mobility. Kumar demonstrates that the modalities through which the upper OBCs express their domination include supra-village networks, landholdings, caste associations and participation in electoral democracy through party politics. Importantly, money and muscle are also used to exclude other marginalized groups, including other OBCs, all of which resonates with findings from other studies of panchayats in UP (Dutta 2012). Kumar concludes that by placing many diverse castes into the inclusive category of OBC, the reservation system perpetuates the inequalities that the category was originally meant to redress. Despite radical changes in the rural power structure of UP, lower OBCs and many SCs remain marginal in local politics. Kumar's findings thus support recent empirical research on social exclusion and inclusion in institutions of local governance in India (Baviskar and Mathew 2009) which sees panchayati raj as neither a magic bullet nor a white elephant, but rather as one important forum among many in which political contestations can play themselves out in both time-tested and unpredictable ways.

Tanka B. Subba's contribution focuses on a process that in a sense constitutes an 'invisible' backdrop to the analyses by Kumar, Samuelsen and Nielsen, namely, the governmental processes of enumeration and classification that produce categories like SC, ST and OBC. These processes are crucial, as they determine which population groups are included in or excluded from the policy of reservations. Focusing on the case of Sikkim, Subba describes a situation where several castes and communities have increasingly demanded inclusion into the ST list so as to become eligible for reservations. Subba examines the workings of the Sinha Committee and the Roy Burman Commission to explore why some communities are included and others excluded, and the principles on which these decisions are arrived at. Having himself been part of the Sinha Committee,

Subba provides a compelling insider's account of how such committees work and how their recommendations are received and viewed by those in power. This process appears just as messy, contested and strongly embedded in power relations as one might expect, and the end result is not unlike that which Myron Weiner ([1989]1997, 488) described two decades ago: while most communities want reservations for themselves, reservations have often left all communities dissatisfied – beneficiaries because they believe the reservations are not satisfactorily administered, and those who are excluded because they view the system as discriminatory.

Moving from the field of politics to the economy, Sumeet Mhaskar's study focuses on the economic exclusion of Muslim's in Mumbai. Mhaskar points out that while we know from observation that economic liberalization in India post-1991 has not contributed to the dissolution of social institutions in the labour processes in the *formal* economy, we know very little about how exclusion works in 'the economy of 88 percent' (Harriss-White 2003, 2), that is, in the informal economy where the large majority of Indians navigate. Mhaskar begins by mapping out the historical role and position of Muslim weavers in the city's once booming textile industry, which has long since fallen into decline, leading to many Muslims being laid off since the 1970s. Where do these Muslim ex-millworkers go in search of work? Mhaskar asks. What openings exist for Muslims in the city's informal economy? Mhaskar's large-scale survey reveals that Muslims mainly flocked to occupations in which their community was already dominant, including mainly hard manual labour within industry, repair and processing. In addition, they faced little if any discrimination within low-status fields of occupation that caste Hindus would not enter, such as waste paper and scrap metal collection. In contrast, Mhaskar documents how few Muslims could find work in sectors dominated by other communities, especially OBC or high-caste Hindus. Unlike the situation described by Nielsen in West Bengal, the politics of Mumbai has been strongly influenced by Hindu extremist and nativist (and anti-Muslim) forces like the Shiv Sena, who have effectively contributed to a generalized feeling of suspicion and mistrust towards Muslims. Local politics in this way produces latent tensions in interpersonal relations between communities, and makes it extremely difficult for Muslim workers to strategically navigate their economic exclusion from spheres of productive activity other than those already available to them.

Resources and Development

Looking back at the idea of development in post-independent India Partha Chatterjee argued that

> A developmental ideology [...] was a constituent part of the self-definition of the post-colonial state. The state was connected to the people-nation not simply through the procedural forms of representative government; it also acquired its representativeness by directing a programme of economic development on behalf of the nation [...] which connected the sovereign powers of the state directly with the economic well-being of the people. (Chatterjee 1997, 277)

Nehru, who was also the first chairman of the Planning Commission, in many respects epitomizes the long history in India of envisioning a pivotal role for the state in the distribution and allocation of resources. Nehru's vision was closely tied to megaprojects such as steel plants or dams, which he hoped would become the new temples of modern India. Behera's contribution in the book's final section focuses on how this Nehruvian dream has turned sour for project-affected populations in Odisha, as he documents the adverse impact of a megadam project. Byrne, Carter and Chakravarti present a more positive instance of a development intervention in Karnataka which, and in spite of its shortcomings, allowed hitherto socioeconomically excluded villagers to build up certain capacities. Finally, Seeberg presents a compelling portrait of the ailing Shankar as he unsuccessfully struggles to navigate the world of public health services. This section thus moves progressively from the macro to the micro level. All three contributions deal with cases of deprivation, marginalization and the reproduction of inequalities. They also discuss the situation of Adivasis/Scheduled Tribes, which is often overlooked in the caste-focused literature on social exclusion.

In his study of the Upper Indravati Hydroelectric Project, Deepak K. Behera paints a very bleak picture of the impact of the dam on local Adivasis. The planning of the project goes as far back as the1950s, while construction work funded by the World Bank started only in the 1980s. Behera documents how the communities affected by the dam were not only displaced, but also excluded from planning and decision-making forums, as well as from any meaningful rehabilitation and resettlement. The result is a situation of multiple exclusions and a further marginalization of the already marginalized Adivasi community. Looking at these processes from an anthropological point of view, Behera explores the dynamics that generated social exclusion or promoted resilience among the project-affected population. He also examines the economic and social impact of multiple exclusions, including the dismantling of traditional production systems, the desecration of ancestral sacred zones, graves and places of worship and the disruption of family and kinship systems and networks. While Behera thus focuses largely on the breakdown of social networks and livelihoods as a consequence of displacement, he also identifies the small attempts made by the Adivasis at navigating their new conditions through, for example, finding work as wage labourers in the construction of the dam or seeking inclusion into the list of Project-Affected People.

Compared to Behera's dismal scenario, Sarah Byrne, Devanshu Chakravarti and Jane Carter are more optimistic about the potential of development interventions to engineer inclusion (or to mitigate the negative impact of an already constructed dam). In their extended case study of a foreign-aided watershed development initiative, the authors look at the evolving dynamics of the project in terms of agency and structures, that is, between individuals and their different communities and villages. All compete over scarce resources such as water as they try to corner the benefits accruing from various national and international development schemes. Byrne, Carter and Chakravrti do not only look at the material incentives offered by such development interventions; they also examine the role and functioning of the newly established institutional spaces created by the intervention itself. They focus particularly on water management committees facilitated by the project that include all households on the basis of gender equality. They ascribe to the committees a major role in creating opportunities for common villagers to articulate, contest and even overcome exclusionary social practices. Supplemented by loan facilities, the committees, which required new forms of local cooperation to function, offered avenues for the poor and hitherto socioeconomically excluded villagers to build up capacities in terms of livelihood support, including the acquisition of livestock as well as long-term watershed structures. In this regard, the new institutional arrangements became spaces for change.

Jens Seeberg's contribution focuses on the history of a single individual and his aspirations and constraints. Shankar is poor and lives in a *basti* (slum), and his untimely death from tuberculosis forms the saddening backdrop of the narrative and analysis. Public health in India illustrates several disparate trends with common intersecting claims of improving the lives of the Indian poor (Roalkvam 2012, 254); but from Shankar's point of view, the engagement with health services is an almost Kafkaesque experience, as he finds himself unable to properly avail himself of and complete the proper treatment. While certain provisions to make treatment available to the TB patient are in place, barriers to enter and partake in the health care system – staffed by more or less sympathetic doctors – are high. This often causes desperation on the side of poor patients, who may seek alternative (but less efficient) forms of treatment. Other factors contributing to Shankar's tragic fate outlined by Seeberg include the marginal position of his community, alcoholism, malnutrition, the pressing need to make a living through hard labour (which makes it impossible to follow the treatment schedules) and Shankar's own apathy. Seeberg's account describes the obstacles Shankar faced and his ultimately unsuccessful struggle to navigate in, around and through them, which pushes Shankar into an increasingly isolated and desperate condition. As Seeberg argues, Shankar's individual position within his own highly stratified poor neighbourhood may be read as standing metonymically for Indian society at large, where the promise of inclusive growth remains unfulfilled in spite of the country's unprecedented economic transformation.

The chapters that follow in *Navigating Social Exclusion and Inclusion* focus on the diversity of fields within which social exclusion and inclusion may be produced, navigated and engineered. The analyses are firmly rooted in rich ethnographies that seek to broaden the debate on social exclusion in contemporary India and beyond by illuminating how structures, agents and practices intertwine to reconstitute relations of power and inequality in a multitude of settings.

References

Alam, Mohd Sanjeer. 2010. 'Social Exclusion of Muslims in India and Deficient Debates about Affirmative Action: Suggestions for a New Approach'. *South Asia Research* 30 (1): 43–65.

Appadurai, Arjun. 2004. 'The Capacity to Aspire: Culture and the Terms of Recognition'. In *Culture and Public Action*, edited by Vijayendra Rao and Michael Walton, 59–84. Palo Alto: Stanford University Press.

Baviskar, B. S. and George Mathew, eds. 2009. *Inclusion and Exclusion in Local Governance: Field Studies from Rural India.* New Delhi: Sage.

Borooah, Vani K. 2010. 'Social Exclusion and Jobs Reservation in India'. *Economic and Political Weekly* 45 (52): 31–5.

Chatterjee, Partha. 1997. 'Development Planning and the Indian State'. In *State and Politics in India*, edited by Partha Chatterjee, 271–97. New Delhi: Oxford University Press.

Das, N. K. 2009. 'Identity Politics and Social Exclusion in India's North-East: The Case for Re-distributive Justice'. *Bangladesh e-Journal of Sociology* 6 (1): 1–17.

de Haan, Arjan. 2004. 'Conceptualising Social Exclusion in the Context of India's Poorest Regions: A Contribution to the Quantitative–Qualitative Debate'. Paper presented at the conference Q-squared in practice: Experiences of Combining Qualitative and Quantitative Methods in Poverty Appraisal, Toronto, March.

Dumont, Louis. (1970) 1980. *Homo Hierarchicus: The Caste System and Its Implications*. New Delhi: Oxford University Press.

Dutta, Sujoy. 2012. 'Power, Patronage and Politics: A Study of Two Panchayat Elections in the North Indian State of Uttar Pradesh'. *South Asia: Journal of South Asian Studies* 35 (2): 329–52.

Gayer, Laurent. 2002. 'The Globalization of Identity Politics: The Sikh Experience'. Paper available at http://www.sciencespo.fr/ceri/sites/sciencespo.fr.ceri/files/artlg_0.pdf (accessed 15 March 2013). Article published on the webpage – the website also has an English version.

Harriss-White, Barbara. 2003. *India Working: Essays on Society and Economy*. Cambridge: Cambridge University Press.

Hasan, Zoya. 2009. *Politics of Inclusion: Castes, Minorities, and Affirmative Action*. New Delhi: Oxford University Press.

Hickey, Sam and Andries du Toit. 2007. 'Adverse Incorporation, Social Exclusion and Chronic Poverty'. CPRC Working Paper 81. Manchester: Chronic Poverty Research Centre.

Jenkins, Robert. 2006. 'Social Exclusion of Scheduled Caste Children from Primary Education in India'. Draft paper. New Delhi: UNICEF India.

Kakar, Sudhir and Katharina Kakar. 2007. *The Indians: Portrait of a People*. New Delhi: Penguin Viking.

Kjosavik, Darley Jose and N. Shanmugaratnam. 2004. 'Integration or Exclusion? Locating Indigenous Peoples in the Development Process of Kerala, South India'. *Forum for Development Studies* 31 (2): 232–73.

Madsen, Stig Toft and Kenneth Bo Nielsen. 2009. 'The Political Culture of Factionalism among Hindu Nationalists in Denmark'. *Critical Asian Studies* 41 (2): 255–80.

______. Forthcoming. 'Hindutva and Its Discontents in Denmark'. In *Migration and Religion in Europe: Perspectives on South Asian Experiences*, edited by Ester Gallo. Farnham: Ashgate.

Mathur, Saloni. 2000. 'History and Anthropology in South Asia: Rethinking the Archive'. *Annual Review of Anthropology* 29: 89–106.

Mathew, Biju and Vijay Prasad. 2000. 'The Protean Forms of Yankee Hindutva'. *Ethnic and Racial Studies* 23 (3): 516–34.

Michelutti, Lucia. 2008. *The Vernacularisation of Democracy: Politics, Caste and Religion in India*. New Delhi: Routledge.

Oommen, T. K. 2010. 'Social Exclusion and the Strategy of Empowerment'. In *The Politics of Social Exclusion in India:. Democracy at the Crossroads*, edited by Harihar Bhattacharyya, Partha Sarkar and Angshuman Kar. London: Routledge.

Pai, Sudha. 2002. *Dalit Assertion and the Unfinished Democratic Revolution: The Bahujan Samaj Party in Uttar Pradesh*. New Delhi: Sage.

Pocock, David F. 1957. 'Inclusion and Exclusion: A Process in the Caste System of Gujerat'. *Southwestern Journal of Anthropology* 13 (1): 19–31.

Popper, Karl R. 1966 (1962). *The Open Society and Its Enemies: Complete Volumes I and II*. Retrieved from http://ambidextrouscivicdiscourse.com/wp-content/uploads/2010/10/Karl-Popper-Open-Society-and-Its-Enemies.pdf (accessed 16 February 2012).

Roalkvam, Sidsel. 2012. 'Stripped of Rights in the Pursuit of the Good: The Politics of Gender and the Reproductive Body in Rajasthan, India'. In *Development and Environment: Practices, Theories, Policies*, edited by Kristian Bjørkdahl and Kenneth Bo Nielsen, 243–56. Oslo: Akademika Publishing.

Sen, Amartya. 2000. 'Social Exclusion: Concept, Application, and Scrutiny'. Social Development Papers No. 1, Office of Environment and Social Development Asian Development Bank. Manila: Asian Development Bank.

Sonowal, C. J. 2008. 'Indian Tribes and Issue of Social Inclusion and Exclusion'. *Studies of Tribes and Tribals* 6 (2): 123–34.

Sreekumar, T. T. 2007. 'Cyber Kiosks and Dilemmas of Social Inclusion in Rural India'. *Media, Culture & Society* 29 (6): 869–89.

Thorat, Sukhdeo. 2011. 'Social Exclusion Framework: Its Relevance to Address Inter-Social Group Inequalities and Deprivation of Discriminated Groups'. Inaugural address delivered at the International Seminar on Social Exclusion: Meanings and Perspectives, Centre for the Study of Social Exclusion and Inclusive Policy, University of Hyderabad, 23–25 March.

Thorat, Sukhdeo and Prakash Louis. 2003. 'Exclusion and Poverty in India: Scheduled Castes, Tribes and Muslims'. Report prepared for Department for International Development, New Delhi.

Verma, H. S., ed. 2005. *The OBCs and the Dynamics of Social Exclusion in India.* New Delhi: Serials Publication.

Vigh, Henrik. 2009. 'Motion Squared: A Second Look at the Concept of Social Navigation'. *Anthropological Theory* 9 (4): 419–38.

Weiner, Myron. (1989) 1997. 'India's Minorities: Who are They? What do They Want?' In *State and Politics in India*, edited by Partha Chatterjee. New Delhi: Oxford University Press.

World Bank. 2011. *Poverty and Social Exclusion in India.* Washington, DC: World Bank.

Part I

SPACES AND VALUES

Chapter 2

COSMOPOLITANISM OR IATROGENESIS? REFLECTIONS ON RELIGIOUS PLURALITY, CENSORSHIP AND DISCIPLINARY ORIENTATIONS

Kathinka Frøystad

In Kanpur I once heard a joke: Three men – an American, a Japanese and a Pakistani – entered a dodgy bar to have drink and a chat while peeping at the beautiful women who passed their time at the counter. The men sat down at a table and were soon engrossed in a lively conversation. Suddenly the American got up and stood to attention, straight as a soldier. 'Why did you do that?' the others wanted to know. 'Well', he replied, 'I just saw a woman passing by wearing a red, white and blue miniskirt, the same colours as the American flag.' The men resumed their conversation. Half an hour later, the Japanese stood up in salute. He had just seen a woman in a tight white dress with red polka dots, which had reminded him of the Japanese flag. When he sat down again, the conversation continued. In the midst of their third round of drinks, the Pakistani suddenly got up from his chair, bent down on his knees and began to do *namaaz* (worship). Now, what had *he* seen? At this point the joke teller leant closer and lowered his voice, as if to underline the political sensitivity of the punch line he was about to deliver. Seconds later the men around us roared in laughter. Once the mirth subsided, the joke teller warned me against ever recounting this joke in public, and certainly not within earshot of Muslims. Not only could it be dangerous, he cautioned, it would also be illegal.

This event occurred during the peak of the Babri Masjid controversy in 1992, and the joker and his friends were middle-class Brahmin, Khattri and Punjabi supporters of the campaign to 'reclaim' the Babri Masjid to construct a glorious Ram temple on its premises.[1] In most of my earlier work I have treated such jokes as local instances of the anti-Muslim discourse that dominated Indian politics at the time, a discourse in which India's 13 per cent strong Muslim minority frequently were termed 'Pakistanis' to allude that their loyalty to Pakistan and Islam surpassed their Indian patriotism (see Frøystad 1994; 2005). In this chapter, I recontextualize them in the light of India's censorship legislation, asking whether the ban on jokes and other expressions that offend religious sensibilities promotes inclusion, exclusion or both at the same time.

My shift of perspective is prompted by the global controversy over comparable expressions following the publication of the infamous cartoons of Prophet Muhammad by the Danish newspaper *JyllandsPosten* in September 2005,[2] a controversy that grew particularly vocal in Denmark and Norway. In the years that followed, popular opinion crystallized around three overall positions. One faction, dominated by conservative Muslims, held that such images ought to be banned on the grounds that they denigrate the Prophet, violate the Norwegian and Danish blasphemy laws and feed into a broader context of post-9/11 anti-Muslim attitudes that makes them border on hate speech. The second faction, dominated by right-wing intellectuals, editors and journalists, argued that any democracy worthy of its name must permit unpleasant satire as part of religious critique, that freedom of expression is the main feature of a democratic form of governance and that hate-speech legislation and human rights alike were meant to protect individuals rather than religions and ideologies.[3] The middle-ground faction, dominated by left-wing intellectuals and secular Muslims, argued that provocative expressions that target a religious minority with limited political power in their countries of domicile are disrespectful and unnecessary, though they should not necessarily be illegal as such. Interestingly, both the second and third factions claimed to represent the legacy of classical liberalism. While heated confrontations between these positions dominated the talk shows and tabloids, a more principled debate was also unfolding in Denmark and Norway: Should the blasphemy legislation be abolished or retained, and if so, in what form? Sweden had abolished its blasphemy section as early as in 1970, and Great Britain – which had only protected Christian beliefs – followed suit in 2008. During the cartoon controversy, the campaigns for abolishing the Danish and Norwegian equivalents gained considerable momentum, but the sections are still in place as I write these lines, albeit in a dormant form.[4]

To follow this controversy as a social anthropologist with long-standing interest in interreligious relations in India was an eerie experience. More than that, it provided a new point of departure for approaching India's religious plurality. Thus, in a recent book chapter, I discussed how India has balanced freedom of expression on the one hand with harmony-motivated censorship on the other since the ban of Salman Rushdie's novel *Satanic Verses* in 1988 (Frøystad 2010).[5] My empirical foundation was India's numerous 'censorship dramas' since the Rushdie case,[6] and my conclusion was that though this kind of censorship appears to have promoted considerable interreligious civility, it has also invited plentiful unwarranted proscription verdicts, judging by the many bans that later were overturned by the Supreme Court. During the course of writing, I became acutely aware of how much easier it was to gather information about controversial censorship cases than about uncontroversial ones, given the unequal press coverage they attracted. Worse, assessing the extent to which proscription of offensive expressions had succeeded in maintaining interreligious respect and social harmony was virtually impossible. These banal observations prompt some reflections on the significance of research methods and disciplinary orientations in investigating the outcomes of this kind of proscription. Thus, in the present chapter, I compare the two most influential perspectives through which censorship of offensive expressions in India has merited attention so far. The first suggests that they reflect a cosmopolitan legislation that serves to include India's religious minorities in a common nationhood; the second suggests that they inadvertently promote social exclusion in the long run and thus have 'iatrogenic' effects.[7] As it turns out, the first position is dominated by normative political philosophers, the second, by South Asianist historians. This is hardly a coincidence, and in the following pages, I examine why it is so. As such, this chapter is primarily a literature review that aims to (1) identify some methodological blind spots that need to be considered in future research into this matter, and (2) suggest that in contexts of proscription, inclusion and exclusion – or cosmopolitanism and iatrogenesis, as I term these positions here – are neither mutually exclusive positions nor a matter of good and bad scholarship, but a matter of perspective and simultaneity.

My use of the terms 'inclusion' and 'exclusion' in this chapter is inspired by the German social philosopher Axel Honneth and his celebrated work *The Struggle for recognition* (1995). Though Honneth does not make explicit use of these concepts, I nevertheless read his book as a treatise on the interconnection between exclusion practices of different kinds and the common structures that promote them. Inspired by G. W. F. Hegel's Jena lectures and George Herbert Mead's I–Me theory, Honneth argues that all kinds of exclusion are rooted in a lack of recognition (or *Anerkennung* in German). An inclusive society depends on recognition at three different levels, he argues: recognition within the family to build self-confidence, recognition by means of legislative fairness to build self-respect, and recognition within civil society to develop self-esteem. In the present discussion, I am mainly concerned with the latter two levels. In India, the kinds of exclusion that Honneth had in mind are usually discussed in terms of more specific concepts. For instance, caste-related exclusion is usually discussed in terms of discrimination and persistent practices of untouchability, economic exclusion in terms of the specific social structures that perpetuate poverty, and exclusion based on religious denomination in terms of marginalization or religious nationalism. But even in these bodies of scholarship, the inclusion/exclusion concepts have proven useful when thinking *across* such contexts (see, for example, Bhattacharyya, Sarkar and Kar 2010). It is true that such a wide conceptualization reduces the value of inclusion/exclusion as clear-cut analytical concepts, as Øyen (1997) and Sen (2000) have pointed out, but they nevertheless remain valuable as sensitizing concepts (cf. Blumer 1954) that help identify structural similarities of social conflicts that usually are discussed one by one. On this note, I now turn to the legal framework that aims to secure all the religious communities in India equal recognition and inclusion in a common nationhood by proscribing offensive expressions akin to the joke I heard in Kanpur.

The Indian Penal Code

At least four of the sections in the Indian Penal Code (IPC) limit the circulation of expressions that may be offensive on religious grounds. These sections are specified in

Chapters 8 and 15 respectively, and to give an idea of the wide phenomena they cover, I quote them quite extensively:

88 [153A. Promoting enmity between different groups on grounds of religion, race, place of birth, residence, language, etc., and doing acts prejudicial to maintenance of harmony

(1) Whoever-

(a) by words, either spoken or written, or by signs or by visible representations or otherwise, promotes or attempts to promote, on grounds of religion, race, place of birth, residence, language, caste or community or any other ground whatsoever, disharmony or feelings of enmity, hatred or ill-will between different religious, racial, language or regional groups or castes or communities, or

(b) commits any act which is prejudicial to the maintenance of harmony between different religious, racial, language or regional groups or castes or communities, and which disturbs or is likely to disturb the public tranquillity (…)]

shall be punished with imprisonment which may extend to three years, or with fine, or with both.

89 [153B. Imputations, assertions prejudicial to national-integration

(1) Whoever, by words either spoken or written or by signs or by visible representations or otherwise,-

(a) makes or publishes any imputation that any class of persons cannot, by reason of their being members of any religious, racial, language or regional group or caste or community, bear true faith and allegiance to the Constitution of India as by law established or uphold the sovereignty and integrity of India, or

(b) asserts, counsels, advises, propagates or publishes that any class of persons shall, by reason of their being members of any religious, racial, language or regional group or caste or community, be denied or deprived of their rights as citizens of India, or

(c) makes or publishes any assertion, counsel, plea or appeal concerning the obligation of any class of persons, by reason of their being members of any religious, racial, language or regional group or caste or community, and such assertion, counsel, plea or appeal causes or is likely to cause disharmony or feelings of enmity or hatred or ill-will between such members and other persons,

shall be punished with imprisonment which may extend to three years, or with fine, or with both. (…)]

145 [295A. Deliberate and malicious acts, intended to outrage religious feelings of any class by insulting its religion or religious beliefs

Whoever, with deliberate and malicious intention of outraging the religious feelings of any class of 146 [citizens of India], 147 [by words, either spoken or written, or by signs or by visible representations or otherwise], insults or attempts to insult the religion or the religious beliefs of that class, shall be punished with imprisonment of either description for a term which may extend to 148 [three years], or with fine, or with both.]

> *298. Uttering, words, etc., with deliberate intent to wound the religious feelings of any person*
> Whoever, with the deliberate intention of wounding the religious feelings of any person, utters any word or makes any sound in the hearing of that person or makes any gesture in the sight of that person or places, any object in the sight of that person, shall be punished with imprisonment of either description for a term which may extend to one year, or with fine, or with both.
>
> (Government of India 2010, square brackets in the original)

The dual numbering reflects the many revisions that the IPC has been subject to over the years and the continued use of the original numbering in contemporary political discourse. Drafted by Lord Macaulay in 1837, passed into law in 1860 and enacted two years later, the IPC was heavily modelled on British law. Its rationale was to provide a uniform law for the vast subcontinent that had just been politically unified, but which remained subject to a confusing legal plurality. According to Skuy (1998), Indian law had until the 1860s consisted of parliamentary charters and acts, Indian legislation (after 1833), East India Company regulations, English common law, Hindu law, Muslim law and several bodies of customary law, and the way in which these judicial systems interacted had not always been clear. Believing Indians to be exceptionally sensitive to intimidations and transgressions – particularly if bearing on caste, religion and women – Macaulay devoted a separate IPC chapter to curbing speech acts of this kind (Ahmed 2009). Section 295A was a later addition: having been unable to prosecute the anti-Muslim Arya Samaj tract Rangila Rasool (The Colourful Prophet) under Section 298,[8] the colonial government added a section in 1927 that made the prosecution of written texts easier than under the other IPC sections at the time (Ahmed 2009, 182), and sections 153A and 153B were later additions still (Dhavan 2008, 160, n. 40). A marked contrast to the British model must nevertheless be noted: Whereas the British blasphemy legislation only protected Christian beliefs as held by the Church of England, the Indian legislation gave equal protection to all religious beliefs, thereby anticipating the principle of religious equidistance that was to become the hallmark of the Indian legislation after Independence. The gradual expansion of these sections has equipped India with censorship legislation which now includes insults on the grounds of religion, race, place of birth, residence, language, caste, community, regional groups 'or on any ground whatsoever'. They also include offences expressed in the verbal, in writing, by signs, visual representations or 'otherwise'. And though they primarily are directed against intentional insults, section 153A also includes unintentional ones. Even without the clauses in quotation marks, these are sweeping sections indeed.[9]

The joke I heard in Kanpur that day would have violated no less than three of these sections if it had been recounted in a more public setting: It would have violated paragraph 153A on the grounds that it could have promoted disharmony in the midst of the political storm over Babri Masjid; it would have violated paragraphs 295A and 198 on the grounds that it insults the Prophet and the religious beliefs of Muslims; and it would even have violated paragraph 153B if its suggestion that Muslims are more loyal to their religion than to their nation-state had been more explicit. Yet, the most inflammatory potential of this joke was not its allusion to disloyalty. Nor was it the suggestion that even the most pious Muslim may drink booze and enjoy looking at skimpily dressed women as soon as he is out of sight of his coreligionists. Nor even was it the dubiousness of doing *namaaz* in an intoxicated state or in an improper place. The main offense appeared in the punch line, which made such an objectionable suggestion about Prophet Muhammad that it would have dwarfed the cartoon in *JyllandsPosten* had it been accompanied by a visual illustration. In the months and years that followed, I amused myself by flipping through Indian joke books whenever I visited a bookstore, to see whether I could find this or other Muslim jokes in print. Until the mid-2000s, I did not. Instead, I came across countless jokes about Sikhs – so-called *sardar* jokes – many of which revolved around the archetypical slow-witted boys Santa and Banta.[10] While there may have been many reasons why *sardar* jokes were more acceptable than Muslim jokes,[11] it was clearly of significance that Muslim jokes ridiculed religious beliefs and practices more frequently than *sardar* jokes, which made them more offensive. Even so, the question remains: From which perspective should we approach a legislation that criminalizes such jokes? While broadening the discussion from malicious jokes to additional kinds of offensive expressions, I open this discussion by summarizing some of the recent scholarship that primarily treats Indian censorship as a means to encourage social inclusion.

Inclusion and Cosmopolitanism

In the past decade, social inclusion has commonly been discussed under the idiom of cosmopolitanism, at least as far as philosophy, anthropology and sociology go. Originally a Greek word, cosmopolitanism means 'citizen of the world' (from *cosmos*, world, and *polites*, citizen). Whereas the everyday use of the word often invokes international sophistication and a certain degree of upper classness, its academic usage primarily refers to a global orientation, openness to heterogeneity and willingness to engage with those perceived as the 'Other' (cf. Mehta 2000, 620). The Ghanaian-British philosopher Kwame Anthony Appiah (2002; 2006), for instance, relates it to the benefits of regular everyday conversation across ethnic and social boundaries, while his American colleague Martha Nussbaum (2002) conceptualizes it as a mode of thought in which one follows the Greek Stoics in imagining oneself as surrounded by concentric circles of affiliations, from family to humanity, and striving to include the outer circles in one's concern.[12] The application of this framework to Indian contexts is still at an early stage, whether explicitly (e.g. Pollock 2002; Parry 2008) or by means of related frameworks (Gilmartin and Lawrence 2000; Gottschalk 2000; Flueckiger 2006; Williams 2007). Even rarer is the explicit engagement with India's legislation in promoting a cosmopolitan, inclusive society, though I know at least three scholars who have commented on this issue by treating it as a cosmopolitan inclusion of India's minorities in a plural state characterized by mutual respect and recognition. One is Martha Nussbaum.

Nussbaum is a political philosopher with a long-standing interest in India, though she is not a specialist on India as such. In *The Clash Within: Democracy, Religious Violence and India's Future* (2007) she aims to sensitize her fellow Americans to one of India's main political tensions: the tug-of-war between 'pluralists' and 'purists' and the challenge it poses to the growing lay acceptance of Huntington's 'clash of civilizations' thesis in the USA.[13] Whereas the pluralists promote political principles and moral codes acceptable to people who differ in terms of religion, region and ethnicity, thus representing a position she elsewhere describes as cosmopolitan, the purists advocate policies and moral codes specific to their own social category, which they strive to make universal. One of her examples is the anti-Muslim violence in Gujarat in 2002, where she not only emphasizes the plight of the victims and the monstrous actions of the perpetrators and bystanders, but devotes equal attention to the countess students, activists and scholars who did their utmost to assist the riot victims, bring the guilty to justice and challenge anti-Muslim discourses in Gujarat and elsewhere. Likewise, her chapter on the Hindu Right concentrates just as much on its 'human face' as on its most vehement anti-Muslim representatives, actions and texts. While Nussbaum's perspective offers a refreshing change from the dystopian views that dominated South Asianist scholarship until recently (cf. Frøystad 2005), the question here is what she has to say on India's balance between freedom of speech and interreligious respect.

Nussbaum's chapter on the Constitution is titled 'A democracy of pluralism, respect, equality' and sets the stage by quoting its preamble:

> WE, THE PEOPLE OF INDIA, having solemnly resolved to constitute India into a SOVEREIGN SOCIALIST SECULAR DEMOCRATIC REPUBLIC and to secure to all its citizens:
> JUSTICE, social, economic and political;
> LIBERTY of thought, expression, belief, faith and worship;
> EQUALITY of status and of opportunity;
> and to promote among them all
> FRATERNITY assuring the dignity of the individual
> and the unity and integrity of the Nation;
> IN OUR CONSTITUENT ASSEMBLY this twenty-sixth day of November, 1949, do HEREBY ADOPT, ENACT AND GIVE TO OURSELVES THIS CONSTITUTION.
>
> (Government of India 2007, capitals in the original)

In this way, Nussbaum draws our attention to the strong constitutional emphasis on inclusionary values such as equality, fraternity, dignity and common nationhood.[14] Proceeding to its substantial content, Nussbaum is particularly impressed with the unusual explicitness with which the Indian Constitution specifies the citizens' fundamental rights and equality. For instance, it establishes equality before the law (Article 14), prohibits discrimination (Article 15), guarantees equality of opportunity in employment (Article 16), abolishes untouchability (Article 17) and contains no less than six articles that establish religious liberty and equality. This, Nussbaum argues, is one of the main reasons why India has succeeded reasonably well in protecting vulnerable minorities, withstanding severe crises and stabilizing its democratic form of governance – to the extent that the Indian constitution has become a model for other countries in the developing world, including

Bangladesh and South Africa (Nussbaum 2007, 123). This being said, Nussbaum also notes its unresolved problems, including the divided Personal Law, the suspension of the citizens' fundamental rights during the Emergency and the paradoxes of India's quota-based affirmative action. But all in all, Nussbaum praises India's constitution for promoting social inclusion, commenting that democracy 'is not simply about majority voting; it is, more fundamentally, about respect for each and every person' (Nussbaum 2007, 128). On this point she is not only in agreement with Axel Honneth´s emphasis on legislative recognition, but also with John Rawls, whose theory of justice has been one of her main inspirational sources throughout her career.[15]

Nussbaum does not proceed to discuss the IPC and its proscription of offensive expressions, but her position is nevertheless discernible from other works. In principle, Nussbaum is strongly committed to free speech, given its importance in sustaining a critical public culture (cf. Nussbaum 2008, 86). In her view, the Gujarat violence was a case in point, given the way India's extensive freedom of expression enabled the public to 'argue back' at the state government and its Hindu nationalist propaganda (Nussbaum 2007, 331). Nonetheless, Nussbaum acknowledges that different nation states may require different degrees of free speech given their dissimilar histories and circumstances. In an article on Amartya Sen's capability concept, she states that 'A free speech right that suits Germany well might be too restrictive in the different climate of the United States' (Nussbaum 2003, 42), which indicates that she ranks respect and inclusion higher than freedom of speech if these values are in conflict (cf. Charlesworth 2000). When I sent her an e-mail to ask whether this would imply that she supports the censorship sections in the IPC (without necessarily defending every word), she responded affirmatively (on 25 November 2010) on the grounds that much religious harassment in India poses an imminent risk of violence. For Nussbaum, then, the Indian proscription of offensive expressions is a necessary measure to limit interreligious violence. Before I comment on the analytical underpinnings of this position, let me briefly mention two other scholars who defend India's harmony-motivated censorship for similar reasons.

Thomas Hylland Eriksen is a social anthropologist who has devoted much of his career to the study of ethnicity, nationalism, identity politics and globalization. With field experience from Trinidad, Mauritius and Norway, Eriksen is no specialist on India, but like Nussbaum he has a long-standing interest in the country through reading and supervision.[16] When the cartoon controversy erupted in 2005, Eriksen was one of the first scholars to reflect on its implications for anthropological theorizing on cosmopolitanism. In this connection, he briefly contrasted the widespread publication of the Muhammad cartoons in Europe with the Indian ban on Salman Rushdie's novel *Satanic Verses* in 1988. The explosive potential of *Satanic Verses* was the way in which Rushdie had interwoven his tale of two Indian migrants to England with a fable of the origin of Islam so unflattering that its initial Muslim readers denounced it as hate literature, history falsification and offensive against Prophet Muhammad (Malik 2009, xvi). When the Indian organization Jamaat-e-Islami came to know about the plans to publish the novel in India, they launched a vocal campaign against it. The turning point came when Syed Shahabuddin, then a member of Parliament from the Janata Dal, supported its critique in the *Times of India* and requested Prime Minister Rajiv Gandhi to ban the book. It had not yet been published in India, but Rajiv Gandhi complied by using The Customs Act to ban the import of foreign copies and the book remains banned till date. In Eriksen's (2011, 315) view, Rajiv Gandhi's move was 'a clear victory for a cosmopolitan attitude that transcends mere liberalism and acknowledges that difference necessitates respect'.[17] The alternative, he suggests, would have been to publish it, watch the protests and ask how many lives the book was worth (Eriksen 2007, 194). This reasoning bears a striking resemblance to that of Nussbaum, except for the fact that Nussbaum refers to the legislation and Eriksen to its application in a particular context.

The Canada-based philosopher Ashwani Kumar Peetush presents a similar perspective. His argument is general rather than India-specific, though his Indian background and interest in Sanskrit and Indian philosophy suggests a strong Indian influence in his thinking. In plural societies, he argues, unlimited freedom of expression may reinforce social marginalization. If your social community is regularly mocked and demeaned in public, it creates a 'chilling climate of subtle discrimination' (Peetush 2009, 177). Growing up in such conditions tends to produce fear, isolation and social alienation, which in turn may foster low self-esteem and even radical resistance. In both cases, the result is a marginalization of the already marginalized (Peetush 2009, 182), which in the long run undermines the kind of society in which a democracy based on equal participation can flourish. India, he argues, is one of the non-European countries that recognizes the harm of hate-speech and other kinds of hurtful expressions.

The view that India's proscription of offensive expressions is a necessary means to promote social inclusion is by no means only an academic exercise. It is also the majority view of India's policymakers, legislators and lawyers, judging by the infrequency with which the present legislation is questioned in the public sphere. In a recent statement, the Supreme Court argues as follows:

> This is the age of democracy and equality. No people or community should be today insulted or looked down upon, and nobody's feelings should be hurt. This is also the spirit of our Constitution and is part of its basic features. [...] In such a country like ours with so much diversity – so many religions, castes, ethnic and lingual groups, etc. – all communities and groups must be treated with equal respect, and no one should be looked down upon as an inferior. That is the only way we can keep our country united.[18] (Supreme Court of India 2008)

This statement was made to clarify whether the use of derogatory caste labels such as *chura-chamar* was punishable according to the Scheduled Caste and Scheduled Tribes (Prevention of Atrocities) Act, 1989 when addressing individual Dalits,[19] but its general wording makes it relevant far beyond contexts of caste. What it displays, I suggest, is an unusually explicit affirmation of the very constitutional values that Nussbaum praised for their inclusivity. That being said, the Supreme Court is not necessarily a unitary institution devoid of opposing viewpoints, as we will see in the next section.

Returning to the scholarly arguments, at least three common features stand out. First, none of them are South Asianists. True, they all know the country fairly well – Nussbaum through frequent visits and several minor studies, Eriksen through his interest for and supervision of research into South-Asian matters, Peetush by his family origin and leisure interests. Nonetheless, none possess the detailed, multifaceted regional knowledge that a specialization on India tends to give. Second, their arguments are strongly normative in the sense that they primarily pertain to how an inclusive plural society *ought* to be founded rather than to how a given plural society (here, India) actually works in practice. What we see in Nussbaum's and Eriksen's cases are descriptive analyses of an Indian event or set of events to make a general, normative point. In Nussbaum's case, the point is that we all have a 'purist' within us that we must struggle to constrain; in Eriksen's case, that living in a multicultural society requires a certain degree of respect; and in Peetush's case, that sustained offensive expressions affect one's self-worth in a way that results in marginalization or radicalization. Third, these scholars share an acute awareness of far murkier alternatives than the management of religious plurality in India. Though not always explicit in the texts I quoted above, the comparative dimension is nevertheless evident as an undertone that provides a strong moral compass in their thinking. The implicit comparative dimension also shines through in their wider social concern. As Boynton noted in the *New York Times Magazine* on 21 November 1999, Nussbaum expressed an early desire to 'join the underdogs and to fight for justice in solidarity with them' and was later to engage deeply with social justice from a feminist perspective. Eriksen has shown more public engagement than any of his Norwegian colleagues in questions of immigration and multiculturalism (cf. Eriksen 2010; Howell 2010), while Peetush is concerned with the hidden assumptions that 'exclude non-liberal non-Western groups from important [...] arenas [in Western states such as Canada]', as he expressed it in a newsletter of the College of Arts and Sciences at Northeastern Illinois University in 2004. All in all, their overall message appears to be that though India certainly has experienced its share of interreligious violence, it nevertheless has some legal structures in place that lower the risk not only of genocide of the kind that tore Yugoslavia apart (see Bailey 1996 for a similar argument), but also of the marginalization of religious minorities that we currently see in Pakistan, Israel and most of the Middle East. This, at least, is what I read between the lines.

The strength of this perspective lies in its awareness of far grimmer scenarios, though the comparative dimension could well have been made more explicit and systematic. Nonetheless, it also has a major weakness in its empirical selectivity and occasional lack of concrete empirical descriptions altogether. Let me now shift to a radically different perspective which holds that India's censorship legislation contributes to *exclude* India's religious minorities in the long run. This perspective is dominated by historians and historical anthropologists who have examined how the Indian constitution and censorship legislation have been put to use in practice. In contemporary anthropological parlance, one would probably describe it as a shift of attention from state institutions and legislative frameworks to their various 'state effects' (cf. Trouillot 2001). So far, virtually all the studies along this line have identified negative consequences of India's legal protection against offensive expressions, and in the next section I suggest that this is a direct result of the empirical material they have prioritized.

Exclusion and Iatrogenesis

Proscription of offensive expressions has been a marginal topic in the historical and anthropological scholarship of India. In recent years, however, censorship legislation has begun to attract more attention – not just because of the cartoon controversy in Europe, but primarily because of the growing number of censorship controversies within India itself. In 2002, a panel on censorship in South Asia was organized at the annual meeting of the American Anthropological Association. Seven years later the workshop anthology *Censorship in South Asia* (Kaur and Mazzarella 2009) saw the light of day, with contributions by historians and anthropologists, case material from India, Pakistan and Nepal and censorship cases pertaining not only to offensive expressions but also to violations of state security and public decency. Which details does this volume give on the proscription of offensive expressions in India?

I begin with Christopher Pinney's historical examination of the proscription of expressions that could provoke religious hostility in Colonial India. His emphasis is on the Code of Criminal Procedure of 1889 and the Press Act of 1910 rather than on the IPC, but the points he makes are also relevant for the political dynamics that the IPC may give rise to. The Code of Criminal Procedure prohibited seditious material that gradually came to include contempt against Her Majesty the Queen, while the Press Act mainly targeted the circulation of images, which recently had picked up due to the proliferation of printing technology (Pinney 2009, 30). Central to Pinney's argument is the view that, in combination, these acts led to an unprecedented circulation of religious images with political connotations. Since images with explicit political critique could not be published without considerable risk of imprisonment or heavy fines, these acts made politics 'spill over' to the religious domain in a radically new way. One example concerns the posters that were circulated during the Cow Protection Movement in the late nineteenth and early twentieth century. To help popularize the sacred status of the cow beyond the upper castes, protect cows from being slaughtered and make the cow a unifying symbol for Indian nationhood, the movement produced a series of visual images to mobilize support. Visual images proved an effective mobilization strategy for a gigantic country in which the art of reading and writing still was confined to a numerically modest elite. Many of these posters portrayed the cow as a mini cosmos that embodied the whole Hindu cosmology with all its main deities and kings in its belly, a maternal imagery that still recurs in the expression *gau mata* (mother cow). In several of these images the cow was threatened by a beastly man who lifts his sword against it. Some versions named this character Kaliyug, the present era of chaos and destruction in the classic Hindu cyclical understanding of time; other versions left the beast unnamed. Named or not, he was often believed to be a Muslim butcher or a symbol of the Muslim minority as a whole, an interpretation that the colonial government feared would provoke violent clashes between Hindus and Muslims. Consequently they proscribed all the posters that contained this beastly character and ordered it removed from all the subsequent versions of the mother cow posters. To Pinney, these posters exemplify the way in which religious images came to acquire political content, and the way in which the strict colonial ban on political images inadvertently motivated ill will between people of different religious denominations.

He does not flesh out the ensuing animosity, presumably because he expects his readers to be familiar with the arguments that the Cow Protection Movement formed the seed of the Hindu Nationalist Movement and its anti-Muslim ideology, and that violent clashes between Hindus and Muslims had been extremely rare until the decades of the Cow Protection Movement.[20] Pinney also argues that the *gau mata* posters and similar images contributed to mythologize and allegorize politics: what was unsayable in public found refuge in mythological images, expressions and nowadays in films, while simultaneously blurring the distinction between past and present. All in all, Pinney's conclusion is that the colonial government inadvertently aggravated the problem it had attempted to resolve by banning offensive images and political critique.

To underline his point, Pinney metaphorically summarizes such effects as iatrogenic. Composed by the Greek words for physician (*iatros*) and origin (*genesis*), iatrogenesis denotes an illness that comes about as a direct result of the physician's intervention. According to Edward Hooper (2000, in Pinney 2009), a prime example of iatrogenesis was the way in which the 1976 Ebola epidemic in the northern Congo was aggravated by the mission hospital. Former outbreaks had been curtailed by the local custom of dispersing from the localities affected by disease, but now the locals flocked to the mission hospital instead, where the beds were close and the medical instruments were insufficiently clean, thus resulting in mass contagion. In this way the Ebola outbreak was seriously aggravated by the measures that had been taken to curtail it. Pinney's iatrogenesis metaphor captures remarkably well the arguments I proceed to discuss below as well, which is why I also employ it to help identify a perspective that contrasts the cosmopolitanism framework of the previous section.

Asad Ali Ahmed's chapter, which covers colonial India as well as present-day Pakistan, identifies additional questionable outcomes. In his rich material from small-town Kamonke near Lahore, Ahmed describes how the blasphemy sections in the Pakistan Penal Code (PPC) – which in contrast to its Indian forerunner only protects Muslim beliefs – contributed to aggravate sectarian strife. Religious life in Kamonke was primarily organized by two Muslim sects, the Ahl-i-Sunnat (Barelwi) and the Ahl-i-Hadith (AIH). The former included music and song in its devotional practice and arranged lively annual celebrations of the Prophet's birthday, while the latter emphasized a more solemn practice by imitating the life of the Prophet, whose birthday it preferred to mark by praying for forgiveness rather than by celebrating with flying colours. In 2000 a visiting *ulema* of the AIH criticized the Ahl-i-Sunnat unusually sharply in his forgiveness speech,[21] ridiculing its religious practices and arguing that Satan did not have to celebrate as he had 'entrusted that task to the Ahl-i-Sunnat' (Ahmed 2009, 186). The *ulema* was promptly charged under section 295-C in the PPC, and this is how Ahmad summarizes the sequence of events:

> In fact, the AIH had first registered a case against the Barelwi *ulema* under sections 295-A and 298, charging them with wounding and outraging religious feelings. The Barelwis then returned the charge with interest, filing a return complaint under sections 295-A, 298-A, and 295-C; that is, outraging religious feelings, making derogatory remarks about holy persons, and blaspheming against the Prophet respectively. (Ahmed 2009, 186, italics added)

Meanwhile spokespersons from the rivalling sects arranged lectures and wrote pamphlets to denounce their opponent's interpretation of Islam, occasionally by resorting to burlesque parodies. To curtail the passion the police and local administration set up a peace committee, and eventually the sects were persuaded to withdraw their cases. Nonetheless, the turbulent period between transgression and withdrawal had deepened the sectarian cleavage considerably. According to Ahmed, this dynamics is reminiscent of the way in which religio-political movements crystallized around court-cases in Colonial India. The Cow Protection Movement, for instance, gained considerable impetus when the Allahabad High Court denied sacred status to cows (Freitag 1989, 150 in Ahmed 2009, 173). Moreover, to succeed in a court case, the plaintiffs had to 'prove' to the court that their religious sensibility had been hurt, which led them to demonstrate and exaggerate their emotionality in a way that accentuates the performative aspect of censorship dynamics. In this way Ahmed joins Pinney in concluding that censorship of offensive expressions can produce detrimental structures of exclusion in the long run.

The editors of *Censorship in South Asia*, Raminder Kaur and William Mazzarella, suggest a third iatrogenic outcome of censorship, which is an inflation of transgressions caused by a desire for publicity. Here they primarily have in mind how Hindi film directors incorporate scenes with increasingly explicit sexual content, such as in the *Choli ke peeche kya hai?* song-and-dance scene from Subhash Ghai's film *Khalnayak* (1993), which hardly would have raised an eyebrow today.[22] Similar motivations may also promote transgressions of religious sensibilities, they suggest, continuing that the documentary filmmaker Anand Pathwardan frequently has been accused of deploying this strategy to market himself as a fearless political critic and activist. Several of his films – including *Ram ke Naam* (1992), *Father, Son and Holy War* (1996) and *War and Peace* (2002) – were banned by various district administrations or censor boards and were not released until they were cut or appealed to the courts.[23] Filmmakers are not alone in profiting from provocations; the media do so as well. As Kaur and Mazzarella see it, the recent explosion in new commercial media that India has encouraged since 1992 has paved the way for an unprecedented media competition that makes it necessary to shout ever louder, with the result that 'the boundaries of public civility and decorum are constantly being challenged' (Kaur and Mazzarella 2009, 3). Though religious transgressions by no means is a necessary outcome of media commercialization,[24] Kaur and Mazzarella are not alone in drawing attention to this tendency in India.

Mini Chandran identifies a fourth worrisome trend, which she refers to as the 'democratization' of censorship. Whereas the agents of censorship ideally are state governments and the courts, contemporary censorship is increasingly enforced by mobs that resort to violence unless their demands for censorship are met (Chandran 2010). Chandran exemplifies this trend with the pressure to ban James Laine's research on the seventeenth-century Maratha king Shivaji (Laine 2003). Laine's alleged offence had been to quote some historical jokes and views on Shivaji to which some current champions of this royal hero objected. Even though the Delhi branch of Oxford University Press agreed to withdraw the Indian edition, the research institute that had assisted Laine during his library studies was vandalized and irreplaceable manuscripts destroyed. The legal battle that followed lasted all the way until July 2010, when the Supreme Court eventually lifted the bans that had been imposed by lower courts and the state government of Maharashtra. Being a scholar of English literature Chandran is mainly concerned with books, but if she had widened the scope of her argument, she might also have included the case of T. J. Joseph, professor at a private Christian college in Kerala. In May 2010 he was attacked by activists from the extreme Muslim organization Popular Front of India, who pulled him out of his car and chopped his right hand off. The motive was that he had given his students an exam questionnaire which the organization claimed to have contained derogatory remarks about the Prophet. Even though Joseph had apologized and the college had agreed to suspend him, the court's decision to release him on bail angered the activists so intensely that they took the law into their own hands (Carvalho 2010). Indeed, violent censorship demands are even more disturbing than Chandran claims, and by treating them as a form of 'democratization', she hints at their affinity with the well-known democratic paradox in India: the more kinds of people who take part in political processes, the less democratic the country becomes (Kaviraj 1991; Widmalm 2010).[25]

This concludes the main academic examination of the proscription of offensive expressions in India so far, but the present section would be incomplete without including Rajeev Dhavan. A senior advocate who regularly fights cases in the Supreme Court, Dhavan has published extensively on Indian censorship, and his arguments offers an interesting extension of the iatrogenesis position while simultaneously reminding us of the fallacy of treating the Supreme Court as a unitary institution. In his book *Publish and Be Damned* (2008) Dhavan expresses deep worry about the implementation of India's censorship legislation, which he criticizes for lack of consistency. In Dhavan's view, the approach has varied from judge to judge, resulting in a judicial system in which the ruling varies from state to state and according to the constellation of judges, even in the Supreme Court (2008, 25 and 143). While Dhavan probably could be said to underestimate the significance of regional and temporal contexts to the potential harmfulness of a particular expression, we should also note that the importance of such contexts has diminished somewhat due to the time-space compression (cf. Harvey 1989, 250) that characterizes our globalized age, as the cartoon controversy amply demonstrates. Dhavan also doubts the wisdom of the censorship legislation itself, suggesting that expressions that merely are offensive ought to be decriminalized and confronted by democratic discourse instead, while retaining the illegality of expressions that put 'people, their property and their habitat in serious risk of injury' (2008, 141). Exactly where he would draw the line in practice is not quite clear except that he criticizes the ban of Laine's and Rushdie's books but applauds the resolute proscription of the Danish Muhammad cartoons and the firm reactions against the Indian media that ignored it. For Dhavan, 'the entire [cartoon] controversy was an exercise in intentional hate speech, designed to provoke, incite and wound the sentiments of the Muslim community' while the repeated re-publication 'was clearly done with a malevolent intent to keep the campaign alive' (2008, 235, see also 2006). Despite his unequivocal stance in the cartoon case, Dhavan advocates a much higher proscription threshold than many Supreme Court judges, and the contrast to the aforementioned Supreme Court statement on the use of caste terms is striking.[26] For the present argument, however, the point I want to make is that Dhavan's concern that extensive censorship sections may lead to a judicial lack of consistency tallies remarkably well with the iatrogenesis perspective of virtually all the scholars who have examined the concrete effects Indian censorship empirically so far.

The scholarly arguments in this section share at least five characteristics. First, they are authored by regional specialists with extensive knowledge of India (or Pakistan in Ahmed's case) and its political past. Second, they appear to be intended for a readership that shares this regional specialization. Though none were as explicit about their readership as Nussbaum, the scarce contextual information they give is revealing: even in the *Censorship in South Asia* volume published in the US, the contextual information is limited to the concrete legislation and certain highly specific historical details, whereas familiarity with India's religious composition, history of ethno-religious violence and secular constitutional framework are taken for granted. Third, with the exception of Kaur and Mazzarella's introduction, the contributions are all based on specific events that unfolded at a particular time and at a particular place. As such, they represent a descriptive-analytical mode of research that differs widely from the normative approach that dominated the studies I discussed in the cosmopolitanism section. Fourth, their comparative dimension is diachronic (concerning former censorship regulation within India) rather than synchronic (concerning censorship regulation in other parts of the world). This is even so in the Censorship volume, which does not explicitly compare the cases of India, Pakistan and Nepal despite having included chapters on all these countries. This point is significant since it promotes the identification of trends and phases within each country but not the imagination of murkier alternatives which is so prominent in normative philosophical thinking. And fifth, their choice of case material is squarely focused on the course of events that precipitated and followed the censorship controversies they examined, leaving the everyday conditions of the religious communities involved out of the analysis.

In my view, the strength of this perspective lies in its detailed engagement with concrete instances of censorship. As I argued above, the main lacuna of the normative research that dominated the cosmopolitanism position was its lack of attention to the concrete application of the censorship legislation and its repercussions on interreligious relations. But the studies that have begun to fill this void have evidently generated blind spots of their own. I have already mentioned their lack of comparative glances to non-Indian situations, which tends to magnify conflicts at the expense of amiable interreligious relations (cf. Frøystad 2009). This tendency is reinforced by a lack of explicit attention to the wider minority–majority situation in which censorship controversies arise. Without contextual descriptions of this kind, the reader acquires little understanding of the wider concerns that may motivate censorship demands, for instance by serving as a proxy for discontent over unequal employment opportunities or repeated xenophobic slur. As a result those who agitate for a ban can easily come across as 'bad guys'. This tendency is further reinforced by the narrow focus on exceptional events of the kind that dominate the news media, police records or legal records rather than on the regular flow of life that makes the censorship dramas stand out as 'events'. Of course, journalistic and archival sources will remain invaluable to any scholar who examines the proscription of offensive expressions empirically, but the heavy reliance on this kind of sources requires more problematization than in the works quoted above. A final problem concerns the implicit monocausality of these studies. Pinney, for example, goes far in suggesting that India's ethno-religious violence is a direct outcome of the implementation of the censorship legislation in the Code of Criminal Procedure and the Press Act insofar as he remains silent about the most commonly quoted factors in this regard, namely the establishment of separate electorates for Hindus and Muslims followed by the gradual crystallization of 'Hindu' and 'Muslim' as separate social identities. Combined, these blind spots make the iatrogenesis conclusion a virtually inevitable outcome of the methodological toolbox of the authors in this section. Of course, iatrogenic outcomes are certainly real and will continue to merit critical discussion, but the analysis that documents them is no less partial than the normative research it aims to complement.

Concluding Remarks

Two perspectives. Two Greek words.[27] Which of them provides the best description of social realities in India? As I have argued, it would be a fallacy to entirely dismiss normative research as lofty romanticism while accepting all empirical examinations of censorship dynamics as unquestionable truths. More specifically I want to emphasize the following two points.

First, the reason why political philosophers and historians have drawn so dissimilar conclusions about the outcome of proscribing offensive expressions has less to do with the quality of their research as with their disciplinary orientations and methodological reflexes. Much would be gained if scholars who examine such a topic would engage more with each other's work, reflect more on their own methodological underpinnings and devise future studies of proscription effects that lower the risk of blind spots such as those I described in the preceding pages. For some scholars a rigorous, systematic comparison will hopefully be an optimal strategy. For others a risk analysis may be an interesting way forward. For historians and anthropologists such as myself I recommend a broader portrayal of the local majority/minority context to enhance the understanding of why censorship activists act the way they do instead of devoting all their attention to their 'victims'.[28] This must include a note on power structures: it is not insignificant whether the religious communities in question enjoy the same legal status (as in the USA and India) or not (as in Pakistan, Norway and Denmark), nor the extent to which their members are adequately represented in the government, parliament, courts, police, media and other formal institutions of power. There are several ways forward, and in the coming years we will hopefully see the emergence of studies that are more fine-tuned than those which currently comprise the cosmopolitanism and iatrogenesis factions.

Second, social exclusion and inclusion are not necessarily mutually exclusive phenomena but coexist more often than we think. Personally I find it fruitful to think of social exclusion/inclusion as contradictory social processes that dominate different social orders and time frames. For instance, the proscription of religio-political posters described by Pinney may well have succeeded in maintaining a certain social order and thus promoted inclusion on a short-term basis despite contributing to an exclusionary discourse in the long run. Similarly, the politics of preferential treatment in India and elsewhere has clearly contributed to include marginalized groups in the formal employment sector at the same time as it has caused resentment that has marginalized them in other ways. Even in the wake of the cartoon controversy it is difficult to entirely dismiss the argument that the publication of offensive images such as Westergaard's Muhammed cartoon serves to include Scandinavian Muslims in a public culture of political satire. Social exclusion and inclusion often go hand in hand, and what we need to examine is which of these processes that gains the upper hand in which contexts and time frames. I acknowledge that such questions make the social exclusion/inclusion concepts even more elusive than Øyen and Sen hold them to be, but unfortunately this does not make them less important.

Given all these considerations, to what extent would it be prudent to divulge the punch line of the joke with which I began? I did quote it once, before the proscription of offensive expressions became such a hot potato. Had I repeated it here, the book you now hold in your hand (or perhaps read on your screen) would undoubtedly have been illegal in India. Yet the main concern that holds me back is my feeling that it would do more harm than good to quote it again. Call it self-censorship if you will; I prefer to think of it as a token of respect and recognition. Frankly, it was not *that* funny either, and the reason why the men around me laughed so hard may well have less to do with the quality of the joke than with their thrill of playing with fire.

Acknowledgements

Following the Exclusion/inclusion workshop in Århus in June 2010, which forms the basis of the present volume, an intermediate version of this chapter was presented at a workshop titled 'Democracy and Censorship', cohosted by the Norwegian Centre for Human Rights and the Beacon for Freedom of Expression, at the Second International Conference on Democracy as Idea and Practice, University of Oslo, 13–14 January 2011. I am thankful to the participants of both workshops as well as to Thomas Sajan and the editors of this volume for useful comments to earlier drafts, though the responsibility for remaining shortcomings is mine alone.

Notes

1 The Babri Masjid – a medieval mosque in the North-Indian town of Ayodhya – was demolished a few months later, precipitating massive riots in Kanpur and several other North-Indian cities, as well as in Mumbai. For details on the background, dynamics and aftermath of the Babri Masjid controversy, van der Veer (1994) and Hansen (1999) are useful places to begin. The controversy has since been left to the judicial system, and in September 2010 the Allahabad High Court ruled that the property be equally divided between the Hindu Mahasabha (representing the Ram Lalla and Ram Chabutara areas), Nirmoni Akhara (representing the Sita ki Rasoi area), and the Sunni Waqf Board (representing the erstwhile Babri Masjid). The verdict was appealed, but the final judgement from the Supreme Court is still years ahead when the present volume goes to press.

2 In the months and years that followed, the cartoonist, publisher and a Swedish artist who made drawings along the same lines were subject to several threats and attacks. Meanwhile the cartoons were republished by additional Scandinavian newspapers, partly because each threat and protest had renewed their news value, but also because several editors wanted to mark the

unacceptability of using violence to curb their freedom of expression. For further details on the course of events, see Klausen (2009).

3 See Flemming Rose (2010) for a detailed elaboration of this position. Rose is the cultural editor of *JyllandsPosten*, where the Muhammad cartoons first were published.

4 There has been no successful prosecution under these laws since 1938 in the case of Denmark and 1912 in Norway. Though *persons* from religious minorities remain proteted by the hate-speech legislation in these countries – § 266 b in the Danish Penal Code and § 135a in the Norwegian Penal Code – these sections do not cover the denigration of religious symbols, beliefs or characters of veneration.

5 An updated version in English will appear in a volume on Indian democracy edited by Arild Engelsen Ruud and Geir Heierstad for Orient BlackSwan.

6 The term 'censorship drama' reflects my inspiration from the British social anthropologist Victor Turner, who devised a stronger attention to 'social dramas' during ethnographic fieldwork to uncover fundamental societal values and value conflicts, and to push anthropological theorizing in a more processual direction than before (for details, see Turner 1974). My own variant of this perspective was considerably more distanced given my reliance on press coverage, but also more systematic due to the numerous 'dramas' I examined in search of patterns.

7 The iatrogenesis metaphor will be introduced in more detail below.

8 Published in Lahore in 1927, The Rangila Rasool was a severe critique of the personal life of Prophet Muhammad. The acquittal of its author and publisher by the Lahore High Court caused remarkable uproar among Muslims in Punjab.

9 One may nevertheless note the absence of gender-related insults in the list – presumably because gender-offensive expressions have not yet been a threat to India's social order. Rape, seduction and misuse of public office for these purposes are however specified in other parts of the Indian Penal Code.

10 The centrality of sardar jokes in North-Indian humour was also evident in Hindi movies, many of which included a Sikh comical character. Comical characters could also be casted as Punjabi Hindus or low-class parvenus who unuccessfully attempted to emulate a high-society life style (see Frøystad 2006 for a discussion of the latter group).

11 One was that the Sikh separatism of the 1980s had been replaced by a conflict over the status of Muslims in India, a conflict where the Babri Masjid became a central turning point.

12 Nussbaum does not specify what kind of social relations these circles consist of, which frees her model from a Greek or Euro–American bias. Her call for a cosmopolitan outlook should not be interpreted as an argument against social attachments; in a later text (2008) she suggests that the Stoics might have gone too far in trying to uproot them.

13 I presume Huntington's argument to be well known given the numerous political references made to it following the 9/11 attack in New York, the ensuing US/NATO warfare in Iraq and Afghanistan and the sharpened anti-Muslim discourse throughout in the USA and Europe alike. Readers unfamiliar with Huntington and his arguments may consult Huntington (1993; 1996).

14 The latter is even more explicit in the Hindi version, which reads *Ham, bharat ke log, bharat ko ek banane ke lie, tatha uski samast nagarikon ko…* ('We, the people of India, to make India one and its inhabitants united…').

15 In *Upheavals of Thought* (2009), Nussbaum also discusses the importance of recognition herself, but without referring to Honneth.

16 Full disclosure: Eriksen served as my supervisor when I wrote my doctoral thesis in 1995–2000.

17 Malik, in contrast, sees Rajiv Gandhi's decision as an instrumental appeasement of his Muslim voters prior to the elections that followed a month later (2009), a viewpoint he shares with the Hindu Right. Eriksen's position on the Indian proscription of *Satanic Verses* does not imply that he advocates a similar ban on the Muhammad cartoons in Europe, as the facsimile of the Muhammad cartoons on the front page of an earlier version of his paper suggests.

18 Syntax in the original.

19 In terms of etymology, *chura* refers to the stigmatized *balmiki* or *bhangi* caste traditionally associated with sweeping, cleaning and the removal of excreta, whereas *chamar* is the equally stigmatized caste of erstwhile leather workers and shoemakers. Used in combination, these words acquire a pronounced denigrating effect.

20 In Indian textbooks the first communal riot is often dated to 1909, when Hindus and Muslims clashed following the colonial establishment of separate electorates for Hindus and Muslims. However, there are also records of earlier clashes, the first probably being the 1714 Holi riot in Ahmedabad discussed by Najaf Haider (2005).

21 An *ulema* (or *ulama*) is an advanced Muslim legal scholar and teacher.

22 *Choli ke peeche kya hai?* ('what is behind my sari blouse?') became a huge hit. Madhuri Dixit's alluring female character who asks what is behind her sari blouse and underneath her *chunari* (scarf/veil) was sufficiently indecent for attracting a writ petition in the Delhi High Court even though the seductress modestly continues that what she has underneath her blouse and *chunari* is her heart, which she will 'give to you, my friend, my love' (Bhowmik 2009).

23 Further details on the censorship of Anand Pathwardhan's films may be found in Bhowmik's detailed study of film censorship in India (2009, 21–25).

24 An obvious counterexample is the USA. Despite its thoroughly commercialized public domain and lack of proscription of offensive expressions (though hate speech is criminalized), religious offenses of the kind discussed in this chapter are remarkably rare.

25 Mini Chandran, personal communication 25 February 2011. Widmalm's chapter will also appear in English in Arild Engelsen Ruud and Geir Heierstad (eds): *Democracy Indian Style* (working title). New Delhi: Orient Blackswan.

26 Even more striking, perhaps, is the self-publication of a book titled *Islam: A Concept of Political World Invasion by Muslims* by another Supreme Court advocate, R. V. Bhasin. The book was banned by the Maharashtra Government, and the Bombay High Court stayed the ban in 2007 (Deshpande 2010), but this does not prevent the book from circulating on the Internet.

27 In parenthesis, I note the persisting prestige of Greek when a new analytical concept or metaphor is to be launched. To the extent we really need classical languages for this purpose, perhaps we South Asianists should begin to make our point of departure in Sanskrit?

28 For want of better terms I take inspiration from David Riches' (1986) 'triangle of violence'– victim, perpetrator, witness – which could well be extended to include a broader set of actors and institutions in the study of censorship, each deserving analytical attention.

References

Ahmed, Asad Ali. 2009. 'Spectres of Macaulay: Blasphemy, the Indian Penal Code, and Pakistan's Postcolonial Predicament'. In *Censorship in South Asia: Cultural Regulation From Sedition to Seduction*, edited by Raminder Kaur and William Mazzarella, 172–205. Bloomington, IN: Indiana University Press.

Appiah, Kwame Anthony. 2002. 'Cosmopolitan Patriots'. In *For Love of Country?* edited by Martha C. Nussbaum and Joshua Cohen, Boston: Beacon Press.

_______. 2006. *Cosmopolitanism: Ethics in a World of Strangers*. New York: W. W. Norton and Company.

Bailey, F. G. 1996. *The Civility of Indifference: On Domesticating Ethnicity*. Ithaca, N.Y.: Cornell University Press.

Bhowmik, Someswar. 2009. *Cinema and Censorship: The Politics of Control in India*. Delhi: Orient BlackSwan.

Blumer, Herbert. 1954. 'What is Wrong with Social Theory?' *American Sociological Review* 19 (1): 3–10.

Carvalho, Nirmala. 2010. 'Kerala, Hand Severed of Christian Professor Accused of Blasphemy'. *AsiaNews.it* 7 May.

Chandran, Mini. 2010. 'The Democratisation of Censorship: Books and the Indian Public'. *Economic and Political Weekly* 45 (40): 27–31.

Charlesworth, Hilary. 2000. 'Martha Nussbaum's Feminist Internationalism'. *Ethics* 111 (1): 64–78.

Deshpande, Swati. 2010. 'Free to Criticize Religions but Not with Hate: Court'. *Times of India*, 7 January.

Dhavan, Rajeev. 2006. 'Limits of Free Speech'. *Times of India*, 16 February.

______. 2008. *Publish and Be Damned: Censorship and Intolerance in India*. New Delhi: Tulika Books.

Eriksen, Thomas Hylland. 2007. 'Ytringsfrihet og globalisering: karikaturstriden og kosmopolitiske verdier'. In *Frihet*, edited by Thomas Hylland Eriksen and Arne Johan Vetlesen, 175–198. Oslo: Universitetsforlaget.

______. 2010. 'Minoritetsdebatt på tomgang'. *Samtiden* 2010 (2): 86–97.

______. 2011. 'The Globalization of the Insult: Freedom of Expression Meets Cosmopolitan Thinking'. In *From Transnational Relations to Transnational Laws: Northern European Laws at the Crossroads*, edited by Anne Hellum, Shaheen Sardar Ali and Anne Griffiths, Surrey: Ashgate.

Flueckiger, Joyce Burkhalter. 2006. *In Amma's Healing Room : Gender and Vernacular Islam in South India*. Bloomington, IN: Indiana University Press.

Freitag, Sandria B. 1989. *Collective Action and Community: Public Arenas and the Emergence of Communalism in North India*. Berkeley: University of California Press.

Frøystad, Kathinka. 1994. *Murer mot muslimer: stereotypier blant hinduer i et praksisteoretisk perspektiv*. Unpublished Master's thesis, Department and Museum of Social Anthropology, University of Oslo.

______. 2005. *Blended Boundaries: Caste, Class, and Shifting Faces of 'Hinduness' in a North Indian City*. New Delhi: Oxford University Press.

______. 2006. 'Anonymous Encounters: Class Categorisation and Social Distancing in Public Places'. In *The Meaning of the Local: Politics of Place in Urban India*, edited by Geert De Neve and Henrike Donner, 159–181. Oxon: Routledge/UCL Press.

______. 2009. 'Communal Riots in India as a Transitory Form of Political Violence: Three Approaches'. *Ethnic and Racial Studies* 32 (3): 442–59.

______. 2010. 'Balansekunst: mellom ytringsfrihet og harmonibegrunnet (selv)sensur. In *Demokrati på indisk*', edited by Arild Engelsen Ruud and Geir Heierstad, 179–211. Oslo: Unipub.

Gilmartin, David and Bruce D. Lawrence, eds. 2000. *Beyond Turk and Hindu: Rethinking Religious Identities in Islamicite South Asia*. Gainsville, FL: University Press of Florida.

Gottschalk, Peter. 2000. *Beyond Hindu and Muslim: Multiple Identity in Narratives from Village India*. New York: Oxford University Press.

Government of India. 2007. The Constitution of India. Available at http://lawmin.nic.in/coi/coiason29july08.pdf (accessed 4 March 2010).

______. 2010. Indian Penal Code. Available at http://www.sdobishnupur.gov.in/Acts%20and%20Rules/Dictionery/0915.pdf (accessed 4 March 2010).

Haider, Najaf. 2005. 'A Holi Riot of 1714: Versions from Ahmedabad and Delhi'. In *Living Together Separately: Cultural India in History and Politics*, edited by Mushirul Hasan and Asim Roy, 127–144. New York: Oxford University Press.

Hansen, Thomas Blom. 1999 *The Saffron Wave: Democracy and Hindu Nationalism in Modern India*. Princeton, NJ: Princeton University Press.

Harvey, David. 1989. *The Condition of Postmodernity: An Enquiry Into the Origins of Cultural Change*. Cambridge, MA: Basil Blackwell.

Honneth, Axel. 1995. *The Struggle for Recognition: The Moral Grammar of Social Conflicts*. Cambridge: Polity Press.

Hooper, Edward. 2000. *The River: A Journey Back to the Source of HIV and AIDS*. Harmondsworth, UK: Penguin.

Howell, Signe. 2010. 'Norwegian Academic Anthropologists in Public Spaces'. *Current Anthropology* 51 (S2): S269-S277.

Huntington, Samuel P. 1993. 'The Clash of Civilizations?' *Foreign Affairs* 72 (3): 22–49.

_______. 1996. *The Clash of Civilizations and the Remaking of World Order*. New York: Simon & Schuster.

Kaur, Raminder and William Mazzarella. 2009. 'Between Sedition and Seduction: Thinking Censorship in South Asia'. In *Censorship in South Asia: Cultural Regulation from Sedition to Seduction.*, edited by Raminder Kaur and Willam Mazzarella. Bloomington, IN: Indiana University Press.

_______. eds. 2009. *Censorship in South Asia: Cultural Regulation from Sedition to Seduction*. Bloomington, IN: Indiana University Press.

Kaviraj, Sudipta. 1991. 'On State, Society and Discourse in India'. In *Rethinking Third World Politics*, edited by James Manor, New York: Longman.

Klausen, Jytte. 2009. *The Cartoons That Shook The World*. New Haven, CT: Yale University Press.

Laine, James W. 2003. *Shivaji: Hindu King in Islamic India*. New York: Oxford University Press.

Malik, Kenan. 2009. *From Fatwa to Jihad: The Rushdie Affair and Its Legacy*. London: Atlantic Books.

Mehta, Pratap Bhanu. 2000. 'Cosmopolitanism and the Circle of Reason'. *Political Theory* 28 (5): 619–39.

Nussbaum, Martha C. 2002. 'Patriotism and Cosmopolitanism'. In *For Love of Country?* edited by Martha C. Nussbaum and Joshua Cohen, 3–20. Boston: Beacon Press.

_______. 2003. 'Capabilities as Fundamental Entitlements: Sen and Social Justice'. *Feminist Economics* 9 (2–3): 33–59.

_______. 2007. *The Clash Within: Democracy, Religious Violence, and India's Future*. Cambridge, MA: The Belknap Press of Harvard University Press.

_______. 2008. 'Toward a globally sensitive patriotism'. *Daedalus* 137 (3): 78–93.

_______. 2009. *Upheavals of Thought: The Intelligence of Emotions*. Cambridge: Cambridge University Press.

Parry, Jonathan. 2008. 'Cosmopolitan Values in an Indian Steel Town'. In *Anthropology and the New Cosmopolitanism*, edited by Pnina Werbner, 325–43. Oxford: Berg.

Peetush, Ashwani K. 2009. 'Caricaturizing Freedom: Islam, Offence, and the Danish Cartoon Controversy'. *Studies in South Asian Film and Media* 1 (1): 173–88.

Pinney, Christopher. 2009. 'Iatrogenic Religion and Politics'. In *Censorship in South Asia: Cultural Regulation From Sedition to Seduction*, edited by Raminder Kaur and William Mazzarella, 29–62. Bloomington, IN: Indiana University Press.

Pollock, Sheldon. 2002. 'Cosmopolitan and Vernacular in History'. In *Cosmopolitanism*, edited by Carol Breckenridge, Sheldon Pollock, Homi K. Bhabha and Dipesh Chakrabarty, Durham: Duke University Press.

Rao, Ursula. 2010. 'Neoliberalism and the Rewriting of the Indian Leader'. *American Ethnologist* 37 (4): 713–725.

Riches, David. 1986. 'The Phenomenon of Violence'. In *The Anthropology of Violence*, edited by David Riches, 1–27. Oxford: Basil Blackwell.

Rose, Flemming. 2010. *Tavshedens Tyranni*. Århus, DK: JyllandsPostens Forlag.

Sen, Amartya. 2000. *Social Exclusion: Concept, Application, and Scrutiny*. Social Development Papers no. 1. Manila: Asian Development Bank.

Skuy, David. 1998. 'Macaulay and the Indian Penal Code of 1862: The Myth of the Inherent Superiority and Modernity of the English Legal System Compared to India's Legal System in the Nineteenth Century'. *Modern Asian Studies* 41 (3): 615–31.

Supreme Court of India. 2008. Criminal appeal no. 1287 of 2008; Swaran Singh & Ors vs State. http://www.indiankanoon.org/doc/531612/ (accessed 4 January 2010).

Trouillot, Michel-Rolph. 2001. 'The Anthropology of the State in the Age of Globalization: Close Encounters of the Deceptive Kind'. *Current Anthropology* 42 (1): 125–38.

Turner, Victor W. 1974. *Dramas, Fields and Metaphors: Symbolic Action in Human Society*. Ithaca: Cornell University Press.

van der Veer, Peter. 1994. *Religious Nationalism: Hindus and Muslims in India*. Berkeley: University of California Press.

Widmalm, Sten. 2010. 'Hvor mye folkelig deltakelse kan Indias demokrati håndtere'. In *Demokrati på indisk*, edited by Arild Engelsen Ruud and Geir Heierstad, 231–56. Oslo: Unipub.

Williams, Philippa. 2007. 'Hindu-Muslim Brotherhood: Exploring the Dynamics of Communal Relations in Varanasi, North India'. *Journal of South Asian Development* 2 (2): 153–176.

Øyen, Else. 1997. 'The Contradictory Concepts of Social Exclusion and Social Inclusion'. In *Social Exclusion and Anti-Poverty Policy*, edited by Charles Gore and Jose B. Figueiredo, Geneva: International Institute of Labour Studies.

Chapter 3

DEPENDENT HUSBANDS: REFLECTIONS ON MARGINAL MASCULINITIES[1]

Radhika Chopra

Across a transcultural spectrum of representations, the figure of the househusband is lampooned as a virtual standup comic act with brooms and aprons – stage props of domesticity – signaling a surrender of masculinity. Humourists have had a field day with *blokus domesticus* (McMahon 1998), nowhere more explicit than cartoon strips and ribald humour. Burlesque images on the Internet cast the house-proud househusband smiling at a food processor or in a state of ecstasy over a shining floor.[2] In one of the cartoons, the caricature is completed by the counter image of the wife/feminine partner reading a financial newspaper, waiting topless for her househusband to iron her business shirt. The sexual imagery heightens the loss – indeed the docile sacrifice – of masculinity and the transference of power to the feminine 'alter' ego. The semiotics of househusband cartoons naturalises negative relations between the doing of domestic work and the slaughter of a male self. So persuasive is this image that it has become the privileged representation in a global discourse of degraded masculinities (Krimmer 2000; Wentworth and Chell 2005). The representation has acquired the nomadic ability to occupy spaces in cultural territories where it does not belong, so that right across the world, the term 'househusband' immediately connotes a marginal man and a socially disqualified masculinity.

In this chapter I focus on the inappropriately placed husband in the Indian family, more particularly on the figure of the North Indian *ghar jawai* – the husband who lives with his wife's family – represented in kinship ideology as a person 'out of place' (Douglas 1966; Strathern 1987) Living in the wrong home is a source of intense shame for the man and his wider kin, for shame travels beyond the individual to contaminate a whole set of associated others. I argue that it is not the performance of domestic work but incorrect residence that defines the degradation of the *ghar jawai*. Unfortunately, the seamless translation of the term *ghar jawai* as househusband elides the cultural specificity of shame and degraded masculinity and places an inaccurate emphasis on the conjugal couple implied in the term 'househusband'. In the North Indian context, the conjugal couple is not the central twosome. The primary vis-à-vis of the *ghar jawai* is his wife's father, upon whom the *ghar jawai* is dependent. The relationship of dependence and authority between the two men subverts the normative structure of kinship hierarchies that place wife givers as subordinate to wife takers and is the key to understanding the figure of the uxorilocal[3] son-in-law. The structure of North Indian patriliny and patriarchy rests on the transfer of women and the immobility of men. Localized understandings of the system of exogamy, documented in detailed studies of North Indian kinship (Madan 1966; Östör, Fruzzetti and Barnett [1982] 1992; Vatuk 1972) and specifically, of Punjabi kinship structures (Leaf 1972; Hershman 1981) position daughters as *paraya*, or stranger, sent away to become part of their husband's homes. Relations of exogamy are the source for abuse in North India. So, for example, the kinship term for wife's brother (*sala*), a hierarchical 'inferior', is an insult used to convey hierarchies between men (Madan 1975; Nicholas 1965; Hershman 1981). Giving daughters/sisters away to 'other men' in exogamous exchange generates a fraught relationship that surfaces in a whole slew of crude and gendered invective, more pithy and fierce than the light hearted humour of househusband jokes. The fierce invective of *bahen chot* – literally, screw your sister – targets the brother who forfeits his sister to other men. The insult seemingly 'forgets' the fact that marriage rules compel the brother to do so. I say 'seemingly' forgotten because in fact it is the compulsion inherent in the rule that spices the insult. Within such a clearly stated patrilineal context the 'giving' or 'sending' away of a man as a *ghar jawai* would be a deeply problematic issue for it would equate the giver both as hierarchical inferior and the target of potential sexual insult, a deeply ambiguous situation for the entire set of kin. Sending a son away, however, to become a member of his wife's family is viewed as a source of deep embarrassment for his patrilineal kin. In Punjabi, the derogatory proverb *Sohre ghar jawai kutta / bhen ghar bhai kutta* (a cur in his father-in-law's home! / a cur in his sister's marital home!) refers to just such an unacceptable movement by men living with their fathers-in-law, or brothers moving into the homes of their sisters. Anthropological and popular translation of the *ghar jawai* as househusband may be a linguistic convenience, but in fact eclipse the intensity of the debasement of the *ghar jawai*. Almost all the evidence (Diwan 2004; Hershman 1981; Singh 2004) suggests that economic compulsion is the reason for the inversion of the marriage rule and living with shame is offset by monetary gain, if not directly for the *ghar jawai*, then at least for his children. I discuss the transactions between shame and economics in greater length below. Suffice to say at this juncture that the inversion is not readily spoken of, precisely because the 'cost' of shame cannot be – in fact must not be – equated with the economics of honour. Instead, as I argue here and elsewhere (Chopra 2009; 2011), shame is disguised as the sacrifice a son makes to sustain his father's house.

In the first part of this chapter I briefly look at the writings on the househusband as a figure in broadly European and North American cultures and kinship, moving to cinematic representations to highlight the specificity of exclusions and precise meanings that emerge from distinct cultural locations. I then analyse the kinship structure and practice of North India, paying particular attention to the *ghar jawai* of the North Indian state of Punjab, to consider the 'shame' and degradation that haunt the *ghar jawai* and his family. In the final section I ask if the issue of marginality and exclusion are 'fixed' in defining the status of the *ghar jawai* and his paternal family, or whether we need to consider life history of the *ghar jawai* as a context in which the stigma of shame fades. Here, I focus on transnational migrations of men as imported husbands and ask if movement enables a 'forgetting' of shame and the possibility of recouping masculine personhood.

Studies of social exclusions primarily forefront the analysis of groups; however, I argue that biographies and life histories provide a particular way of analysing the trajectories of social exclusion to inclusion. It is in the biography of the *ghar jawai* that I locate my understanding of marginality of socially excluded men. My concern throughout is to think through the ideas of degraded masculinities as specific to their cultural contexts and not as free-floating signifiers of gender identity or social exclusion. It is my contention that the inappropriate translation – or rather the mistranslation – of *ghar jawai* as househusband denies the possibilities of recouping lost masculinity or the chance of any movement toward reincorporation into a collectively accepted and socially included persona. Though the ribald cartoon humour of the househusband cartoons is a rather pale reflection of the intense hostility implicit in the insults directed toward *ghar jawai*, it is precisely this extreme debasement inherent in the insult that provides a space for reflection on, and the possible retrieval of, socially excluded masculinity.

Marginal Husbands in Cinema

It is pertinent to identify the context where the term 'househusband' is most aptly used. Writings on the social and political economy of late twentieth century households convincingly argue that the househusband is a product of 'companiate marriage' in a postmodern age (Anderson et al. 1994; Giddens 1993; Lasch 1997), where heterosexual partners share the responsibilities of paid work and family care. In the transformation of the household economy and the domestic sphere, the primary players are the conjugal couple. The more optimistic discourse of companionate marriage presents the late twentieth century 'new man' within a harmonious – though reshaped – domesticity. It is his caricatured doppelganger self, the househusband, upon whom the anxieties of lost masculinity are centred. Both the affirmative and the cynical versions of new men are interestingly located within the confines of conjugality and the nuclear household, and these are the precise contexts for the writings on the post-industrial family and the cartoon text.

Satires distorted image of conjugality and the debased househusband does not remain unremarked; it is countered by the discourse of postmodern fatherhood. Fathers *in* the family, not just earning *for* the family, produce the man as simultaneously a 'caring father' and a 'better mother'. Hollywood versions of new fathers in *Kramer vs. Kramer* (1979), *Three Men and a Baby* (1987) *and Mrs Doubtfire* (1993) took satire on and then turned it around into a recuperation of mislaid masculinity, affirming the masculine self through the tasks of parenting. Recuperation and affirmation required the complete vanquishing – indeed in *Kramer vs. Kramer* and *Three Men* it is the virtual vanishing – of the mother figure, the displacement and substitution of the two parent family model by the father as *über* parent (Chopra 2001). The presence of the child restores the seminal position of man, the father. Conflated with fatherhood, the ignominious househusband is reinstated with honour intact.

The *ghar jawai* of early Indian cinema was a parodic figure. The 1925 classic *Ghar Jamai*, a comedy of manners, focused on an out-of-work man who seeks a 'position' as a *ghar jamai* in the home of a rich spinster. The film made no attempt to create an empathetic character, but played on the idea of misplaced masculinity. Director Homi Master remade this popular film, with sound, within a decade of its silent era release. Later cinematic representations, however, tried to pry open the issue of degraded husbands. In 1992 a film, also called *Ghar Jamai*, starred a popular Bombay cinema star, Mithun Chakraborty. The film had all the elements of Bombay cinema financing, with actor Prem Chopra playing yet another of his villainous roles, and lyrics by the popular music director brothers, Anand and Milind Shrivastav (universally known and adored as Anand Milind). Unlike its 1925/1935 predecessors, director Arun Bhatt created Mithun Chakraborty as an impoverished but morally upright man, and a reluctant *ghar jamai*. It is at the insistence of his millionaire father-in-law, who cannot bear to see his daughter live in a lower middle class home, that the protagonist moves into his wife's home and takes over his father-in-law's business, getting rid of corrupt employees. The narrative is driven by a mistrustful mother-in-law and a villainous accountant, whom Anil must overcome. The *ghar jamai* triumphs over his degraded status to become the hero of this family drama. A lesser known, but similar themed Bengali *Gharjamai*, directed by Anup Sengupta in 2008, also has the *ghar jamai* riding to the rescue to save the heroine and the family business.

Finally, the hugely successful (and very expensively produced) *Namaste London* (2007) starring established Bombay cinema actors Akshay Kumar, Katrina Kaif and Rishi Kapoor, added a twist to the issue. Akshay Kumar became a transnational *ghar jawai*, invited by his father-in-law (played by Rishi Kapoor) to 'teach' his pretty but Westernized daughter (Katrina Kaif, who grew up in London) how to be Indian.

In all the films, economics is never far from the surface, though the 'intention' in becoming a *ghar jawai* is always positioned as a dilemma both for the individual man and for viewers. The playoff between economic gain and shame is the narrative driver for all the cinematic *ghar jawais*. But what is equally interesting is the way the single life cycle becomes the frame through which to 'view' shifts of social value. It is this latter aspect of individual biography that is pertinent, especially for those 'roles' that are statistically and socially infrequent precisely because they are aberrant. How does the conscious adoption of an aberrant status enable us to understand exclusion as well as the process of reinstatement? This, in part, is the crux of my exploration of the aberrant and 'socially excluded' figure of the *ghar jawai*.

Social Structures and Counter Constructions

The processes of loss and reinstatement of masculinity presented by the househusband-as-father are inappropriate to the cultural circumstance and social construction of the *ghar jawai* of North Indian kinship structures. Very briefly, the structure of North Indian patriliny and patriarchy, within which Punjabi kinship is framed, rests on the transfer of women and the immobility of men. Here, residence is intrinsic to the construction of personhood, and sons are highly valued members of the patrilineal family. Parables of prodigal sons sent away by furious fathers are not common to Punjabi folklore. On the contrary, being a son of the house is a matter of immense significance in a boy's biography and simultaneously shapes the life history of his family. The explicit proverb *putr jamiya, pair jamme* (a boy's birth secures a woman's status in her conjugal home) suggests that his birth is as much an event in his mother's life cycle as it is in his own. A son is viewed as a visible symbol of the prosperity of households and represents the idea of protected spaces – the home and the field – shielded by the presence of males.[4] In Punjabi kinship the patrilocal home is critical to the formation and assertion of masculine personhood: the wife's family must reinforce this primacy, not dispute it.

In the structure of North Indian marriage preferences and residence patterns, the wife moves into her husband's home, of which she becomes a member, socially, morally and legally. Despite the structural pattern, giving daughters/sisters away to 'other men' in exogamous exchange generates a fraught relationship that surfaces in sexualized abuse between men, explained above. The figure of the *ghar jawai* as the 'given away' son, who follows the postmarital residence trajectory of his sister, is therefore an interesting anthropological enigma. My interest in the *ghar jawai* is rooted in my concern with masculinity and the formation of gendered identities, but also rests on the puzzle of why a family would choose to convert a loved and valued son to the degraded position of a *ghar jawai*.

Surprisingly, little ethnography exists on the *ghar jawai*, but the little that does elucidates some key issues. The term itself is fairly commonly used across the Indian subcontinent, though variations – *khana damad* or *ghar damad*, and colloquially *ghar jamai* – are also widely understood. Though terms of reference may be similar, the processes entailed in becoming *ghar jawai* are various.

Western Indian practices cast the figure of the *ghar jawai* as a 'servitor'. The Bhilala tribe of central and western regions of India, said to be descendants of Bhils and Rajputs, adopting practices of both, formalize the underlying principle of servitude inherent to the position of being a *ghar jawai* in the practice of 'marriage by service'. Bhilala men who cannot pay the bride price offer themselves as servitors to their future fathers-in-law before becoming accepted as *ghar jawai* (Singh 2004, 307). Contract and servitude travel as ideas across regions, and while servitude may not be as explicit in every Indian context, the position of the *ghar jawai* as a dependent and a person who 'reproduces' the household of his wife's kin rather than his own patriliny through the labour of his body, surfaces quite clearly. Representing this social 'truth', the *ghar jawais* of Indian cinema lay bare the business economics of the relationship.

In urban family firms, the *ghar jawai* may not reside with his wife's family; but his active involvement and participation in his father-in-law's business casts him as an 'inadvertent' *ghar jawai*. I say inadvertent because here, the term expands beyond the context of residence. Anthropological studies of North Indian kinship terminology pay attention to the expanded contexts of kin terms like *bhai* (brother), *behen* (sister) or *sala* (wife's brother) to nonkinship contexts (Dumont 1966; Vatuk 1969). The use of the term imparts a sense of the familial to an alien context, and at the same time converts strangers to fictive kin members. The family firm as a site actively simulates the domestic – indeed, it is often spoken of as an expansion of the home into the workplace. The husband who is a member of his wife's family business is viewed as inappropriately located in his father-in-law's domain, and therefore tainted as *ghar jawai* (Sonpar 2005). The plethora of practices around the *ghar jawai* generates a discourse of degradation, servitude and shame that underscores the social exclusion and dependent position of the *ghar jawai*.

As stated earlier, kinship structures that conceive the place of primary residence as intrinsic to the construction of personhood (in whatever terms location and person may be constituted), sons are highly valued members of the patrilineal family, and patrilocality is stressed in every possible way, including, though not limited to, a share in house sites and homesteads. In her discussion of the nature of person, Strathern outlines the different order of attachment and detachment with respect to particular kin that constitute 'person' and identity, and 'are visible in the different ties he or she has with others' (Strathern 1987, 275). To detach a son from his patrilocal residence is to make him 'out of place' (Douglas 1966). The move from valued son in his own home, an honoured guest (*parohna*) in his affinal home, to the decimated uxorilocal husband living in his wife's home as *ghar jawai* reduces his ability to be appropriately male precisely because he is incongruously placed as dependent on his affines.

Unlike the househusband, in Punjab – and in North India more generally – the primary reason for a man to move to his wife's father's home is inheritance of property, not the performance of housework (though the management of land and property might be entailed in doing work 'for the home'). Hershman briefly suggests that the *ghar jawai* in Punjab is a phenomenon among landed rural families, who may not have sons to farm their land and therefore invite the son-in-law to conduct the affairs of the family (Hershman 1981, 73–80), though this is not a first option and distant agnates or collateral kin are usually preferred. Customary law places the *ghar jawai* as a conduit for the real heir to property – his own son – who acquires fuller and more complete rights in his grandfather's property, while a *ghar jawai* may benefit only tangentially. While neither the *ghar jawai* nor his children are expected to change their patronymic or their lineage name, the purpose of the institution of the *ghar jawai* is to benefit the daughter's son and not leave land and property untended. The *ghar jawai* is 'brought into the house with the sole objective that he would procreate an heir…for the appointer [and is] *merely a medium* by which the son born to the daughter of the proprietor to whom he is married succeeds to the property of the proprietor' (Diwan, Jain, and Peeyushi Diwan 2004, 39–40; italics mine). Taken together, custom and practice present the *ghar jawai* as a muted category of person, effeminized by the loss of dominion, a mere instrument in the reproduction of rights in property. Jeffery, Jeffery and Lyon (1989) describe the position of the *ghar jawai* as the mirror image of the new *bahu* (daughter-in-law) in her husband's home, dependent on and subservient to her conjugal kin. They also suggest that precisely for this reason, the status of being *ghar jawai* is unappealing, even if it entails personal economic gain for the individual man and his children.

Rightly speaking and properly translated, the *ghar jawai* is a live-in son-in-law, not a househusband. The primary relationship is between son-in-law and father-in-law, and the father-in-law is the key male figure against whom the *ghar jawai's* position is qualified. Within a masculine discourse, it is not the satiric, lighthearted cartoon images of the househusband that frames the *ghar jawai* – it is abuse. The severity and deeply sexualised allusions inherent in abuse shape the shame of the *ghar jawai* vis-à-vis other men. The intensity of the insult draws attention to the critical differences between the househusband and the live-in son-in-law. Sexual humour and abuse configures the father-in-law's phallocentric authority as absolute and the incoming son-in-law as the ass licker of a superior male,[5] literally swinging from his father-in-law's penis, completely reversing the relations of avoidance and deference between patrilocally located sons-in-law and their wives' fathers.

So intense is the abuse that it runs throughout the life of a *ghar jawai*. In part, this is because he is seen as usurping the 'rights' of agnates to claim coparcener property. Inheritance of ancestral land remains contested and a *ghar jawai* cannot alienate his father-in-law's ancestral land even if he farms it. The compelling rights of the agnatic community of coparceners in a man's ancestral property bear upon the *ghar jawai's* right to inherit or alienate his father-in-law's property. Property is the reason for the move into uxorilocal residence as well as the reason for the hostility and derision directed toward the *ghar jawai* in rural Punjab, and much of northern India.

Perhaps because a *ghar jawai's* property rights as a 'full' member of his wife's home are so indistinct, a fair degree of effort is spent in sustaining (and claiming) an attachment with the partilocal home. Kinship practices and rituals observed in both homes – the man's natal and his affinal homes – preserve patrilineal identity. A *ghar jawai's* children might reside with their mother's brother, but they carry their father's name, retaining his surname even while living in the home of their maternal grandfather. Upon his death, members of a *ghar jawai* patrilineage mourn his passing.[6] His wife's family maintain an elaborate fiction of a *ghar jawai's* impermanent residence, referring to him as a *paronah*, an honoured guest 'passing through', despite his constant presence in domestic routines and everyday work. This terminological and quotidian disconnect positions the *ghar jawai* as Janus-faced (a term more often used to describe the position of women in exogamous structures), creating an identity that vacillates between honoured guest and dependent person. From the perspective of the *ghar jawai* and his patrikin, the move into degraded personhood is 'explained' as a sacrifice, an obligation and a duty to renounce patrilineal property and, at least in rural North India, to prevent fragmentation of landholdings. The movement is cast as a duty that sons must exhibit toward their families, justified by a string of details about why this move was necessary, or even underplayed by infrequent reference. In either case, of exhaustive excuses or silence, it is considered a troublesome move.

Recouping Lost Masculinity: The Transnational *Ghar Jawai*

Social exclusion, however, is not an absolute or fixed position. Time, space and travel enter to critically reconfigure the figure of the *ghar jawai* in distinctive and more socially accepted directions. Transnational families as a location for live-in sons-in-law are crucial to an understanding of the transformations in the personhood and masculinity of the *ghar jawai*. Fieldwork done among migrant communities in the UK indicates the shifts in the discourses around the *ghar jawai*. South Asian migrant communities view marital import as a way of retaining their links to home and language. Older residents in settled transnational communities, like the West London neighbourhood of Southall,[7] rued the loss of language of their third-generation grandchildren,[8] or the fact that children view the homeland as a tourist site rather than a place imbued with moral value. The loss of language and valued tradition are sought to be recouped by the 'imported' spouse who can impart the morality seen to reside in homeland 'traditions' (Rapport and Dawson 1998; Werbner 1999). While the literature on marriage and migration concentrates primarily on imported brides among South Asian communities (especially Punjabi communities), the imported husband is treated as special category of imported spouse.

Like its Indiacentric equivalent, the writing on the transnational *ghar jawai* is sparse, but telling. One of the earliest discussions is Helweg's (1986) study of Sikh Jat landowners settled in Gravesend in the UK. In a short biographical sketch of Ajay Singh, Helweg draws attention to the uncertainties of being an imported husband. Ajay Singh was brought from a Punjabi village as a *ghar jawai* to wed a Jat Sikh girl, raised in Gravesend. Apart from an international ticket, Ajay's wife's family has a nominal commitment toward their transnational son-in-law, and unlike the 'great Indian wedding', no dowry (gifts to the bridegroom) are given to Ajay. Burdened by cultural illiteracy, faced with alien household tasks like hanging wallpaper, Ajay Singh had to meekly bear the criticisms of his wife's wider kin who dismissed him as 'useless', precisely because he lived with his wife's family as *ghar jawai*. Ajay Singh's father-in-law declared that he would send him back to Punjab if necessary and marry his daughter to another man, convinced that there were enough bridegrooms for a daughter with a UK passport. It is clear that Gravesend Punjabis, and others like them, perfectly understand the value of passports and deploy this precious commodity to keep the *ghar jawai* in place. For the groom's family, access to citizenship outweighs the loss of dowry and the shame of exporting husbands, but for the groom himself, the transnational family seems to be an uncertain space.

Katherine Charsley's (2005) essay on migrant Pakistani men in Bristol who arrive as *ghar damads* (house son-in-laws) is perhaps one of the more detailed descriptions of the experience of being a transnational uxorilocal husband. Her essay focuses on the fragmented masculinity of the *ghar damad* and his debased position, especially vis-à-vis his male affines. In contrast to his wife, surrounded by her own kin, the inmigrating *ghar jawai* is without the support or network of his own patrikin. One of the interesting points Charsley makes is that while a girl is literally primed from her childhood to leave her natal family and home at marriage, a man is unprepared to face the consequences of such a move (ibid., 95–97).

The problem is compounded by the fact that transnational *ghar jawais* literally need to be 'unearthed' from larger narratives of migration. Simon Chamber's documentary film *Every Good Marriage Begins with Tears* (2007) is a biographical narrative of two Bangladeshi migrant sisters who marry 'imported' husbands. In the course of the film, the husbands literally fade away after the sisters divorce them. The film does not follow the husbands' lives at all and we are left to speculate the 'disappearances'. One frame depicts a façade of numerous South Asian restaurants of the neighbourhood suggesting the multicultural landscape into which the 'ex-husbands' vanish, possibly as illegal labour. But I think the inattentiveness in the film suggests a significant aspect in the biography of the transnational *ghar jawai*, namely, that transactions in husbands are not widely discussed. Perhaps this has to do with the negative public opinion that censures the import of marriage partners as signs of inward-looking migrant communities. But equally, it seems to me that the imported husband is juxtaposed with 'illegal' migrants, tainted with the suspicion of a 'false' marriage undertaken for the sake of a visa, an act that locks transnational communities into a discourse of unintegrated 'foreigners' who become conduits for unwanted migrations. Whatever the reason, the modern *ghar jawai* is literally allowed and enabled to 'fade away' into a multicultural landscape.

Most families I interviewed in 2005 and 2006, families who had brought young men to marry their daughters, did not readily speak of such migrations. So while migration imparts a status to transnational families which they deploy in marriage markets of their homelands (Beck-Grensheim 2007) to make advantageous marriages, within the context of their adopted homes, imported spouses, including husbands, remain muted in discussion. I therefore did not interview too many families and men who admitted to bringing in, or being, *ghar jawais*.

Some issues do emerge from the few interviews, however. The possibilities provided by the transnational context may be enabling in the transformation of the *ghar jawai* to household head primarily through establishing a nuclear household. What is perhaps more striking is that the move toward setting up a nuclear household also enables an expansion toward creating an attenuated patrilocal context within the transnational settlement. During the course of fieldwork in Southall, I was told of 'uncles' who came to live in their wives homes. A. Singh of Cranford told me that his father had been brought by his mother's brother who had also arrived in the 1940s as a *ghar jawai*. While his father could not recoup his own loss of status as a man imported by his mother's brother for labour and marriage, his son, A. Singh, went back to his father's village and bought agricultural land and a city house in Jullundur. The buying of land and property restored to him and his patrilineal family the status of substantial landowners in the eyes of the village community. The loss of a landed status had forced the father to become an 'imported spouse', moving into the kinship networks of his mother's brother, and his father's affines. But one generation down the line, the stigma of degradation had been smoothened out and at the time of the interview, A. Singh 'employed' his collateral village kin to tend his agricultural land. 'They're happy; I'm happy,' he told me pragmatically.

Another migrant, a Mr J., formerly a teacher in a Punjabi village school and a postmaster at the Mount Pleasant Road post office in London, played the role of a *bichola* (marriage go-between) for many an incoming *ghar jawai*, including his sister's son. Mr J. did not view this as a problem, neither for himself nor for the incoming husbands. Instead, he saw the process as a transaction that strengthened kinship ties. '*Sadi rishtedari teh rasook bardhe hai*' ('our kin circles and relationships grow like this'), he said.

On the one hand, interviews confirm economics as the compelling circumstance and even migration as *ghar jawai* was viewed as the duty of sons to prevent the fragmentation of precious land.[9] What was equally striking was the restoration of security of property and reputation that *ghar jawais* accomplished 'for family'. It was not clear to me if the entire system of kinship and martial exchanges that are expressed through gift giving, for example, were retained or discarded. In the transnational context, Charsley and Helweg draw attention to the houses 'gifted' to young conjugal couples to set up independent households. Charsley suggests that the nuclear household represents a chance for the *ghar jawai* to amend his everyday dependence on his father-in-law and achieve the status of a household head. But success is not guaranteed and independence may remain an incomplete achievement if the father-in-law who purchases the 'independent' home as gift retains the mortgage. The *ghar jawai*, especially as a young man, is continually negotiating and moving between dependence and autonomy.

By the time I did fieldwork, many former *ghar jawai* had set up nuclear and extended households and were instrumental in enabling the migration of younger men of their patrikin to Southall, simulating a partilineal context for themselves and for subsequent migrants. The juxtaposition of an earlier personhood and a later identity – *ghar jawai* transformed to 'benefactor' – were simultaneous in the narratives and life histories of these men. Lambert's study of locality and relatedness is a particularly interesting framework to understand the creation of kinship contexts, 'used to emphasize the processual and contextually determined character' of relatedness (Lambert 2000, 82). In kinship theory, relatedness is a broad concept that includes fictive and genealogical kinship. I find Lambert's understanding of locality and proximity in constituting 'relatives' useful when thinking about the constitution of transnational patrilocality. Fictive kinship and forms of relatedness are employed by migrants in general. Many come with nothing but a telephone number or an address of a distant relative and it is locality and proximity that transforms the genealogical distance into a more substantive relationship for reckoning kinship support and relatedness. This transformative potential of kinship as processual and contextual is even more important for the migrant *ghar jawai*. While financially dependent on affines, the possibility of a localized patriliny that rests on sentiment and affect, which Lambert characterizes as a form of substance critical for creating relatedness, is of immense value to the otherwise denigrated *ghar jawai*.

The processual creation of a transnational patrilocal context implies forgetting of a past as *ghar jawai*. This forgetting may be deliberate, a response to damaging press reports of imported spouses among South Asian diasporas or the ability to fade away into different cultural landscapes and disavow an awkward identity. Perhaps the absence of competing inheritors of property enables forgetting, for there is no quarrel with rival agnates over ancestral property.

It does seem to me that unlike the transnational *ghar jawai* of the fifties and sixties who, like other migrants, came with the idea of going back 'home', the late twentieth century and early twenty-first century *ghar jawai* have recast their relation to village homes. My interviews suggest that 'going back' is no longer an aspiration. In fact, the village is a 'tourist' destination of sorts, especially for children. For them, rural kin resemble Taj Mahal souvenirs, to be cherished as 'memory' rather than central of to everyday life. But clearly, too, buying property in the village continues and becomes the continuing link between transnational home and village 'place'. Land, the reason for the transformation of son to *ghar jawai*, becomes the base on which resignification and inclusion are accomplished.

Conclusion

From whichever perspective or location – rural or transnational – we look, the figure of the *ghar jawai* is ensnared by economic constraint, financial need and the sense of shame, the antithesis of the 'sense of honour' (Bourdieu 1979). Together, constraint, need and shame produce dispositions that taint the personhood of the *ghar jawai* and his wider kin. But stigma, when inserted in the life cycle, does not remain static. Strategies that counter the 'structure of shame' are intrinsic to 'playing' the rule with actions that slide along a scale of 'more' or 'less' dishonourable. Incongruously, resorting to the conversion of a son to *ghar jawai* because of economic necessity is a perfectly intelligible act for a wider cultural audience of interpreters who may subscribe to the ideology of shame in which the *ghar jawai* is mired, but also represent this as the inevitability of 'fate' occasioned by dire circumstance. Retrospective tolerance weakens the stigma of dependence and degradation, restoring a semblance of normalcy.

In the transnational context, the fact that the *ghar jawai* might become a conduit for future migrations of kin and village folk purges some part of the shame. It is possible, therefore, to argue that while hegemonic discourse assigns the *ghar jawai* to the domain of the abject, practice and processual kinship enable a form of collective miscognition and a partial recouping of misplaced masculinity. At least some aberrations fade into forgiveness.

The discourse of exclusion emphasizes the collective as the bearer of social inequity. Some forms of social exclusion do envisage distinction 'flowing' from individuals to groups. Dumont's now classic study of hierarchy and marriage (Dumont 1957) envisages distinctions between members of a family among the Kallar, where the sons of 'senior' wives are 'purer' than the sons of 'junior' wives, within the same family. The idea of purity that ranks groups percolates into individual lives, he argues. Therefore, the sons of junior wives (and the subset of their family) are positioned as less pure than sons of senior wives, ranked along a scale of purity that otherwise govern social groups like castes. While Dumont's own work does not address the individual per se, my reading of his work suggests the individual as a 'bearer' of purity that flows from individual to group and, it seems to me, produces a 'life cycle of purity'. Building on Dumont, we could argue that in the play of purity, a man who is the son of a junior wife would not be ranked on the same scale as his own son from his senior wife.

Bringing Dumont forward, it is possible to analyse individual migrations as enabling the movement of individuals and wider groups from lower ranks to higher positions. From the little ethnography that exists, it can be argued that the *ghar jawai*, located within a 'structure' of shame and degradation, represents a social nadir. Within the *habitus* of shame, however, a life of a *ghar jawai* shows us that his biography is not a frozen chronicle, but moves from valuing him as a son, to a socially excluded figure, and then toward a respected position in a localized group of patrikin, because he can create a 'home' for migrant brothers. A social flaw may not be entirely forgotten, but it can fade. It is the mobility in the life cycle of the person that enables transformations in the biography of an individual, and it is this 'moving' quality that is lost in the mistranslation of the *ghar jawai* as househusband.

Notes

1 An earlier version of this chapter appeared as '*Ghar jawai* (House Husband): A Note on Mistranslation' in *Culture, Society and Masculinities* 1 (1) (2009): 96–105.

2 http://www.cartoonstock.com/directory/h/house_husband.asp (accessed 15 December 2008).

3 Uxorilocal residence is when a groom moves into the bride's household. Patrilocal residence, also called virilocality, is a pattern where the bride moves to stay in her husband's father's household. In North Indian kinship structures, the focus of this chapter, the primary residence pattern is virilocal. Together, virilocality and patrilineal kinship reckoning accentuate patriarchal authority.

4 In rural Punjab, gender segregated work cycles enable families with sons to undertake a large variety of agricultural tasks that cannot be performed by daughter-only households.

5 Stanley Brandes' analysis of sexual humour and masculine identity is germane to my discussion (Brandes 1980).

6 These kinship practices are reminiscent of Malinowski's account of the matrilineal Trobriand for whom the father is *tomakava* or stranger. Subsequent interpretations of Trobriand rituals reveal the sense of connection maintained between children and the father through the lifespan of both (Blu Sider 1967; Weiner 1976). Despite the elision suggested by kinship terminology, the father is not forgotten. In the same spirit the son who has moved (or been sent away) as *ghar jawai* is always 'remembered' as wholly belonging to his patrilineage.

7 Fieldwork informing this section of the chapter was done in Southall in March 2005, September 2005, and October–November 2006. I am grateful to the Charles Wallace (India) Trust for a grant that enabled me to begin the fieldwork. I am grateful to ICES, Colombo, from whom I received a grant under the Project 'Globalization, National Identity and Violence: Exploring South Asian Masculinities in the New Millennium' that enabled the research to go forward. I would like to thank Prof. John Harris at the LSE for enabling the Visiting Fellowship, and colleagues at the LSE Department of Anthropology for stimulating discussions.

8 To call these children 'third generation' is somewhat of a misnomer, since one of the parents (including the father) may be an imported spouse and therefore a first-generation migrant.

9 Gardner, on the other hand, indicates that Bangladeshi migrant men often leave their less affluent sons-in-law in charge of the home, and while the young husband is converted to a *ghar jawai*, he also becomes the sole decision maker in the absence of his migrant father-in-law. Uxorilocal residence is seen as 'a response to the practical problems posed by migration [...] but uxorilocal residence in the long term is also presented as a sad state of affairs' (Gardner 1995, 167–68).

References

Anderson, Michael, Frank Bechhofer, and Jonathan Gershuny, eds. 1994. *The Social and Political Economy of the Household*. Oxford: Oxford University Press.

Beck-Gernsheim, Elisabeth. 2007. 'Transnational Lives, Transnational Marriages: A Review of the Evidence from Migrant Communities in Europe'. *Global Networks* 7 (3): 271–88.

Blu Sider, Karen. 1967. 'Kinship and Culture: Affinity and the Role of the Father in the Trobriands'. *Southwestern Journal of Anthropology* 23 (1): 90–109.

Bourdieu, Pierre. 1979. *Algeria 1960: The Disenchantment of the World, the Sense of Honour, the Kabyle House or the World Reversed*. Cambridge: Cambridge University Press.

Brandes, Stanley. 1980. *Metaphors of Masculinity: Sex and Status in Andalusian Folklore*. Philadelphia: University of Pennsylvania Press.

Chambers, Simon. 2007. *Every Good Marriage Begins with Tears*. Documentary. Directed by Simon Chambers. London: The Royal Anthropological Institute.

Charsley, Katherine. 2005. 'Unhappy Husbands: Masculinity and Migration in Pakistani Transnational Marriages'. *Journal of the Royal Anthropological Institute* (N. S.) 11 (1): 85–105.

Chopra, Radhika. 2001. 'Retrieving the Father: Gender Studies "Father Love" and the Discourse of Motherhood'. Edited by J. Liddle and C. Wright. In *Journal of the Women's' Studies International Forum* Special Issue 24 (314): 445–55.

Chopra, Radhika. 2009. '*Ghar jawai* (House Husband): A Note on Mistranslation'. *Culture, Society and Masculinities* 1 (1): 96–105.

Chopra, Radhika. 2011. *Militant and Migrant: The Politics and Social History of Punjab*. London, NY, New Delhi: Routledge.

Diwan, Paras, Shailendra Jain and Peeyushi Diwan. 2004. *Law of Adoption, Minority, Guardianship and Custody*. 3rd ed. New Delhi: Universal Law Publishing Company, Indian Personal Law Series.

Douglas, Mary. 1966. *Purity and Danger: An Analysis of Concept of Pollution and Taboo*. London: Routledge and Kegan Paul.

Dumont, Louis. 1957. 'Hierarchy and Marriage Alliance in South Indian Kinship'. Occasional Papers of the Royal Anthropological Institute of Great Britain and Ireland, No. 12. London: Royal Anthropological Institute.

_______. 1966. 'Marriage in India: The Present State of the Question III'. *Contributions to Indian Sociology* 9: 90–114.

Gardner, K. 1995. *Global Migrants, Local Lives: Migration and Transformation in Rural Bangladesh.* Oxford: Oxford University Press.

Giddens, Anthony. 1993. *The Transformation of Intimacy* Stanford: Stanford University Press.

Helweg, Arthur. 1986. *Sikhs in England.* Delhi: Oxford University Press.

Hershman, Paul. 1981. *Punjabi Kinship and Marriage.* Delhi: Hindustani Publishing Corporation.

Jeffery, Patricia, Roger Jeffery, and Andrew Lyon. 1989. *Labour Pains and Labour Power: Women and Childbearing in India.* New Delhi: Sage.

Krimmer, E. 2000. 'Nobody Wants to be a Man Anymore? Cross-Dressing in American Movies of the 90s'. In *Subverting Masculinity: Hegemonic and Alternative Versions of Masculinity in Contemporary Culture,* edited by R. West and F. Lay, 29–44. Amsterdam: Rodopi.

Lasch. Christopher. 1997. *Women and the Common Life: Love, Marriage and Feminism.* New York: W. W. Norton.

Lambert, Helen. 2000. 'Sentiment and Substance in North Indian Forms of Relatedness'. In *Cultures of Relatedness: New Approaches to the Study of Kinship,* edited by Janet Carsten. Cambridge: Cambridge University Press, 81–100.

Madan, Triloki N. 1966. *Family and Kinship: A Study of the Pandits of Rural Kashmir.* New York: Asia Publishing House.

_______. 1975. 'Structural Implications of Marriage in North India: Wife-Givers and Wife-Takers Among the Pandits of Kashmir'. *Contributions to Indian Sociology* (N. S.) 9: 217–43.

McMahon, Anthony. 1998. 'Blokus Domesticus: The Sensitive New Age Guy in Australia'. *Journal of Australian Studies* 56: 147–58.

Nicholas, Ralph W. 1965. 'Factions: A Comparative Analysis'. In *Political Systems and the Distribution of Power,* edited by M. Banton, 21–92. London: Tavistock.

Östör, A., L. Fruzzetti, and S. Barnett, eds. (1982) 1992. *Concepts of Person: Kinship, Marriage, and Caste in India.* Cambridge, MA: Harvard University Press.

Rapport, Nigel, and Andrew Dawson, eds. 1998. *Migrants of Identity: Perceptions of Home in a World of Movement.* New York: Berg.

Singh, Kurmar Suresh. 2004. *People of India: Anthropological Survey of India.* Mumbai: Popular Prakashan.

Sonpar, Shobna. 2005. 'Marriage in India: Clinical Issues'. *Contemporary Family Therapy* 2 (3): September, 301–13.

Strathern, Marilyn. 1987. 'Producing Difference: Connections and Disconnections in Two New Guinea Highland Systems'. In *Gender and Kinship: Toward a Unified Analysis,* edited by J. Collier and S. Yanagisako. Stanford: Stanford University Press, 271–300.

Vatuk, Sylvia. 1969. 'A Structural Analysis of Hindi Kinship Terminology'. *Contributions to Indian Sociology* (N. S.) 3: 94–115.

_______. 1972. *Kinship and Urbanization: White Collar Migrants in North India.* Berkeley: University of California Press.

Weiner, Annette B. 1976. *Women of Value, Men of Renown: New Perspectives in Trobriand Exchange.* Austin: University of Texas Press.

Wentworth, D. K., and Chell, R. M. 2005. 'Gender Identity at Home: Comparing the Role of Househusband to Housewife'. In *Psychology of Gender Identity,* edited by J. W. Lee. Hauppauge, NY: Nova Biomedical Books, 113–26.

Werbner, Pnina. 1999. 'Global Pathways: Working Class Cosmopolitans and the Creation of Transnational Ethnic Worlds'. *Social Anthropology* 7 (1): 17–37.

Chapter 4

EXCLUSION AND INCLUSION: NAVIGATION STRATEGIES AMONG HINDUS IN THE DIASPORA – A CASE STUDY FROM DENMARK

Marianne Qvortrup Fibiger

The concepts of exclusion and inclusion are not only concerned with social or cultural processes where exclusion and inclusion strategies are used in an overall political framework and where individuals or a group of people are either included or excluded in relation to shared privileges. Exclusion and inclusion can also be seen as part of mobility strategies from within, where a group of people use exclusion and inclusion in a situation of cultural discontinuity, trying to find new ways of constructing meaning in a new setting (such changes may be necessitated by modernity, globalization, or a diaspora situation, etc.). In doing so, they also construct a shared understanding of belonging to a specific cultural, ethnic or religious tradition. This is an ongoing process of negotiation during which the understanding of belonging are redefined. This process can be found among all groups of people, irrespective of time or place.

This chapter will argue that these types of negotiations are most prevalent and profound among groups living abroad or in diaspora. In such cases, a tradition (whether religious, cultural or ethnic) becomes part of a society that does not share its history and that played no role in its formation. Therefore, the tradition is confronted first hand with various paradigms and worldviews, which, up until that point, it had not been part of. This does not mean that the tradition is lost; it is simply reshaped and, in this way, it remains part of an identity that connects its members to the country they have left. In this chapter, diaspora as an identity category is understood in its broadest sense, that is, as a transnationally committed community. This means that the tradition's identity changes in relation to its new circumstances, but that it retains roots that bind it to something that defines it as a community in itself. Or, as phrased by Tölölyan (1991, 3), the founding editor of the journal *Diaspora*, 'diasporas are the exemplary communities of the transnational moment.' Being a minority community in diaspora, with shared ties to a country and culture, initiates a process of inclusiveness and exclusiveness, through which the tradition changes according to its new setting, but maintains a shared relation to its place of origin. This is part of an identification process in which members of the tradition, but also other communities, groups, or systems (political, cultural, governmental, etc.) play a role. As Jenkins (2003) writes, 'identification has both to do with similarities as well as differences'.

The point of departure for this chapter is ethnic Hindus (mostly Sri Lankan, but also Indian) in Denmark. Ethnic is used to frame the Hindus who are born as Hindus and see themselves as Hindus in a religious, cultural and ethnic sense. This distinguishes them from the smaller Hindu-inspired groups of ethnic Danes such as the International Society for Krishna Consciousness (ISKCON). In particular, I focus on the Sri Lankan Tamil Hindus. I have followed this group since the mid-1990s and have concentrated on their relation to their own religious tradition. My main interest, as a scholar of the study of religion, has been to examine the development of the religious institution and to investigate the different meanings that the members ascribe to the religious, alias 'cultural', category. Recently, I have focused primarily on the similarities and differences between the generations in an attempt to establish what they consider to be the core elements within the tradition.

Keeping up Hindu Tradition in a New Setting and under New Circumstances

As a minority group living in diaspora, the exclusion and inclusion of elements within the Hindu tradition plays a significant role in constructing a Hindu identity. Hinduism is no longer just a 'way of life', but a 'part of life', and is therefore understood as an entity or a system in itself, which has to be given topicality in the new setting in order for its members to survive.[1]

In this dynamic process of place making in the new surroundings, a more conscious navigation strategy is being followed.[2] The tension between which elements from the tradition should be removed or retained, on the one hand, and on the other hand, which elements from the new society should be adopted, shows us what is at stake at different levels. This also applies in relation to contexts and circumstances, which emphasizes the constructivist aspect of tradition.

The two levels that will be examined in this chapter are: the relation between the local and global Hindu traditions, and the relation between the generations. It is not the ambition of this chapter to provide a profound understanding of all the processes of inclusion and exclusion involved in becoming a citizen of a new society. Instead, this chapter aims to present a few examples of the interrelated dynamics between such processes.

My primary focus will be on the Sri Lankan Tamil Hindu tradition in Denmark and I shall therefore only discuss a small section of this place-making process. The place-making process can also be described as (1) a process of legitimizing the tradition, not only for its members in a new environment, but also for the Danish society, and (2) a process of formalizing the tradition, allowing it to adapt to the new setting and, thus, to be preserved and transmitted through the generations. In India and Sri Lanka, this has mostly been achieved through adhering to orthodox practices (orthopraxis) and through oral communication. However, when it comes to preserving a tradition in a new environment where, until recently, Hinduism had not been a part of its culture, it seems necessary to preserve the tradition in writing. I will demonstrate how customs that were previously in nonwritten form, and which were particularly characteristic of the so-called 'little tradition' or folk tradition, are now written down. As a result of this process, the Sri Lankan Tamil Hindu tradition in Denmark is taken up for reconsideration and the content of the Hindu category or identity is revised and negotiated. In particular, this chapter will examine how a form of shaktism (goddess worship), which was formerly locally based and primarily orally transmitted, is becoming increasingly formalized and text based. It shall also examine how, as a consequence of this, shaktism is changing from a local phenomenon, known only by the Sri Lankan Tamil Hindus in Denmark, to a global phenomenon known among Sri Lankan Tamil Hindus worldwide. In fact, the temple that houses the cult around the Abirami goddess is now a place of pilgrimage for Sri Lankan Tamil Hindus from all over the world. Many negotiations and compromises have taken place in this process, during which some elements have been excluded and others have been included. And the people involved in this process have become increasingly aware of their tradition and their belonging, as well as the boundaries of their tradition. The extent to which a tradition can accommodate exclusion and inclusion, given that the members of the tradition wish to relate to it and preserve it in its new setting, is a fundamental and persistent question when discussing the notion of preserving through change.

With the main focus on exclusion and inclusion processes, this chapter will also argue that, by focusing on a group of Hindus in diaspora, we not only gain an insight into religious transformation and adaption (which provides the religion with local features), but we are also able to identify the features of the Hindu tradition that remain, despite the new setting. Therefore, we can identify the core features of Hinduism, which are otherwise so difficult to classify. These supposed core features can be identified by asking second generation immigrants what they perceive to be the key aspects of their religion, aspects they not only understand as important in their self-understanding as Hindu or Tamil, but also wish to pass on to their children. However, it is also necessary to understand the meaning of the religious institution, that is, the temples, which both first- and second-generation Hindus identify as important places for preserving the tradition in diaspora (Jacobsen and Kumar 2004).

The core features that appear to be transmitted from generation to generation and kept in the religious institution will be called 'cultural memory', as defined by Jan Assmann (2006) and Danièle Hervieu-Léger (2000). According to Assmann and Hervieu-Léger, elements of a tradition retained for more than three generations qualify as cultural memory. It does not mean that these supposed core features are not changed or (re)constructed, but rather that in the minds of the bearers of the tradition, they are understood as essential for their cultural and/or religious belonging.

Collective or Cultural Memory: Presumed Core Features that are Kept through Generations

Jan Assmann (2006) differentiates between communicative memory and collective memory, an important distinction for this chapter. He states that communicative memory occurs in the immediate interaction between people and does not remember more than three generations back. The individual's state of mind or emotional state of being plays an important role in the communicative memory because it helps to preserve the content of the experience (love, anger, disillusion, and so forth) (ibid., 3). But it does not help to preserve a collective memory, which can be transmitted from generation to generation. Therefore, as a survival mechanism in an evolutionary cultural scheme, it is important to store core features of the tradition in the collective memory, since, in contrast to communicative memory, cultural or collective memory remembers back in history and can be either stored in institutions or in text. From Assmann's point of view, cultural or religious texts are a special class of oral or written texts, which can be recalled irrespective of time and place.

In relation to religion, Assmann defines cultural memory as an institutionalization of what he calls 'invisible religion' (with reference to Berger and Luckmann). Invisible religion is understood as the process of individuation and the formation of a personal self. Assmann does not reject invisible religion, he simply aims to understand why we find maintenance of symbolic universes over the generations and a continuity of a special system of meaning and identity (ibid., 37). What interests me is not so much the maintenance of symbolic universes, but rather the recalling or awareness of symbolic universes that can be used in the formation or establishment of a collective memory. Below, I will show how the diaspora situation and the need for establishing a collective memory have changed a formerly local, personal and lay-oriented tradition, which was primarily found among low-caste Hindus in Sri Lanka, to a globally oriented tradition which is now internationally recognized. This has occurred through the formation and use of symbols and texts. In this way, either by referring to an ahistorical and mythological world that is well known among many Hindus or by writing new texts, they have made a formerly orally transmitted tradition fit a new situation, and thereby made it possible that the tradition is stored as collective memory. In other words, it can be argued that the diaspora situation has not only started a process of mobilization, but has also increased awareness of what should be kept as important tradition-bearers in a new setting and under new circumstances. Therefore, traditions that once relied on oral communication and were locally situated are either slowly disappearing or given a form that makes them more transmittable. This does not mean that there is no religious diversity among Hindus in diaspora, but rather that the religious expressions change form in relation to the new circumstances and in relation to who the transmitters of the tradition are, as well as to whom it is transmitted. This is not the same as claiming that the religious traditions and practices originate from the Brahmanical tradition, which has already been noted in other diaspora studies among Hindus (Jacobsen and Kumar 2004). I wish to emphasize that the folk or local traditions are given a new form which allows them to be preserved through generations. That is, at least, what my studies in Denmark show.

Hinduism in the Diaspora

Over the last twenty years or so, the number of academic studies of groups in diaspora has increased tremendously. These studies also focus on the many groups of South Asians and Hindus, represented in most parts of the world, who have settled down and found their way of life in relation to the societies of which they are now a part (Jacobsen and Kumar 2004). This new intake of local studies of diaspora groups not only gives us insight into the complexity and plurality of the Hindu tradition(s) as such, it can also provide us with new knowledge of possible core features of the same tradition. I argue that it is in the diaspora situation, in which the Hindu tradition has a minority status and has to negotiate its way into a new society, that core elements of the tradition become more obvious. This is the case for both the bearers of the tradition and for the researchers.

The tradition is particularly vulnerable in relation to new generations that are struggling with their identity; for example, an identity as both Danish and Tamil/Indian, and being Hindu on new terms. While a permanent reinterpretation process is occurring for the whole group as such, there is also an important generation gap when comparing first- and second-generation immigrants. Like their parents, second-generation immigrants are all Hindus in their self-understanding, but what they assign to this category seems to differ in many aspects. Whereas first-generation immigrants generally try to keep up tradition as they knew it from India or Sri Lanka, second-generation immigrants do not (Fibiger 2011). They reinterpret or select those elements from the tradition that help to engage with the society they are now a part of and link them to the tradition they share with their parents. As mentioned above, these adaption processes of excluding and including provide us with an insight into what can be understood as core elements, which remain in spite of place, especially if compared with different diaspora settings. In this way, the local features as well as the potentially more global ones can be isolated from each other.

As an overall pattern in Denmark, it seems as though the second generation of Hindus withdraw from many of the local or family-based rituals which they categorize as superstition. It would be interesting to decipher whether the following statement is only a locally framed statement, which gives a picture of the Danish Hindu youth, or whether it is general pattern in relation to generations:

> Hinduism is full of superstition. Just look at our parents. As an example, I can tell you that my mother was very engaged in astrology, especially how the planets were placed in relation to each other. Sometimes she said: 'now we are facing a bad period.' And we had to fast or we had to go to the temple to make offerings. It was driving me crazy. Today, I have to admit, I look a bit on it myself – but in contrast to my mother, I consult books about the subject. (Second-generation Sri Lankan Hindu Tamil woman, 27 years old)

This statement is an example of how second-generation immigrants relate themselves to the same tradition as their parents, though not without hesitation. They need proof or a textual authority to support the belief before they allow it to become part of their religious meaning system or approve it as part of the collective memory they share with their parents. It becomes obvious that text matters for the second generation of Hindus in diaspora. Another important thing is the religious institution as the bearer per se of their shared tradition, which, as mentioned above, both the first and second generations of Sri Lankans Tamil Hindus in Denmark can agree upon.

The Hindu Diaspora Group in Denmark

In Denmark, there are approximately 10 thousand Sri Lankan Tamils. There are around 12 thousand ethnic Hindus, of which approximately 9 thousand emigrated from Sri Lanka as refugees, and the rest (approximately 3,000–4,000) emigrated from various parts of India, mostly northern India.[3]

The new settlers had to learn Danish. Their education from India or Sri Lanka was often not recognized, which meant that they either had to do unskilled work or to go through the education system once again, but on Danish terms. In many ways they felt socially excluded. This was also the case in relation to religion; for example, they did not find any political or public understanding or support in relation to building religious institutions or other ways of maintaining their tradition.

Most of the Indians and more than half of the Sri Lankan Tamils living in Denmark have become Danish citizens, but most of them still have a close relation to either India or Sri Lanka, which they still consider as a kind of homeland. And, compared to most of the other refugee and immigrant groups in Denmark, the Indians and the Sri Lankan Tamils are very well integrated into Danish society; most of them are employed,[4] their children are doing well in Danish schools and they often choose to speak Danish to each other.

When it comes to cultural adaption, more and more of both the Tamils and the Indians adopt some of the Danish traditions such as Christmas Eve, but on their own terms. This inclusion of elements from the Danish tradition also makes them more aware of the important hallmarks associated with being Hindu or Indian/Tamil, and it provides us with an interesting example of how inclusiveness and exclusiveness in relation to tradition can have a mutual impact. Because new things are included in the tradition, other things within the tradition are simultaneously emphasized and cherished. As a father of two children told me:

> We do celebrate Christmas with presents and a Christmas tree, decorated with things our children make at school, in our living room, but we don't sing Christmas carols or go to church – some of our Tamil friends in Germany go to church, but we have decided not to. We think it is important that our children get a relation to our temple instead. It's not that they are not allowed in the church – they go there with the school – but just for them to get an idea about where our tradition comes from or belongs to.

This statement touches upon a crucial point when it comes to the relation between adaption and the preservation of tradition. Something changes according to the new setting (adaption), but only to a certain extent and without losing what appear to be the core features within the same tradition (preservation). In this way, the collective memory, despite its continuingly changing form, can still be understood as the caretaker of a supposedly mutually shared tradition. This is what Hervieu-Léger (2000) calls a 'memory chain', used to construct a system of meaning in a new setting.

This can be underlined in the following statements given by second-generation Sri Lankan Tamil Hindus in relation to what they want to transmit to their children:

> I will take the good things from both cultures, and in relation to Hinduism I would like to understand it more before I choose what to give my children from it. (Male, 27 years old)
>
> I don't want my children to become rootless. I do have roots here, but anyway. The Tamil language, but also the temple must play a role. (Female, 24 years old)
>
> The language is something I will transmit to my children. When I was a child myself, I didn't pay much attention to the language, but being 25 years, I now begin to think that the Tamil language is important. (Female, 25 years old)

Through my interviews with second-generation Sri Lankan Tamil Hindus in Denmark (Fibiger 2011), it has become evident how the language, the texts, and the temple institution play an important role in storing tradition and as something they not only relate to in their self-identity, as being Tamil and/or Hindu, but also as something they want to transmit to their children. They consider language important for two reasons: Firstly, they can communicate with their older relatives, both in Denmark and in Sri Lanka, and thereby relate to their shared background. Secondly, they can understand what is said in the temple and they can read the holy stories and texts themselves. The last point is particularly concerned with religious identity and the religious institution, which seems to be the focal point for both generations. The way they relate to the religious institution seems to differ, but both generations agree that the temple is a cultural keeper and broker, an important symbol of the tradition and a place to consult when required. This fits an old Tamil saying, which states that you should not live in a village where there is no temple.

In the following, I will therefore concentrate on the religious institution as an example of place making and storage of collective memory. I will focus on one of the three ethnic Hindu temples in Denmark (two of which are Sri Lankan Hindu temples), using it as an example of this process and showing how the tradition is becoming formalized through textual framing as well as a ritual one. In this way, it both adapts to the Westernized understanding of religion and to the need of second-generation immigrants; and it works as an important storage place for the collective memory, which can be preserved for generations.

First, I will make a short presentation of the two ethnic Hindu groups in Denmark – the Indian Hindus and the Sri Lankan Tamil Hindus – in order to understand the setting in which the Sri Lankan Hindus take part. Because of differences in their national, cultural, and linguistic linking, the two groups constitute two parallel diasporas. They have separate temples and do not mix very much with each other.

The Indian Hindus

The first generation of Hindus came to Denmark in the 1970s. They mostly came from the northern parts of India or from East Africa and were seen as so-called guest workers, meaning they could only stay in Denmark as long as there were jobs. Most of them settled in Zealand, in and around Denmark's capital city, Copenhagen, but some settled in the main cities in Jutland such as Aarhus and Aalborg.

Those coming from East Africa can, in some respects, be understood as a group in itself, since they have emigrated more than once and have, therefore, also brought elements from their establishment in East Africa with them to Denmark. They have, in other words, already been through the process of adaption and their identity or identities can be even more complex and hybrid in relation to belonging and preserving their culture. What in East Africa was considered important for being Indians and Hindus can be understood as an extra lens through which they look at their relation to their tradition in Denmark.

This can form a significant part of their cultural memory in Denmark. It could be claimed that they have a dual identity, relating, on the one hand, to their stay in East Africa and how they or their families tried to preserve tradition there, and, on the other hand, to India as a common reference as homeland. In other words, it could be said that India is moving farther and farther away but, at the same time, it is coming closer, being the common place of reference for all Indian Hindus in Denmark irrespective of whether they came directly from India or from East Africa. The link to India as such – and not to a special state or area in India – becomes their shared point of departure. This is important in discourses regarding the maintenance of local differences in diaspora, especially when it comes to the second or third generation of Hindus in Denmark, where the local linking seems to be displaced by a national linking to India as such. It can play a significant role in their understanding of being Hindu and can lead to a closer linking between Hinduism and nationalism, or to a global form of Hinduism.

This common place of reference is underlined by the name chosen for the only Indian Hindu temple in Denmark: Hindu Bharatiya Mandir,[5] which indicates the common relation to Mother India. The temple is placed at Skovlunde, a suburb of Copenhagen. The building that houses the temple was first rented and later, in the mid-1990s, was bought from the Jehovah's Witnesses who used it as a prayer room. Today, it is filled with the globally recognized deities such as Rama and Sita, Shiva and Parvati, Krishna and Radha, Vishnu and Laxmi, Durga, Ganesha and Hanuman. It has so far not been consecrated and is not open every day. It is only open on Sundays for *satsang* and for the Indian Hindu festivals. The temple, which is a Sanatana Dharma temple, is seen as an important meeting place for the Hindu Indians and as a place for preserving temple worship and offering the children an understanding of the Hindu cult. However, it is not understood as the bearer of the tradition per se. In contrast to the Sri Lankan Tamil Hindus, the Indian Hindus consider the holy texts, such as the Ramayana and the Bhagavad Gita, to be important preservers of their tradition and they can be read everywhere. Or, as one Indian Hindu male expresses it:

> You may say that, in Denmark, we have chosen a few elements from our Hindu tradition that we want to preserve and really do a lot to preserve. For example Diwali; we do everything to celebrate this festival, and we put effort into the celebration – even more than we would have done if we were still living in India. It is also important

that our children visit the temple because there they get knowledge about how to do puja, but also about the importance of our Holy text, which we read aloud in the temple. In the temple we also speak Hindi and Punjabi together and eat traditional Indian food. I must admit though, that we don't go very often. (Male, 50 years old)

The Sri Lankan Tamil Hindus

The first Tamils came to Denmark in 1983 because of the escalating conflict in Sri Lanka. They were mostly men and were categorized ipso facto as refugees. During the 1990's they were reunited with their families in Denmark or they married Sri Lankan Tamil women and began to settle down.

Most of them were located in the middle of Jutland, especially around the cities of Herning, Brande, Holstebro, Skjern, Struer and Tarm, where industry expanded in the 1990s and there was a need for unskilled workers. Another group was located further south in Jutland around the cities of Vejle, Middelfart and Billund, and a few were located in the northern part of Zealand, in and around the suburb of Copenhagen called Farum.

I have been studying the Srilankan Tamil Hindus in Denmark since the mid-1990s and I have followed the establishment and consecration of two of their temples:[6] One is a Vinayakar (Ganesha) temple in the city of Herning. It is very well organized, with an educated Brahmin priest and an eleven-member committee, who see it as their primary role to ensure that all religious rules are kept when it comes to puja or temple worship; this was also noted by a well-esteemed priest visiting from Sri Lanka who was astonished to see that everything was done by the book. It is very clear to everyone that this temple wants to preserve the tradition, or the religiously based collective memory, which they not only know from Sri Lanka but which they also, from what they have heard or read, consider to be correct conduct. In other words, living in a diaspora situation has made them more aware of the tradition based on written texts. In some ways, this temple can be labelled an orthodox temple, with a Brahmin priest and high-caste members (Vellalars) on the committee.

The other temple, which will be examined further as an example of the place-making process, is dedicated to the goddess Abirami.[7] Here it is an autodidact laywoman, Lalitha Sripalan, who functions as a priest, Shakti medium and, consequently, as a healer. Because she does not know Sanskrit and has no religious training or education, she conducts puja in silence and does it according to what she has experienced in her local temple in Jaffna, Sri Lanka, before coming to Denmark. In other words, a local form of shaktism, from a village in Jaffna, is revitalized or continued in Denmark and given form accordingly.

Occasionally, and when required, she is possessed by the shakti energy, or she becomes Shakti and then she is able to perform various kinds of healing for physical and mental conditions. She is also consulted on other matters; for example, she can find the right time for travelling, she can help young people in conflict with parents as well as parents who are struggling with teenagers, or she can even read people's horoscopes and find a suitable partner in marriage, and so on. However, she is mostly known for helping childless women conceive. In this temple there are no affiliated Brahmins and there is no temple committee; but there is a group of devotees who help run the temple.

Today, Lalita Sripalan, now simply called Amma, is not only well known among the Sri Lankan Hindu Tamils in Denmark, but also the Sri Lankan Hindu Tamils abroad as well as ethnic Danes. On the temple consecration days, or the Theer, which is a 15-day festival held in July, more than 2,500 devotees are assembled on one day, and most of these travel from abroad: Norway, Switzerland, Canada, Germany and even Sri Lanka. They see their travel to the Apirami temple in Denmark as a sort of *tirtha* (pilgrimage). What is of special interest is that, over the last couple of years, Amma's role has changed from that of a healer – and, it could be argued, a supplement to the religious belief – to the focal point around which a specific shakta cult is created. The tradition is no longer only transmitted orally, but is now also located in texts and related to a specific temple around which a specific cult has developed. And it seems as though the diaspora situation and the adaption to a Western concept of religion, where text and the institution are important, have given this particular cult options it would never have had if it were situated only in Sri Lanka. It has changed from a local to a global phenomenon. However, because of the growing interest among ethnic Danes over the last couple of years, it has also become more established locally. Despite the fact that the ethnic Danes understand Amma primarily as an alternative healer among other alternative healers, and therefore not as a bearer of a particular tradition, it gives the group of Sri Lankan Tamils, who can be labelled as core members, a feeling of contributing to the Danish society. This acceptance can be understood as the inclusiveness of the tradition in the Danish cultural landscape, which has an impact on changing the tradition in a way that it can be stored as collective memory through generations (Fibiger 2012).

The Abirami Cult as an Example of Establishing Collective Memory

From a theoretical point of view, I find the development of this particular cult very interesting because I see it as an example of how – on a minimalistic scale – a religious community based on an oral tradition is developing a collective memory by becoming institutionalized, by including recurrent rituals and indexical symbols, and by inventing or finding text that can either store this particular cult through history or legitimize the contemporary cult and the people involved by relating it to an ahistoric past or sphere. In this way, the shakta cult around Lalita Sripalan can be stored and thus survive and give meaning to its worshippers, even once Lalita Sripalan passes away. In other words, it can be transmitted from generation to generation in a way that seems to suit both the new setting and the new generation, which was brought up in a society where the understanding of religion is often related to institutions and texts.

I agree that rituals are stable and that the texts, and especially the worshippers' interpretations of these, are more liable to change. However, the texts (as canonical texts, as myths, or songs) with a reference to a mythological, ahistorical past, still play an important role not only in the legitimation of a given cult, but also as a frame in which the ritual can be understood. As Durkheim (1995, 379) writes, 'one is more sure in one's faith when one sees how far into the past it goes and what great things it has inspired. This is the feature of the ceremony that makes it instructive.' In relation to this, Durkheim discusses the importance of memory, arguing that 'how the society imagines man and the world is expressed in the traditions whose memory the mythology perpetuates' (ibid., 379). In other words, it can be difficult to store a collective memory if there are no texts. In relation to the Abirami temple in Brande, this means that new texts are included in a tradition that was (formerly) orally based. However, this does not mean that the oral transmission is entirely excluded; it has simply become framed with texts, rituals and symbols that will live on after Amma's death. In this way, the collective memory is secured, provided there are transmitters of it. In the following section I will briefly outline the development which provides the essential elements in the shaping of a collective memory, where the process has been to include elements that suit the new setting and the need for its bearers and to exclude elements that could be understood as anachronistic, both in relation to those that the tradition should be communicated to and in relation to the society in which it is now placed. I wish to mention four important hallmarks: (1) The development of special *avatara* days (the Danish New Year's Eve and the three following days), where Amma becomes a named goddess as Parvati, Kali, Durga; (2) the development of icons in the temple, where Amma is now depicted as a goddess sitting in the same row as the goddesses known form the mythological texts; (3) the development of praising songs composed by the worshippers themselves and (4) the withdrawal of more globally known mythological texts, such as Abirami Anthadi, who depicts Abirami as Mahadevi (the Great Goddess).

The *Avatara* Day

In the narrative about Lalitha Sripalan or Amma, and as a legitimation of this shakta cult as something special, I see the Danish New Year's eve of 1998, the first *avatara* day, as a crucial turning point. It was on that evening that the first direct and obvious manifestation of a name-given shakti energy became visible through Lalitha Sripalan. She was Parvati, the spouse of Shiva, for three days. And it was not a coincidence that Parvati was chosen or that Parvati chose to be the first direct manifestation. For shaivites, Parvati is the ideal woman and the incarnate mother figure and, therefore, the beginning or foundation of everything. She told the crowd that she was Parvati and she wore her special attributes. This event gave birth to a specific and manifest shakta tradition connected to Lalitha Sripalan, and it gave birth to a very dedicated congregation.

Her three-day Parvati manifestation followed a special pattern which could be interpreted as the birth and foundation of the tradition around Lalitha Sripalan and the special shakta cult in Denmark; but it could also be read as a sign that worship was needed for the shakti energy to be conducted in Denmark. First, Lalitha Sripalan was Parvati as a baby. She was helpless and could not do anything by herself. She was fed, helped to the toilet and dressed. Then she became Parvati as a young woman, later as an adult and in the end, as an old woman. In other words, she lived through Parvati's whole lifespan in three days. But she could not do that by herself. Lalitha Sripalan's husband and son and her devotees helped her through all her stages while they prayed. They were told by the shakti energy that they had to pray with all their heart if Lalitha Sripalan should come into being again and not depart with the old Parvati.

This event was also an important sign for Lalitha Sripalan, irrespective of whether she contributed to it. After this event, she was more aware of her abilities and her autobiography changed in character. New things were emphasized and her life and different life experiences were now looked upon as signs; signs which she did not consider as signs before New Year's Eve 1998. At the same time, the Danish New Year's Eve was not chosen by coincidence. It can be understood both as a cross-cultural day of importance and, of course, as a sign of a new beginning.

This event created a cultic awareness among the devotees and, following the event, Lalita Sripalan was only referred to as Amma. Every subsequent New Year, which is now called the *avatara* day, she becomes a new goddess. And the same three-day pattern is followed.

In the invention of *avatara* days the local tradition is given space both locally and globally; locally because it is only at this temple that the *avatara* days are celebrated, and globally because this local cult is becoming inscribed in a global Hindu context, as news about the goddess spreads internationally. This form of 'coming to being' both locally and globally clearly shows how inclusion and exclusion are used in a navigating strategy. The Danish New Year's Eve is included, while the intrinsic Hindu calendar is excluded.

The Sree Abirami Amman Temple

Until May 2007, the Sree Apirami Amman temple was a rebuilt farm located on Vejlevej 114 on the outskirts of Brande, a town in the middle of Jutland. It was completed and consecrated in 2000. Before that time worshippers used a temple located in the middle of Brande that was a rebuilt public house, bought through private means by Lalitha and her husband in 1996. However, due to problems in the neighbourhood, Lalitha and the local Tamil community agreed to move out of town. They were quoted in the local newspaper as saying that they 'never wanted to cause trouble'. They bought a farm approximately 3 kilometres from the town of Brande. The Sri Lankan Tamil Hindus even said that the new surroundings gave them more independence. And they also obtained the permission to build a 16-meter-tall temple tower (*gopuram*). The construction of the *gopuram* was finished in late 2011. It has been painted yellow so it is easy to recognize when approaching the temple. Upon seeing the temple, the mayor of Brande commented that 'a new tourist attraction is coming to town'. This demonstrates the change in attitude toward the temple after it relocated from the town centre.

From then on, Amma became even more aware of her role and never left the temple premises. The devotees treated her accordingly, helping her, for example, not to touch the polluted soil around the temple by laying out a carpet in front of her when she moved outside the temple.

The building of the new temple and its consecration in May 2007 was a particularly important turning point, which was crucial for the development of a collective memory. When the new temple was consecrated, Amma's new status was shown by her being depicted in the temple alongside the gods; this is what I call indexical symbolization because she was depicted with the same attributes as the well-known goddesses from Hindu mythology. A narrative around her being shakti was slowly emerging, and the pictures from the various *avatara* days were hung on the temple wall.

The Textualization of the Local Shakta Cult in Brande

The final element in the shaping of the collective memory – to live up to both the second-generation immigrants' understanding of religion being text based and to the Western understanding of religion – is the use and composition of texts used under *puja*.

This development began slowly in the beginning of 2000 (when the temple moved to the new premises) with the composition of worshipping texts to Lalitha Sripalan as representing Abirami and later, around 2007, by using internationally recognized texts found on the Internet. These are called Abirami Anthadi, which means 'prayer hymns for Abirami'. Lalitha Sripalan recites stanza 69 while healing:

Riches great, they will get,
Knowledge fine they will get,
A mind that never tires, they will get,
Godly beauty they will get,
Friends who do not deceive they will get,
And all this and more they will get,
From the incense filled flower haired Abirami's,
Slanting sight from her beautiful eyes.

The final stanza in Abirami Anthandi, No. 101, during which Abirami is worshipped as Mahadevi, is sung as a devotional song by the devotees:

Forever they suffer not in this life,
Who worship the mother of us all,
My mother Abirami,
Who created the universe,
Who has the colour of flowers of pomegranate,
Who protects the entire world,
Who has with her the pasangusa,
And the bow made of sugarcane,
And who has three eyes.

The latest development not only connects the local cult to a globally shared Hindu-shakta mythology, it also shapes a collective memory by becoming textualized and symbolized.

Conclusion

From a social constructivist viewpoint it can be stated that tradition is always negotiated and changing in relation to context and situation. Tradition is therefore always on the move and impossible to capture in one solid definition. This statement becomes even clearer when dealing with tradition in a diaspora situation, where the tradition is placed in a new setting. This is not only apparent for the researchers, but also for many of the bearers of the tradition who, by active means, have to adapt the tradition to its new environment while retaining focal points for themselves. By using a social constructivist point of departure, which gives priority to the processes involved in the negotiation of meaning of tradition as a social phenomenon, it becomes of interest how the tradition is used and is referred to in a self-understanding (Beckford 2003, 193–96). And, in the context of inclusion and exclusion in a diaspora situation, it is of interest to decipher which elements are strengthened and which are removed. In this way, we can encircle the elements that are understood as focal points for the members of a tradition, but in a way that constitutes a system of meaning that is relevant to its members in the new setting. Thereby, we can construct a chain of memory which connects the members to a shared tradition and place of belonging.

It is my conviction that diaspora studies not only throw light on how Hinduism has adapted to a new situation, but also show us which elements of the tradition are so central that they survive despite its location. I have therefore used Assmann's idea about collective memory, but I have inverted it to show how collective memory not only looks back, but can also be reinvented in such a way that it suits an entirely new purpose, namely, by preventing the tradition from disappearing. This demands a process of inclusion and exclusion where some elements are preserved and others are excluded; others are reinvented, but in such a way that the tradition continues to exist as a system of meaning for its members.

Notes

1 This is seen in a cultural evolutionist perspective where only the cultural or religious systems that give meaning to its members will survive. In other words, the system is nothing in itself, but only something in relation to the bearers or providers of the system.
2 This is what Amartya Sen (2000, 14) calls active exclusion (as opposed to passive exclusion).
3 Because Statistics Denmark, who register all newcomers to Denmark, do not take religious, but only geographic, affiliation into account, it is difficult to give an exact figure when it comes to religious grouping.
4 Around 67 per cent of all Tamils in Denmark are fully employed, which means that together with the Indians and the Vietnamese, they have the largest number of employees among all immigrant (and refugee) groups in Denmark. Also, the education level among the young Indians and Tamils is high compared to other groups.
5 I have chosen to use the Anglicized form and the internationally common transcription of Sanskrit, Hindi and Tamil without diacritical marks. In that way, I hope to avoid misunderstandings when it comes to pronunciation and translation.
6 Today they have three consecrated temples in Denmark. The latest, a Murugan temple, was consecrated in June 2010 in Middelfart, a small city around 75 km from Herning and Brande. That there are now three temples in Denmark located close to where most of the Sri Lankan Tamil Hindus live shows the importance attached by Sri Lankan Tamil Hindus to the presence of a temple and temple worship.
7 The right translation would have been Apirami, but because the temple itself uses Abirami on signs and on the Internet, I have chosen to follow their translation.

References

Assmann, Jan. 2006. *Religion and Cultural Memory.* Stanford: Stanford University Press.
Beckford, James A. 2003. *Social Theory and Religion.* Cambridge: Cambridge University Press.

Durkheim, Émile. 1995. *The Elementary Forms of Religious Life*. New York: The Free Press.

Fibiger, Marianne Qvortrup. 2011. 'Young Tamil Hindus in Denmark and Their Relationship to Tradition and Collective Memory'. *Finnish Journal of Ethnicity and Migration* (e-journal).

______. 2012 'When the Hindu-goddess Moves to Denmark: The Establishment of a Sakta-tradition'. *Bulletin for the Study of Religion* 41 (3).

Halbwachs, Maurice. 1952. *Les Cadres sociaux de la mémoire*. Paris: PUF.

Hervieu-Léger, Danièle. 2000. *Religion as a Chain of Memory*. Cambridge: Polity Press.

Jacobsen, Knut A., and P. Pratap Kumar. 2004. Introduction to *South Asians in the Diaspora: Histories and Religious Traditions*, edited by Knut A. Jacobsen and P. Pratap Kumar, ix–xxiv. Leiden: Brill.

Jacobsen, Knut A. 2004. 'Establishing Ritual Space in the Hindu Diaspora in Norway'. In *South Asians in the Diaspora: Histories and Religious Traditions*, edited by Knut A. Jacobsen and P. Pratap Kumar, 134–48. Leiden: Brill.

Jenkins, Richard. 2003. *Rethinking Ethnicity*. London: Sage.

Sen, Amartya. 2000. 'Social Exclusion: Concept, Application, and Scrutiny'. Social Development Papers No. 1, Office of Environment and Social Development Asian Development Bank. Manila: Asian Development Bank.

Tölölyan, L. 1991. 'The Nation State and Its Others: In Lieu of a Preface'. *Diaspora* 1 (1): 3–7.

Part II

COMMUNITIES AND POLITICS

Chapter 5

IN SEARCH OF DEVELOPMENT: MUSLIMS AND ELECTORAL POLITICS IN AN INDIAN STATE[1]

Kenneth Bo Nielsen

The Muslim minority in the Indian state of West Bengal, where they comprise approximately 25 per cent of the population, are in many respects excluded from both the developmental and political processes in the state. Muslims score significantly lower on a range of socioeconomic indicators compared to other sections of the state's population, and their representation in the political sphere is poor. However, the past five years have witnessed an increasing mobilization of Muslim groups and organizations seeking to address and overcome this 'development deficit'. As part of this mobilization search of development, these organizations have used the Muslim electorate's – whose vote determines the outcome in somewhere between 50 and 80 of the state's 294 constituencies (Choudhury 2010) – strength of numbers to promote issues of concern to Muslim voters. In doing so, they have succeeded in putting significant pressure on all major political parties in the state, who in recent years have found themselves engaged in an intense political competition that culminated with the ouster of the incumbent Left Front (LF) government at the 2011 state assembly elections. This situation of intense political competition is new to West Bengal. Here, the LF government, which ruled West Bengal from 1977 to 2011, has approached virtually all recent state elections as the odds-on favourite to win. But by 2011 the two major political formations in the state – the LF and an alliance of parties led by the Trinamul Congress (TMC) – were more evenly matched. This competitive context, where every vote in every constituency literally counted, created a space of opportunity for Muslim organizations to more strategically, vocally and unambiguously press their demands for development, and to engage in a process of political bargaining with the contending political parties in order to extract promises and resources in exchange for political support. As a consequence,, both the now ex-Chief Minister Buddhadeb Bhattacharya of the LF, and his principal adversary, TMC chief and current Chief Minister Mamata Banerjee, actively vied and competed for Muslim support during the prolonged campaign leading up to the 2011 elections. Perhaps the most significant outcome of this competition for Muslim support has been a gradual shift in political allegiance among Muslim voters in West Bengal, who have traditionally tended to support the LF, but who lately have increasingly gravitated towards the TMC. In this chapter, I first present a brief outline of why many Muslim voters have historically supported the LF in West Bengal, and why they increasingly came to feel alienated from it. The LF's general failure to include Muslims in the development agenda of the state forms an important part of the explanation, but in addition, a number of symbolically charged events, both in West Bengal and elsewhere in India, have recently transpired to more clearly bring out the everyday marginalization and exclusion of Muslims. These include the publication of the so-called Sachar Committee's (officially, the Prime Minister's High Level Committee) report surveying the state of Muslims in India; the LF's policy of forcefully expropriating agricultural land to make way for industrial sites and the alleged murder-and-cover-up case – with a clear communal tint – of a young Muslim named Rizwanur Rahman. Such symbolically potent events were important in making Muslim voters question the credentials of the LF and to search for political alternatives elsewhere.

Against this backdrop, I proceed to examine how some Muslim organizations and groups increasingly began to demand that the state introduce special measures to overcome the 'development deficit' experienced by Muslims. Highest on the list of special measures was the introduction of reservations and quotas for Muslims in, for example, education and government employment. Tellingly, the LF almost immediately took note of this grievance and – as the coalition then in power – set to work on implementing quotas for Muslims, while also introducing a slew of development initiatives aimed at improving the living standards of Muslim families. The TMC, because it did not hold power in West Bengal prior to 2011, was in no position to offer reservations, although it wholeheartedly endorsed the idea of introducing special quotas for Muslims. Instead, the TMC used its strength in the national parliament, the Lok Sabha, and Mamata Banerjee's control of the Railway Ministry – she served as railway minister from 2009 until she resigned to become chief minister of West Bengal in 2011 – as platforms from which to display its commitment to addressing issues and grievances of concern to Muslim voters. These displays of dedication have included a range of development and infrastructure projects undertaken by the Indian Railways, as well as a host of oftentimes symbolic campaigns and initiatives aimed at portraying the TMC as a credible political alternative in the eyes of Muslim voters. I demonstrate how, and in spite of the LF's introduction of reservations for Muslims, Mamata Banerjee and her TMC have generally managed to increase its stock of Muslim support by both outperforming and outbidding the LF in a game of political one-upmanship. A string of electoral reverses, setbacks and defeats for the LF from 2008 up to the 2011 state assembly elections testify to this. While some may lament this decline of the Indian parliamentary Left and the concomitant consolidation of competitive populism or patronage democracy (Chandra 2003) in West Bengal, I argue that this phenomenon should be understood as the outcome of successful and strategic operations in what Partha Chatterjee (2004) calls 'political society' by a marginalized Muslim electorate in search of development. Central to the theory of political society is the observation that social groups as 'populations' can engage in strategic and contentious bargaining for government welfare and development, inter alia, by manipulating its electoral strength. A fiercely competitive political context, such as has existed in West Bengal over the past five years, is eminently conducive to this kind of popular mobilization among marginalized groups in political society. I return to this point in the conclusion.

The Muslim Electorate and the Left Front

The LF coalition that ruled West Bengal between 1977 and 2011 consists of a number of Left parties. By far the largest constituent is the Communist Party of India (Marxist) (CPM), while the three largest 'junior partners' are the Revolutionary Socialist Party, the Forward Bloc and the Communist Party of India.

It was first and foremost the rural vote that brought the LF to power in 1977. In the decade preceding the 1977 elections, the Left parties, and the CPM in particular, had devoted considerable political time and effort to mobilize and politicize rural constituencies (Ruud 2003). Generally, their target constituencies were marginal rural communities such as sharecroppers and the landless, which included a large proportion of formerly untouchable castes and Muslims. From 1977 onward, the majority of the rural vote generally remained loyal to the Left parties. This included the Muslim vote as well. Muslim voters in West Bengal had, ever since India became independent in 1947, sought to take part in mainstream politics in the state by aligning themselves with the dominant secular national political party, the Congress. At the 1952 elections a large number of Bengali Muslims supported the Congress, and this 'mainstreaming' around a secular party made it almost impossible for more communal parties like the Muslim League to establish any kind of base in West Bengal. Tellingly, when at the 1957 elections the leaders of various Muslim organizations formed a front to contest against the Congress, they had very little success. But from 1977 Muslim voters began rallying around the secular alternative offered by the LF, whose political victories in 1977 and again in 1982, and its various development programmes undertaken for minorities, made it an attractive alternative. Thus, in 1982 the LF won most of the areas with a high concentration of Muslim voters (Dasgupta 2009, 94–5). There were, of course, some significant local exceptions to this pattern, for instance, in the Muslim dominated districts of Murshidabad and Malda, where particular local histories and power configurations continue to guarantee a power base for the Congress. But outside these pockets of non-Left influence Muslim voters have supported the Left parties at the ballot so consistently that according to analyst Irfan Engineer, Muslims in West Bengal 'always voted for the Left Front', even to the extent of bringing about the defeat of Muslim candidates fielded by the non-LF parties (Engineer 1995, 200). Apparently, at election time, loyalty to the LF oftentimes easily overrode communal loyalties.

Irfan Engineer's comment on the political loyalties of the Muslim electorate is indicative of a consensus among Indian political observers that the LF, throughout its extensive spell in power, was consistently able to count on overwhelming Muslim support. The reasons for this support are complex, but among the important factors is the fact that the LF parties generally had both pro-poor and secular credentials. Because of its consistent emphasis on secular politics and its principled opposition to the wave of

Hindu nationalist, chauvinist and anti-Muslim politics that affected large parts of India from the 1980s onwards (cf. Jaffrelot 1999), many Muslims have seen the LF as the political coalition most likely to keep West Bengal free from overt communalism. In addition, the LF's ambitious and progressive rural reform programmes undertaken during the late 1970s and early 1980s significantly improved the living conditions of the West Bengal's poor and marginal communities. By distributing land to the landless and by securing and making hereditary the rights of sharecroppers to tenure and to a fixed share of the harvest, the living conditions of hitherto marginal groups improved considerably. This included Muslim peasant households, who were among the poorest in rural West Bengal. In addition, by decentralizing political power down to the grassroots level by establishing a functioning three-tier system of local governance, the *panchayat* system, the LF provided the poor with a political voice. These marginal groups accordingly tended to cast their ballot in support of the LF.[2]

As recently as during the run-up to the 2006 state assembly elections, media pundits and political commentators argued that West Bengal's poor and marginal groups would once again demonstrate their political loyalty to the LF by securing them yet another electoral triumph. Thus, two prominent analysts of Indian politics who predicted an easy win for the LF, Yogendra Yadav and Sanjay Kumar, based their argument on the observation that since coming into being in West Bengal, the CPM had successfully crafted a social base for itself among marginal farmers, sharecroppers and the landless poor. This class base had been carefully stitched together to form a coalition of socially marginalized groups that included Dalits (formerly untouchable castes), Adivasis (indigenous groups) and Muslims. This social coalition had stood by the LF through all the political change of the last three decades, and that it would do so once again could be taken as read (Yadav and Kumar 2006). Yadav and Kumar's analysis proved correct. The LF not only won its seventh consecutive state assembly elections; it was returned to power with a record majority.[3]

Marginalized Muslims: The Sachar Committee Report and Beyond

In light of this consistent political and electoral support extended to the LF by Muslim voters, the findings of the Sachar Committee, established by the prime minister of India in 2005 to look into the condition of Muslims in India, surprised many.[4] The committee's report, published in November 2006, demonstrated that at the all-India level, Muslims scored significantly lower than their Hindu counterparts on most indicators. Significantly, the Muslim community as a whole cut a particularly sorry figure in key development indicators such as literacy, education, employment and consumption (Alam 2010, 47). The real surprise, however, was that many of these findings also applied to West Bengal, and the report thus demonstrated that while the LF might have secured Muslims a safe existence free from overt communalism, the community had to a great extent been excluded from the development processes of the state.[5] The report presented clear evidence that on most indicators West Bengal's Muslim minority scored significantly lower than other sections of the state's population. A large number of Muslim concentration villages lacked postal and telegraph services, and the report identified a clear inverse association (in small villages) between the proportion of Muslim population and the availability of educational infrastructure. It also found that the proportion of Muslim concentration villages with medical facilities was lower than the proportion of all villages with such facilities. There was, in other words, a distinct bias in public service provisioning in Muslim concentration areas in the fields of education, physical infrastructure and health facilities. In addition, in comparison with other Indian states, the condition of Muslims in West Bengal was found to be particularly bad in some fields. For instance, the mean years of schooling of Muslims was lowest in states like West Bengal (Robinson 2007, 840–42),[6] and the most glaring cases of Muslim deprivation in government jobs were found in the Left-ruled states of West Bengal and Kerala: In West Bengal, only 4.2 per cent of government staff were Muslims as against their population share of 25 per cent.

While the findings of the Sachar Committee did certainly not point out something hitherto completely unknown – at least not to scholars or political activists working on the subject – the publication of the report marked the first time that the facts about the development deficit among Indian Muslims were presented with such comprehensive data. In the words of the noted scholar-cum-activist Ashgar Ali Engineer, it 'articulated for the first time what the common masses of Indian Muslims had always wanted to say about themselves' (in Jodhka 2007, 2996). Significantly, in analysing the issue of Muslim exclusion the report foregrounded the question of citizenship and relegated issues of identity or cultural distinctiveness, and treated 'the Muslim question' as a question of social justice, human rights and the development of the marginalized and excluded (Jodhka 2007, 2998–9). It also gave a new impetus to the not entirely new demands for reservations for Muslims, especially in educational institutions and public employment (Alam 2010).

While the Sachar Committee's report thus gave Muslim voters good reasons to be critical of the LF, several events transpired in West Bengal in the immediate wake of the publication of the said report, which further alienated the Muslim electorate from the LF. In the state's East Midnapur district, the local Haldia Development Authority revealed its plans to expropriate approximately 14,500 acres of mainly agricultural land in Nandigram block. The land would be used to set up a chemical hub and special economic zone (SEZ). The expropriation constituted part of the LF's new policy of acquiring agricultural land for industrial purposes – by force if necessary – that had already been met with considerable local resistance elsewhere in the state (cf. Nielsen 2010).

Nandigram is a Muslim dominated habitation comprised mostly of small and marginal farmers, many of whom stood to loose their land as a result of the land acquisition. The proclamation of the land acquisition plan almost immediately led to a popular uprising against the LF, as many of the affected villagers came together in a movement led by the Bhumi Ucched Protirodh Committee (BUPC), the Committee to Resist Eviction from the Land. The BUPC was formed by local leaders of the TMC along with other organizations, including the Jamiat Ulama-e Hind (JUH), one of the leading Islamic organizations in India. The villagers and BUPC activists drove out both the police and many LF supporters from the villages and took over the administration of the area. They dug trenches and destroyed all roads, paths and bridges to the villages to prevent the administration from going ahead with the land acquisition. The stand-off between villagers and the administration lasted for some two months, after which the LF decided to break the BUPC resistance at Nandigram. A massive operation involving thousands of policemen was launched on 14 March 2007. According to press reports, a group of armed and trained CPM cadres wore police uniforms and joined the police. However, as prior information of the impending action had leaked out, the BUPC had amassed a crowd of several thousand villagers at the entry points into Nandigram, with women and children forming the front lines. In the resulting mayhem at least 14 people were killed and hundreds injured according to the official version. According to locals, at least 50 people were killed, with the rest of the dead bodies being thrown into the Haldi River, some with the head cut off to avoid identification. Of the people who died, a significant number consisted of women and teenagers, mostly Muslims and Dalits (Samaddar 2009, 171–2). Reports of rape of local Muslim women were many, and at a local relief camp established by the Medical Service Centre, more than a thousand patients with serious injuries sought treatment (Sarkar and Sarkar 2008, 45–8).

People across the state responded to the police and cadre atrocities with shock and anger. Among Muslim commentators, Sabir Ghaffar of the Muslim Students Federation wrote that the Muslims in West Bengal had been made the victims of a covert war waged against them by the administration. M. Burhanuddin Qasmi, the editor of the English monthly *Eastern Crescent* said that:

> In order to give effect to his envisioned industrial resurgence of the state Budhadev Bhattacharya has once again purposely chosen and picked up mostly Muslim lands for setting up industries which will displace this minority population from their ancestral land and livelihood. (Qasmi 2007)

And Maulana Siddiqullah Chowdhury, BUPC leader and the president of the West Bengal unit of the JUH added that 'what is happening in Nandigram is a reflection of the real character and outlook of Leftists and their insensitivity towards the poor in general and Muslims in particular' (Qasmi 2007). Perhaps most importantly, a BUPC leader in Nandigram pointed to the deeper psychological impact of the violence let loose on Muslims in Nandigram:

> The only good thing with regard to Muslims is that in the last 30 years of Left rule in West Bengal, they were safe. What happened in Nandigram now puts a question mark on that, too. (Cited in Sivaraman 2009)

Nandigram was not the only place in West Bengal where the LF's land acquisition policy affected Muslim landowners in particular. The district of South 24 Parganas, which has a large agriculture-dependent Muslim population, also witnessed anti-LF mobilization as fears over losing land to Nandigram-like projects spread. For instance, a planned expressway of more than 100 km was set to cut through large tracts of land, several thousand acres in all, owned by Muslim farmers. The reaction in Muslim-dominated areas was one of anger and protest (Choudhury 2010).

Alongside the land acquisition controversies, the alleged murder of a young Muslim man named Rizwanur Rahman became a matter of public concern. Rizwanur had met and secretly married Priyanka Todi, the daughter of an extremely wealthy Hindu businessman. Initially, the marriage was kept secret, but when Priyanka's father learned of the marriage, he was displeased with the fact that his daughter had entered into an intercommunal marriage with a Muslim from a low-income family. Mr Todi allegedly used his influence with top-level police officers, who ostensibly summoned the couple several times and threatened Rizwanur with dire consequences if he did not separate from his wife. On 21 September 2007 Rizwanur was found dead beside a railway track; but even before the post-mortem results had been released, the police commissioner, a high-caste Hindu, created a controversy by stating that it was only natural that the Rizwanur–Priyanka marriage should face opposition, since relationships in which financial and social status did not match were not desirable (Dasgupta 2007). He also said that Rizwanur's death was a simple case of suicide. The covert communal tone of the police commissioner's comment, the police's repeated interference in an intercommunal marriage and the coercion of the Muslim Rizwanur by Hindu police officers were all indicative of a growing communalization or 'Hinduization' of the West Bengal Police. And on the streets of Kolkata, the possibility that Rizwanur had been murdered at the behest of the influential Todi family – and that the police was now complicit in covering up the murder – was both widely discussed and believed. Popular demands that the police commissioner be sacked soon emerged, but were not acted upon by the administration. Evidently, the LF, given its many decades in power in West Bengal, was held responsible for the lacklustre quality of the state's police force; and from the point of view of the LF, matters went from bad to worse when it became known that the chief minister had personally, approximately a year earlier, given his unconditional support and backing to the police commissioner when he had (unsuccessfully) stood as a candidate for the post of chairman of the Cricket Association of Bengal (cf. Mazumdar 2006). The chief minister eventually had the police commissioner removed, but only after a delay of almost four weeks. The administration's poor handling of the Rizwanur case inflicted significant political damage on the LF and, according to senior LF leaders, further alienated Muslim voters (Das 2007).

The series of events described above had, by the time elections for the three-tier *panchayats* were approaching in 2008, created a situation where Muslim support could no longer be taken for granted by the LF. And the LF's fear of declining voter support proved well founded: the LF 'only' won control of 13 of the 17 district level *zilla parishads*, approximately 57 per cent of the block level *panchayat samitis*, and about half of the village-level *gram panchayats* in the state. While such a result would by most standards be interpreted as a comfortable victory, it in fact marked a significant decline in political support for the LF, and made it the worst ever election for the LF in the history of the *panchayat* system in West Bengal.[7] The slump in the LF's share of the votes for the *zilla parishad* showed a striking similarity with the proposed industrialization map of the LF: the LF suffered its worst setbacks in precisely those areas where it had resorted to forcible land acquisition. And in these areas, there had been significant erosion in the Muslim support base of the LF as well (Chattopadhyay 2008).

The LF parties went on to perform even worse at the 2009 Lok Sabha elections, when more voters deserted the LF and flocked to the TMC. The LF won less than half of the seats it had won in 2004, while the TMC upped its tally from a single MP in 2004 to 19 this time. In the run-up to the elections, the TMC had worked particularly hard to improve its image among Muslim voters. It had abandoned the political alliance it had had for several years with the Hindu nationalist Bharatiya Janata Party (BJP) in favour of the more secular Congress, and party supremo Mamata Banerjee had managed to enlist the support of Rizwanur's brother Rukbanur, who campaigned alongside her in the state capital Kolkata. On the campaign trail Rukbanur proclaimed that the firm faith his family and the Muslim community in general had once had in the LF was now gone for good (Banerjee 2009). Evidently, Rukbanur's comment struck a chord among many urban Muslim voters. A Muslim community leader in Kolkata summed up the mood of the Muslim electorate in his locality thus:

> In my college days I knew communists were the people with the best political ideology and were the most trusted saviours of weak or minority communities. Banking on key Muslim votes they have been staying in power for more than three decades. But they have done so little for us – we feel cheated [...] Muslims are not going to trust them [the CPM] that easily and [...] the communists will discover this bitter truth. (Cited in Rahman 2009)

Outside the state capital, in many of the rural localities where Muslims had struggled to oppose the LF's land acquisition policy, they had been aided by local TMC activists, who oftentimes spearheaded the protests. Such tactical moves on the part of the TMC worked to the extent that according to one newspaper report, Muslim voters who had gradually turned their backs on the LF at the 2008 *panchayat* elections now began deserting the Left in droves (*Telegraph* 2010a). Another commentator added that 'the core reason for Mamata Banerjee's success lies in the shift of the Muslim vote from the Left toward her persona' (Akbar 2010), while the *Statesman* (2010) concluded that 'Muslims, who once used to be the party's [CPM] most dependable vote bank has turned away'. According to one estimate, only 37 per cent of the Muslim electorate voted for the LF in 2009 (Basu 2011).

Towards the 2011 State Elections: Seeking Development through Quotas

With the Lok Sabha elections thus concluded, all eyes immediately turned towards the 2011 state assembly elections, which for a time promised to be a closely fought contest. Even minor changes in voter preferences appeared likely to influence the outcome, and with Muslim voters determining the result in perhaps as much as one-fourth of all constituencies, both the LF and the TMC started paying considerable attention to the demands emanating from the Muslim electorate. Muslim organizations and interest groups, in turn, skillfully stepped up their demand for both political inclusion and increased participation in the development of the state; and highest on their list was the demand for reservations in government employment and educational institutions akin to those the Indian state offers to other so-called backward communities. This includes the formerly untouchable castes known as Scheduled Castes (SC), the indigenous Adivasis population known as Scheduled Tribes (ST) and the so-called Other Backward Classes (OBC), a large and heterogeneous category of castes and classes deemed educationally, economically or socially backward.

The idea of special quotas for Muslims in government jobs and education was recommended by the Ranganath Mishra Commission. Constituted in 2004, the Mishra Commission was entrusted with a mandate to suggest criteria for identification of socially and economically backward sections among religious and linguistic minorities; to recommend measures for enhancing the welfare of the said groups, including reservation in education and government employment and to suggest the necessary constitutional, legal and administrative modalities required for the implementation of the commission's recommendations (Ministry of Minority Affairs 2007, 1). The commission submitted its report in 2007 and it was tabled two years later, in December 2009. In its reports, the commission argued, inter alia, that since minorities, and Muslims especially, were very underrepresented in government employment, they should be regarded as backward in this respect. Accordingly, the commission recommended a 15 per cent reservation in jobs and employment for minorities, with 10 per cent earmarked for Muslims (Rajalakshmi 2011, 89). This recommendation, however, proved to be controversial because it seemingly ran counter to the letter and spirit of the Indian Constitution, several articles in which enunciate the principle of nondiscrimination on the basis of religion. This constitutional principle is difficult to reconcile with recommendations for reservations to particular religious minorities. Yet, in West Bengal the commission's recommendations elicited an overwhelmingly favourable response from most quarters. The state's own Minorities Commission backed the idea of introducing reservations – according to its chairman, the time had by 2010 come to adopt 'emergency measures' in the form of reservations to ensure that the exclusion of Muslims in the state did not accelerate any further (Bilal 2010). Many Muslim organizations similarly and loudly demanded reservations, and frequently cited both the Sachar and Mishra reports during their political campaigns. This included the JUH, which, at a large conference in Kolkata in January 2010, demanded reservations for Muslims to solve their educational and social backwardness. JUH's general secretary Siddiqullah Chowdhury said that

> 10% reservation will not be enough to solve the West Bengal Muslim problems. Therefore, we demand 20% reservation because currently only 2.5% Muslims are in government job while they comprise 30% of the total population of the state. We gave ultimatum to the government to take the decision on the matter on earliest because we can not wait any more. We have fed up of promises since last 30 years now government has to step in practically.[8] (Cited in Bilal 2010)

He added that all leading Muslim organizations and groups, including Jam'at Islami Hind, Indian Muslim League, All India Milli Council and Republican Party of India, were with the JUH in this struggle, and that the JUH would hold vehicle rallies to visit all Muslim dominated areas in the state to 'create awareness among the community'. Such efforts would continue until the demand for reservations was fulfilled. The JUH was not the only Muslim organization organizing such public events. Less than two weeks after the JUH conference was held, the Popular Front of India (PFI) started its National Campaign for Muslim Reservation from Kolkata, demanding at least 20 per cent reservation for Muslims in West Bengal. The main event of the PFI rally was to send on its way a caravan, which would move through Muslim dominated districts like South 24 Parganas, North 24 Parganas, Nadia, Birbhum, Malda and end in Murshidabad (Popular Front India 2010).

The LF responded immediately and very favourably to the demand for quotas. It unanimously welcomed the Mishra Commission's recommendations, and one of its minor constituents, the Forward Bloc, urged the chief minister to set an 'example' by introducing Muslim reservations in the state. The LF Chairman indicated that the LF would ensure reservations for Muslims by including many more Muslim castes in the state's list of OBC (*Telegraph* 2010a). West Bengal's OBC list had been prepared in 1994 on the basis of occupations with which social and economic backwardness was associated. In 2003 only eight out of 60 castes in the list were Muslim, and by early 2010 this number had increased only marginally to 12 (Bhabani 2010). But now the LF chairman suggested that the number could be raised from 12 to 37 'or above' (*Telegraph* 2010a), while the chief minister went even further by proposing that the number of Muslim communities on the OBC list be raised to 40 (Bilal 2010). In concrete terms, the LF intended to work out a solution that would set aside 10 per cent of government jobs for socially, economically and educationally backward Muslims. These reservations would be implemented 'at the earliest', the chief minister said (Choudhury 2010). He also indicated that a committee comprising representatives of the Minorities Department, the Backward Class Welfare (BCW) Department, the Minorities Commission, and the BCW Commission would be formed to implement the government's plan (Ummid 2010).

The Muslim response to the LF's offer of 10 per cent reservation was mixed. While some adopted a wait-and-see attitude, others were unequivocal in their dismissal and asked for more. An editor of a Kolkata-based Urdu daily labelled the LF's offer an electoral gimmick, while the *imam* of Kolkata's Nakhoda Mosque, Maulana Md. Shafique, said that

> We are not satisfied with the announcement. We demanded 20 per cent reservation for Muslims in West Bengal and it is possible […] [And] if the government offers reservation facility to the Muslims only in government jobs, it will not benefit the community as a whole. They should first ensure quality education for backward Muslims […] If Muslims are deprived of quality education, how can they apply for government jobs? (Cited in Bhabani 2010)

When no progress had been made in terms of implementation two months after the LF had first signalled its good intentions to work for reservations for Muslims, various Muslim groups renewed their agitation. The West Bengal chapter of the Students Islamic

Organisation of India (SIO) launched a statewide 10-day campaign on the issue. The SIO president said that

> We demand the implementation of Ranganath Mishra Commission report at the national level. In West Bengal, where Muslims are more than 25% we want 20% reservation to the economically backward sections of the Muslims [*sic*] community cutting across castes. (Cited in Falahi 2010)

JUH President Siddiqullah Chowdhury similarly reiterated his stand that 20 per cent reservation in jobs and educational institutions should be granted to Muslims, and added that the 20 per cent quota should be extended to also include the posts of elected representatives in both the state assemblies and the Lok Sabha (*Indian Express* 2010). His demand was accompanied by a stern warning. Speaking at a conference on 'Why are reservations necessary for Muslims in West Bengal?' he warned that the trouble the LF was facing with controlling insurgent Maoist groups in parts of West Bengal would pale in comparison with what was in store if the LF failed to extend reservations to Muslims:

> In West Bengal only a few Maoists thrashed the administration in certain areas of Midnapur District. They are continuing the agitation for development of those areas. Muslims in West Bengal are nearby 30% and more than 2.5 *crore*.[9] If, like Maoists, they start agitation, the State Government cannot stop them [...] the ruling Left Front government should declare reservations for Muslims in West Bengal, otherwise Muslims will throw them out of power.[10] (Cited in Haque 2010a)

The demand for special quotas for Muslims was thus widely supported and bargained for with a unanimous voice by a host of Muslim organizations.[11] In response, the chief minister, at a political rally held in May 2010, reaffirmed his commitment to implementing reservations in government jobs for Muslims:

> One *crore* Muslims will get reservation by June. Muslims will be entitled to 10 per cent reservation in government jobs [...] My logic is simple, if the Scheduled Castes and Tribes enjoy this right, why should the Muslims be deprived of it? (Cited in NDTV 2010)

While the LF thus enthusiastically endorsed the idea of introducing quotas for Muslims, it had to find ways to bypass the legal hurdles created by the fact that the Indian Constitution does not allow for the implementation of quotas on the basis of religious identity. Thus, rather than introducing a potentially unconstitutional 10 per cent 'Muslim quota', the LF, in September 2010, chose to include an additional 41 Muslim communities in the OBC category, bringing the total number of Muslim communities in the OBC list to 53. It then subdivided the OBC category further into a 'backward' and a 'more backward' section, and placed 49 of the Muslim communities in the 'more backward' section, thus making the 'more backward' section predominantly Muslim. Lastly, they announced that while the 'backward' communities would henceforth be entitled to 7 per cent reservation, the 'more backward' communities would be entitled to 10 per cent reservation. According to a senior official in the state BCW department, the 53 Muslim communities now included in the OBC category covered more than 86 per cent of the Muslim population in the state (Sifynews 2010). Months later, the LF expanded the scope of reservations by reserving 17 per cent of all seats in government and government-aided colleges for OBC students (*Hindu* 2010) and introduced a similar 17 per cent reservation for OBC candidates in the three-tier *panchayat* system (Dutta 2010). Muslims stood to benefit tremendously from both policies.

Further Policy Initiatives by the LF

In addition, the chief minister emphasized the need for addressing the 'housing problems' of the Muslims. Few Muslims reside in the new, large townships coming up in the state and to address this lack of access, the chief minister suggested establishing separate housing colonies for Muslims (*Hindu* 2011b). The LF also increased the total allocation for the West Bengal Minorities Development and Financial Corporation (WBMDFC) dramatically. In 1998 the WBMDFC had been allocated Rs. 7 *crore*; in 2010 it received Rs. 425 *crore*, with the maximum increase coming since 2007. As one journalist noted laconically, this increase in government spending on minority issues seemed to be inversely proportional to the decrease in the LF's vote share (Sengupta 2010b). And lastly, the LF's list of candidates for the 2011 state elections included 57 Muslims, up from 44 in previous elections. Yet even these generous policy initiatives would turn out to be insufficient to win back the support of Muslim voters. Some Muslim organizations and groups flatly dismissed the LF's promises as too little, too late, or as last minute electoral gimmicks designed to lure back Muslim voters (*Times of India* 2010c; All India Muslim Majlis-e-Mushawarat 2011). And yet, other Muslim organizations explicitly came out in support of Mamata Banerjee. The following example, based on a report in the *Times of India* (Gupta and Banerjee 2010), is indicative of the persistent dissatisfaction with the LF, and concomitant support for the TMC, prevalent among certain Muslim organizations and clerics during the run-up to the 2011 state elections.

Rallying behind Mamata at Furfura Sharif

In April 2010 Muslim clerics and community leaders received Mamata Banerjee at Furfura Sharif, one of the most important Muslim pilgrimage sites in West Bengal. Throughout the meeting, the clerics criticized the LF regime and pledged their support for Mamata Banerjee. The political meeting-cum-rally marked the laying of the foundation stone of a 20 km railway link between Dankuni and Furfura Sharif. The 75-year-old Peer Abdul Para Siddiqui of the Furfura Darbar Sharif recalled that he had heard talk of such a railway connection ever since his childhood; but only now, during Mamata Banerjee's tenure as railway minister, was it set to finally materialize. She, accordingly, was the guest of honour.

In front of a crowd of several thousand people Maulana Noor-ur-Rehman Barkati, the *imam* of the Tipu Sultan mosque in Kolkata, said

> The 'Reds' have destroyed Bengal. The *janata* [people] is with Mamata and it is high time we made her the Chief Minister. She is the undisputed queen of Bengal and only she can save the state from complete ruin.

Peerjada Toha Siddiqui, the director of the Furfura Darbar Sharif, then went on to vividly describe how the Muslim community had been mistreated by the LF for so many years:

> When it came to putting up flags and banners, you needed us. When you wanted bombs made and hurled, you needed us. When it came to brandishing pistols and shooting people, our help was required. When you needed to fill up the Shahid Minar or Brigade Parade Ground [popular sites for political rallies in Kolkata], you wooed us. Later, you sat on high pedestals and enjoyed while we suffered. It is time we 'kick' you down. For 33 years, you have played football with us. Now it is time for us to play football [...] I can only assure Mamata that of the 30 million Muslims in the state, at least 25 million are on her side. Just because we are not directly involved in politics does not mean that we do not understand politics. We have had enough of *dekchhi, hochchhe, hobey* [lit. 'I see, it is happening, it shall be done.' Implies empty or false promises]. We don't want any more of that. Jyoti Basu [LF chief minister of West Bengal from 1977 to 2000] had finished us off and Buddhadeb Bhattacharjee followed in his footsteps. Don't use us any longer!

Toha Siddiqui then asked Mamata Banerjee to provide jobs for Muslims: 'Even menial ones will do,' he added. Mamata Banerjee promptly promised to develop Furfura Sharif into 'what it deserves to be', and hinted that she would provide railway connectivity 'to many locations'. She added that she hoped that no one would hamper the development projects she intended to introduce, and also pledged to name the station at Furfura Sharif after Maulana Md. Abu Bakr Siddiqui, the social and religious reformer who founded the Order of Furfura Sharif and whose tomb is located within the Furfura Sharif itself.

The speeches delivered at Furfura Sharif bring out the kind of support Mamata Banerjee received from Muslim organizations and clerics during the run-up to the 2011 state elections. Elsewhere in the state, top clerics similarly criticized the LF and urged Muslims to vote for the TMC. Some even announced that they would pray for Mamata's victory (News One 2011). The meeting at Furfura Sharif also demonstrates how the articulation of Muslim interests generally centred on 'secular' issues like jobs, infrastructure and development. At Furfura Sharif and elsewhere (e.g. Gupta 2010), Mamata Banerjee endorsed and promised to deliver on such demands and followed up on such promises. Thus, in January 2011 she again met with Toha Siddiqui, this time at her Kolkata residence where the two discussed the progress of the railway line. Toha Siddiqui said to the press that the Muslims now regarded Mamata as their friend, adding that 'in the past 34 years we have been left further and further behind. If this continues for another five years we will be in further trouble' (*Times of India* 2011a). Mamata Banerjee returned to Furfura Sharif in February to assure locals that she wanted the Muslim community to progress and prosper, while also warning them that the reservations offered by the LF were nothing but a hoax and 'one of the several lies' the LF spoke daily (*Hindu* 2011a).

Yet, it is also clear that issues like dignity and respect figured prominently in, for example, Toha Siddiqui's speech. In her campaign to promote herself as a credible political choice for Muslim voters, Mamata Banerjee accordingly – in addition to promising to usher in development – took care to project herself as a dedicated, caring and respectful leader, mindful of the concerns and values of the Muslim community. In doing so, she did not refrain from invoking religious sensibilities and symbolism. The final section examines the TMC's response to Muslim mobilization, and looks more closely at some of the strategies deployed by Mamata Banerjee to attract Muslim voters.

TMC's Campaign to Attract Muslim Voters: Development and Dignity

In addition to supporting the demand for Muslim quotas in education and employment, Mamata Banerjee lobbied for Muslim quotas in other spheres as well. Thus, when in March 2010 the central government put to vote in the Upper House of Parliament, the Rajya Sabha, a new Women's Bill that would extend 33 per cent reservations to women in all state assemblies and the two houses of Parliament,[12] she met with leaders of the JUH and the All India Muslim Personal Law Board prior to the vote. She promised that she would do her best to put pressure on the central government to carve out a special quota-within-the-quota for Muslim women. Yet, because Mamata Banerjee was herself a part of the central government, she could not be seen to vote against her own government's bill. Instead, she engineered the departure of her party's two Rajya Sabha MPs, who left parliament shortly before the vote on the bill took place (Kasturi 2010). Mamata explained that while she was all for the Women's Bill in principle, she did not feel that it, in its present form, properly addressed the concerns of backward Muslims (Chatterjee 2010). She reiterated this stand when the Women's Bill, after being passed by the Rajya Sabha, was to be placed in the Lok Sabha.

More generally, Mamata Banerjee used the platform provided by the Lok Sabha to express her dedication to West Bengal's Muslim voters. In August 2010 she demanded in the Lok Sabha that the government provide more advertisement to Urdu newspapers, and open an Urdu university and Urdu academies everywhere in the country. She also demanded a comprehensive plan for the development of the language and increased reservations for Muslims. While doing so, she quoted several lines of Urdu poetry – as she had likewise done when presenting the railway budget – adding that 'Urdu is such a sweet language. I love it like anything' (in Joshi 2010) and 'I love *shayari* [Urdu poetry]; it's so powerful' (in Yadav 2010). Weeks later, TMC MPs followed up by seeking the implementation of a 17-year-old Supreme Court order asking the government to give salaries to *imams* of government-aided mosques. According to TMC MP Sudip Bandyopadhyay, the proposal was spawned by the fact that *imams* in *West Bengal* were facing an economic crisis (*Hindustan Times* 2010, emphasis added). Later, the MP also demanded that *imams* across India be provided with salaries at government scales, while the TMC's Minority Cell Chairman added that the party would launch a campaign on the issue of higher salaries for both *imams* and *muezzins* (Indiareport 2011).

In addition, Mamata used her tenure as railway minister from 2009 to 2011, and the resources this placed at her disposal, to cater to the West Bengal electorate in general, and to Muslim aspirations in particular. Within a seven-month period in the latter part of 2010 she inaugurated or laid foundation stones for no less than 120 railway projects in her home state (Jha 2010). She ensured that notices were posted in Urdu (alongside English and Hindi) on the notice boards in the Railway Ministry; allowed candidates to take rail recruitment tests in Urdu; waived the Railway Recruitment Board examination fee for applicants with a minority background; extended students' travel concessions to *madrasas*, higher *madrasas* and senior *madrasas* and increased the frequency of trains to areas in West Bengal with high Muslim concentration (*Telegraph* 2010c). Her ministry also produced two railway advertisements, carried in 15 Bengali newspapers on the eve of Eid, with pictures of Mamata wearing a *hijab*, her eyes closed in devotion and her two palms joined together open and spread out in a gesture of offering *namaz*. The background contained Islamic motifs like the crescent moon, a star and the outlines of a mosque. The advertisements promoted railway projects inaugurated in West Bengal under slogans such as 'Joy comes alive on Eid – A real development indeed' and 'Nursing College in Garden Reach – Railway's Gift on Eid'. Thus, railway projects executed by the ministry were projected and portrayed as Mamata Banerjee's more or less personal gift to West Bengal's Muslims.

The Muslim population of Kolkata also received special attention during the run-up to the municipal elections in 2010. During her campaign, Mamata, while speaking in Muslim-dominated areas, warned Muslim voters that the CPM was a communal, that is, anti-Muslim, party. She claimed to have secret information that the LF, assisted by a section of the police, would foment communal trouble and unleash violence after the polls. Graffiti with similar messages also appeared in such areas (*Times of India* 2010a). The extent to which such rhetoric was in any way significant in producing a TMC victory at the Kolkata municipal elections is questionable; but the TMC did score a spectacular win. And the Muslim vote was certainly instrumental, as it continued to shift away from the LF towards the TMC (Chattopadhyay 2010, 31). While TMC won in 95 of Kolkata's 141 wards, it won in 14 of the 18 Muslim-dominated wards in the city, while of the 28 wards with a 'substantial' Muslim presence, it won 22 (*Statesman* 2010). After the election many Urdu newspapers celebrated TMC's win. The Kolkata-based *Akhbar-e-Mashriq* devoted the entire front page and several inside pages to hailing Mamata Banerjee's victory and, in a show of support for her, ran the headline '*Ghuroor Gharat*' ('The End of Arrogance') accompanied by a caption of joyous TMC supporters. Many papers also published Urdu couplets hailing her victory.

To indicate that she was sincere with regard to addressing issues of importance to Muslims, Mamata Banerjee ostensibly contemplated making a Muslim the mayor of Kolkata, a city which had not had a Muslim mayor since independence. Already prior to the election, the name of Javed Khan, the leader of the opposition in the outgoing Kolkata Municipal Corporation (KMC), was aired by TMC leaders as a potential candidate (*Telegraph* 2010b). A senior TMC leader said that selecting Khan would be a good choice as it would send the right message to voters:

> A minority leader for the post of Mayor is a great idea. It will project a good image of our party to the over 26 per cent minority voters in the state. The minority vote is crucial for us in the Assembly polls next year. (*Expressindia* 2010)

When 'shadow mayor' Javed Khan surprisingly failed to win reelection, other Muslim candidates like Bobby Hakim and Javed Khan's wife Rafat emerged as potential mayoral candidates (Roy 2010). Eventually Sovan Chatterjee – an upper-caste Hindu – was appointed mayor, but Farzana Alam was made deputy mayor, Manzur Iqbal the leader of the TMC municipal party, Bobby Hakim one of three deputy leaders (*Times of India* 2010b) and Rizwanur Rahman's mother Kishwar Jahan was appointed to the new and influential 'advisory committee' established to oversee the KMC's functioning (*Thaindian News* 2010). Mamata Banerjee had first met Kishwar Jahan after her son's death and had since then met her often. Some eight months before the municipal elections, she had visited the house of Kishwar Jahan during Eid, and from there she had proceeded to visit several other Muslim-dominated areas of Kolkata (Sodhan 2009). When Eid came around in 2010, she vowed to place her supporters on the streets of Kolkata to prevent a CPM-backed union, which had planned a complete strike and shutdown in the city, from disrupting this important Muslim holiday.

Lastly, as the 2011 elections approached, the TMC sealed an alliance with JUH Working Committee Member Maulana Badruddin Ajmal (also an MP of the All India United Democratic Front of Assam) to strengthen its pro-Muslim credentials (Paul 2010). And when the TMC-led alliance released its list of candidates, it contained 63 Muslim candidates, six more than the LF. The TMC's strategy worked. Not only did it secure a solid electoral victory by winning, together with its alliance partners, 227 seats against the LF's 62, it also won in 90 of the state's 125 constituencies that have sizeable Muslim populations. And the new state assembly will have 59 Muslim MLAs (up from 46), corresponding to about 20 per cent of the assembly.

Conclusion: Political Society and the Search for Development

The Muslim search for a stake in the development trajectory of West Bengal described here has seemingly yielded rich dividends. The assertiveness and rising political voice of Muslims groups and organizations managed to put the concerns and desires of the Muslim electorate high on the political agenda among all major political parties in West Bengal in the years leading up to the recently concluded 2011 state assembly election. While collective political action by Muslim groups is of course not a recent phenomenon in the Indian context, the current emergence of a strong Muslim voice is the outcome of complex social and political processes that are characterized by a series of engagements with the state. In this regard, the reports of first the Sachar Committee, and later of the Mishra Commission, constitute important events. Both reports analysed and made sense of the Muslim question in the language of development and participation.

They thereby facilitated the transformation of Muslims from a community with particular religio-cultural characteristics and boundaries, into a 'population' that could be identified, described and analysed using the language of the modern state. This language of classification in turn also made Muslims available to a range of engagements by various (state) agencies and development interventions (Jodhka 2007, 2998). The idea that governmental classifications, technologies and performance create populations as empirical categories that define the targets of policy is integral to Partha Chatterjee's oft-cited theory of political society. In his *The Politics of the Governed* (2004), and in a series of related articles, Chatterjee has suggested that once conjured into being by the activities of governmental functioning, population groups may come together to act politically in and on the uncertain terrain of political society, understood as a sphere of contentious popular political action distinct from 'bourgeois' civil society proper (cf. Chatterjee 2001, 172). This creates a field of continuous negotiation between population groups and government authorities, and the better organized the population group, the better it can play the game of strategic political negotiations (Chatterjee 2004, 138). Hence, the success of claims made in political society depends almost entirely on the ability of a population group to mobilize sufficient support to influence the implementation of governmental policy in its favour. Importantly, successful mobilizations in political society are often premised on the strategic manipulation of *relative electoral strength* (Chatterjee 2004, 61, emphasis added). Actions in political society are thus directed towards government welfare and development and are embedded in the dynamics of electoral democracy.[13]

The Muslim groups and organizations, whose voices have been presented here, have effectively negotiated the terrain of political society as they have bargained strategically with not only the then incumbent LF government, but also with the state government-in-spe, that is, the TMC. In doing so, they have sought to appear, in both discourse and practice, precisely as a population: they have pressed their demands for development not as particular organizations or groups, but in the name of the entire Muslim population of West Bengal. Concomitantly, they have also projected Muslims as a population that tends to vote *en bloc*. Undoubtedly, this manipulation of *relative* electoral importance was facilitated by the intense competition for political support between West Bengal's two leading coalitions, the LF and the TMC-led opposition. It is noteworthy that other 'populations' likewise made good use of this highly competitive political context. The Matua Mahasabha – an organization of the formerly untouchable Matua caste with more than ten million followers in West Bengal – headed by its spiritual leader Binapani Devi, cleverly offered to make Mamata Banerjee the chief patron of the All India Matua Mahasabha in 2010. Mamata Banerjee accepted and went on to promise a new railway station for Binapani Devi's village, along with a stadium and a railway hospital. She also nominated Binapani Devi's son as a candidate for the 2011 state elections.[14] Not to be outdone, the LF offered the Matuas land on which to build a research organization, and instituted a scholarship in the name of the Matua Mahasabha's founder (Jacob 2011). And in what may well have been a unique event during the campaign leading up to the 2011 elections, the Matua Mahasabha managed to bring together on one stage political leaders from the TMC, the LF, the Congress and the Hindu nationalist BJP. Attending Matua voters could then judge for themselves *in situ* which party made the most credible and attractive offers. Similarly, the Kurmis – an OBC community numerous in certain parts of West Bengal – and their organization, the Yuba Chhatra Kurmi Sangram Committee (YCKSC), raised the demand that *all* parties planning to contest in areas where the Kurmis were dominant (42 constituencies in all, according to the YCKSC) should nominate candidates from the Kurmi community (*Times of India* 2011b). Evidently, when political competition increases, so does the importance of each vote, which in turn makes it possible for organized groups in political society to bargain hard for promises of patronage and access to development programmes and quotas. Importantly, such strategic operations in political society involve, I believe, a *critical* assessment on the part of marginalized groups of the different candidates' capacity for and willingness to introduce the desired development policies. By *critical* I mean that political support is not simply for sale to the highest bidder. Mamata Banerjee has, for instance, previously and without much success tried to attract Muslim voters through extravagant promises not unlike those she made during the run-up to the 2011 elections. Thus, when campaigning for the 2001 state assembly elections, she – at a National Convention for Upliftment of the Muslims – promised 50 per cent reservations in jobs for Muslims in the Calcutta Municipal Corporation, whose name she also decreed should henceforth be written in Urdu (alongside Bengali and English). She also promised to give Urdu second-language status in areas where Muslims constituted 10 per cent or more of the population, and she threatened to pull out of the BJP-led central government, of which the TMC was then part, the minute the BJP threatened to harm Muslim interests (Ashfaque 2000a; 2000b). Yet such promises did not then cut much ice among Muslim voters, who – given her alliance with the Hindu nationalists – doubted her sincerity and dedication. Evidently, the strategic manoeuvring by groups in political society is highly sensitive to the larger context in which politics is played out. This time, however, Mamata Banerjee in a more focused manner designed policies aimed at proving her dedication to including Muslims in the development trajectory of West Bengal. She also parted ways with the communal BJP and instead, forged an alliance with other secular partners like the congress. And to further strengthen her pro-Muslim credentials she adopted a series of symbolic expressions intended to signal sincerity and respect, such as quoting Urdu poetry, wearing a *hijab*, and offering *namaz*. This suggests that while the search for development forms the cornerstone of the politics of the Muslim organizations analysed here, their mobilization also centred on issues of dignity and respect, which is perhaps why, for instance, the state and cadre violence perpetrated on Muslims in Nandigram could acquire such symbolic importance among some Muslim voters. Muslim voters in West Bengal also demonstrated their critical and strategic approach to politics by generally *not* voting for the candidates of the minor United Social Democratic Front (USDF), a coalition of small parties that included several explicitly pro-Muslim parties along with a party led by the JUH's Siddiqullah Chowdhury. Knowing full well that the USDF would be an insignificant player after the election, the TMC seemed the wiser choice to most.

With the 2011 elections only just concluded, it is too early to say whether the Muslim mobilization in search of development will continue to yield results in the future as well. Yet, Muslim voters and organizations have already been increasingly drawn into the ambit of political society, from where their aspirations and desires have been forcefully articulated. It is likely that they will continue to navigate political society and thereby leave their mark on the future development trajectory of West Bengal.

Notes

1 Earlier versions were presented at the workshop on 'Social In- and Exclusion in Contemporary India and Beyond' at Aarhus University, Denmark, in June 2010; at the workshop on 'Practices and Experiences of Democracy in Post-Colonial Localities' at the '2nd International Conference on Democracy as Idea and Practice' in Oslo, Norway, in January 2011; and at the international seminar on 'Social Exclusion: Meanings and Perspectives' at the University of Hyderabad, India, in March 2011. I thank the participants for their comments. A version of this chapter was published in 2011 in *Forum for Development Studies* 38 (3) and is reprinted here with permission. I am particularly grateful to G. Krishna Reddy, Radhika Chopra, Arild Engelsen Ruud, Pamela Price, Staffan Lindberg and *Forum for Development Studies*' two anonymous reviewers for their constructive criticism. A special thanks also to Abhijit Dasgupta, Uwe Skoda and Stig Toft Madsen for their careful reading of the preliminary draft.

2 There are, however, competing explanations for why rural poor and marginal communities have supported the LF. See Bhattacharyya (2009).

3 In 2006 the LF also benefited from the fact that the TMC, the leading opposition party at the time, was in disarray and was considered by many to be on the decline as a political force in West Bengal (Nielsen 2011, 174).

4 For a brief overview of the key features of the Sachar Committee's report, see Basant (2007).

5 The marginalization of Muslims in Bengal did not originate with the coming to power of the LF. As far back as 1871 W. W. Hunter (2002, 138–206) wrote of how colonial rule increasingly adversely affected the Muslim community. The question of reservations for certain sections of Muslims was also raised from time to time during colonial rule (Dasgupta 2009, 92). What the Sachar Committee Report did was rather to underline the failure of the LF to address these historically produced inequalities.

6 Contrary to a widely held negative stereotype, most Muslims do not reject the value of education per se. According to Zakir Husain (2005) both literacy and education are in demand among Muslims in West Bengal. However, Muslim boys in particular tend to lose interest in education because they perceive a bias against them in the labour market. And similarly, the belief that their children will not get jobs leads Muslim parents to devalue the importance of education (Borooah 2010, 33). In terms of primary completion rates the difference between Muslims and other communities appears to not have diminished in the wake of the publication of the Sachar Committee report. If anything, it has continued to widen (Husain and Chatterjee 2009).

7 For instance, the LF's total tally of *gram panchayats* decreased in all 17 districts. A comparison with the previous *panchayat* elections also brings out the decline in support for the LF. In 2003 the LF had won in 15 of 17 *zilla parishads* and had gained a majority in 85 per cent of the *panchayat samitis* and 72 per cent of the *gram panchayats*.

8 Syntax in the original.

9 One *crore* is 10 million.

10 Syntax in the original.

11 Other organizations that have similarly demanded reservations are, inter alia, Naya Zamana West Bengal, Muslim Youth Federation, TMC's Minority Cell, All India Minority Forum, and the Indian National League (Haque 2010b).

12 Existing legislation already provides for 33 per cent reservation for women in the three-tier *panchayat* system as well as in urban municipal bodies.

13 Arild Engelsen Ruud (2011) similarly reports from neighbouring Bangladesh how rural voters see the delivery of development and welfare as perhaps the key function of democracy.

14 Successfully – Devi's son won.

References

Akbar, M. J. 2010. 'Muslim Factor in Mamata Banerjee's Victory'. *Arab News*, 6 June. Online: http://arabnews.com/opinion/columns/article62028.ece (accessed 25 October 2011).

Alam, Mohd Sanjeer. 2010. 'Social Exclusion of Muslims in India and Deficient Debates About Affirmative Action: Suggestions for a New Approach'. *South Asia Research* 30 (1): 43–65.

All India Muslim Majlis-e-Mushawarat. 2011. Resolutions for special meeting of MMM, New Delhi, 15 January. Online: http://www.mushawarat.com/news.asp?id=545 (accessed 25 October 2011).

Ashfaque, Mohammad. 2000a. 'National Convention for the Upliftment of the Muslims'. *Milli Gazette*, 1 December. Online: http://www.milligazette.com/Archives/1–12–2000/Art7.htm (accessed 25 October 2011).

______. 2000b. 'Wooing Time'. *Islamic Voice* 14 (168). Online: http://www. islamicvoice.com/december.2000/politics.htm (accessed 25 October 2011).

Banerjee, Aloke. 2009. 'CPM Can't Take Muslim Vote Bank for Granted'. *India Today*, 19 April. Online: http://indiatoday.intoday.in/site/Story/37618/Elections:%20East/CPM+can%E2%80%99t+take+Muslim+vote+bank+for+granted.html (accessed 25 October 2011).

Basant, Rakesh. 2007. 'Social, Economic and Educational Conditions of Indian Muslims'. *Economic and Political Weekly* 42 (10): 828–32.

Basu, Joyeeta. 2011. 'Bengal Diary: Buddholand Awaits Mamatadi'. *Sunday Guardian*, 29 March. Online: http://www.sunday-guardian.com/analysis/bengal-diary-buddholand-awaits-Mamatadi (accessed 25 October 2011).

Bhabani, Soudhriti. 2010. 'West Bengal Muslims Divided Over Job Reservation'. *Thaindian News*, 11 February. Online: http://www.thaindian.com/newsportal/politics/west-bengal-muslimsdivided-over-job-reservation_100318405.html (accessed 25 October 2011).

Bhattacharyya, Dwaipayan. 2009. 'Of Control and Factions: The Changing "Party-Society" in Rural West Bengal'. *Economic and Political Weekly* 44 (9): 59–69.

Bilal, Manzar. 2010. 'India: Demand Grows for Reservation for West Bengal Muslims'. *The Muslim News*, 2 February. Online: http://www.muslimnews.co.uk/news/news.php?article=17499 (accessed 25 October 2011).

Borooah, Vani K. 2010. 'Social Exclusion and Jobs Reservation in India'. *Economic and Political Weekly* 45 (52): 31–5.

Chandra, Kanchan. 2003. *Why Ethnic Parties Succeed: Patronage and Ethnic Headcounts in India*. Cambridge: Cambridge University Press.

Chatterjee, Mohua. 2010. 'Didi Wants Sub-Quota for Muslims in Women's Bill'. *Times of India*, "6 April. Online: http://timesofindia.indiatimes.com/india/Didi-wants-sub-quota-for-Muslimsin-Womens-Bill/articleshow/5764942.cms (accessed 25 October 2011).

Chatterjee, Partha. 2001. 'On Civil and Political Society in Post-Colonial Democracies'. In *Civil Society: History and Possibilities*, edited by Sudipta Kaviraj and Sunil Khilnani, 165–78. Cambridge: Cambridge University Press.

______. 2004. *The Politics of the Governed: Reflections on Popular Politics in Most of the World*. Delhi: Permanent Black.

______. 2008. 'Democracy and Economic Transformation in India'. *Economic and Political Weekly* 43 (16): 53–62.

Chattopadhyay, Suhrid Sankar. 2008. 'People Are Trying to Give Us a Message'. *Frontline* 25 (12). Online: http://www.flonnet.com/fl2512/stories/20080620251203600.htm (accessed 25 October 2011).

______. 2010. 'Another Jolt'. *Frontline* 27 (13): 30–31.

Choudhury, Anirban. 2010. 'Muslims, Marxists and Mamata'. *Hindustan Times*, 15 February. Online: http://www.hindustantimes.com/rssfeed/kolkata/Muslims-Marxists-amp-Mamata/Article1-508914.aspx (accessed 25 October 2011).

Das, Sanchita. 2007. 'Bengal Seeks Housing Quotas for Muslims in Run-Up to Local Poll'. *Livemint.com*, 5 November. Online: http://www.livemint.com/2007/11/05004443/Bengal-seekshousing-quota-for.html (accessed 25 October 2011).

Dasgupta, Abhijit. 2009. 'On the Margins: Muslims in West Bengal'. *Economic and Political Weekly* 44 (16): 91–6.

Dasgupta, Rajashri. 2007. 'Hide Your Love Away'. *Times of India*, 4 October. Online: http://timesofindia.indiatimes.com/Opinion/Editorial/LEADER_ARTICLE_Hide_Your_Love_Away/articleshow/2426738.cms (accessed 25 October 2011).

Dutta, Ananya. 2010. 'West Bengal Raises Quota for OBC Muslims'. *Hindu*, 25 December. Online: http://www.hinduonnet.com/thehindu/thscrip/print.pl?file=2010122560740300.htm&date= 2010/12/25/&prd=th& (accessed 25 October 2011).

Engineer, Irfan. 1995. 'Politics of Muslim Vote Bank'. *Economic and Political Weekly* 30 (4): 197–200.

Expressindia. 2010. 'Winds of Change May Blow in a Mayor from Minority Community'. 1 June. Online: http://www.expressindia.com/latest-news/winds-of-change-may-blow-in-a-mayor-from minority-community/627619/ (accessed 25 October 2011).

Falahi, Mumtaz Alam. 2010. 'SIO Launches Muslim Reservation Campaign in West Bengal'. *TwoCircles.net*, 21 April, http://www.twocircles.net/2010apr21/sio_launches_muslim_reservation_campaign_west_bengal.html (accessed 25 October 2011).

Gupta, Jayanta. 2010. 'Crowd Swings to Didi Development Pitch'. *Times of India*, 31 October. Online: http://timesofindia.indiatimes.com/city/kolkata-/Crowd-swings-to-Didi-development-pitch/articleshow/6844206.cms (accessed 25 October 2011).

Gupta, Jayanta, and Falguni Banerjee. 2010. 'Muslim Clerics Vow Support to Mamata'. *Times of India*, 14 April. Online: http://timesofindia.indiatimes.com/city/kolkata-/Muslim-clerics-vowsupport-to-Mamata/articleshow/5799190.cms (accessed 25 October 2011).

Haque, Zaidul. 2010a. 'WB Muslims Likely to Form New Group for Reservation'. *Radiance Weekly*, 11 April. Online: http://www.radianceweekly.com/198/5175/STRIP-AWAYIMMUNITY-TO-POLICE–in-Gujarat-like-Situations/2010–04–11/Report/Story-Detail/WB-Muslims-Likely-to-Form-New-Group-for-Reservation.html (accessed 25 October 2011).

______. 2010b. 'West Bengal: 834 Lower Division Clerks Recruited, Only 16 Muslims'. *TwoCircles.net*, 21 April. Online: http://www.twocircles.net/2010apr21/west_bengal_834_lower_division_clerks_recruited_only_16_muslims.html (accessed 25 October 2011).

Hindu. 2010. '17 % Quota for OBC Students in West Bengal'. 24 December. Online: http://www.thehindu.com/news/national/article972589.ece (accessed 25 October 2011).

______. 2011a. 'Reservation for Muslims by Left Front Govt. a Hoax: Mamata'. 4 February. Online: www.hindu.com/2011/02/04/stories/2011020459520300.htm (accessed 25 October 2011).

______. 2011b. 'Housing Needs of Muslims Must Be Addressed: Buddhadeb'. 28 February. Online: http://www.hindu.com/2011/02/28/stories/2011022851960200.htm (accessed 25 October 2011).

Hindustan Times. 2010. 'Polls Put Imam Salary in Focus'. 22 August. Online: http://www.hindustantimes.com/News-Feed/newdelhi/Polls-put-imam-salary-in-focus/Article1–590068.aspx (accessed 25 October 2011).

Hunter, W. W. 2002. *The Indian Musalmans*. New Delhi: Rupa & Co.

Husain, Zakir. 2005. 'Analysing Demand for Primary Education: Muslim Slum Dwellers of Kolkata'. *Economic and Political Weekly* 40 (2): 137–47.

Husain, Zakir, and Amrita Chatterjee. 2009. 'Primary Completion Rates across Socio-Religious Communities in West Bengal'. *Economic and Political Weekly* 44 (15): 59–67.

Indian Express. 2010. 'Muslim Group Asks Trinamool to Clarify Stand'. 11 March. Online: http://www.indianexpress.com/news/muslim-group-asks-trinamool-to-clarify-stand/589458/ (accessed 25 October 2011).

Indiareport. 2011. 'Bengal Failed to Utilise Central Funds for Muslims: TC'. 30 January. Online: http://www.indiareport.com/India-usa-uk-news/latest-news/987668/National/1/20/1 (accessed 25 October 2011).

Jacob, Shine. 2011. 'Political Parties Woo Matua Community'. *Business Standard*, 28 April. Online: http://www.business-standard.com/india/news/political-parties-woo-matua-community/433761/ (accessed 25 October 2011).

Jaffrelot, Christophe. 1999. *The Hindu Nationalist Movement and Indian Politics, 1925 to the 1990s*. New Delhi: Penguin.

Jha, Srinand. 2010. 'Promises at Dead-End'. *Hindustan Times*, 6 December. Online: http://www.hindustantimes.com/StoryPage/Print/635187.aspx (accessed 25 October 2011).

Jodhka, Surinder S. 2007. 'Perceptions and Receptions: Sachar Committee and the Secular Left'. *Economic and Political Weekly* 42 (29): 2996–9.

Joshi, Poornima. 2010. 'Mamata "Hosts" Urdu Soiree in Lok Sabha'. *India Today*, 6 August. Online: http://indiatoday.intoday.in/site/Story/107984/mamata-hosts-urdu-soiree-in-lok-sabha.html (accessed 25 October 2011).

Kasturi, Charu Sudan. 2010. 'Mamata Boycott with Eye on Minorities'. *Telegraph*, 9 March. Online: http://www.telegraphindia.com/1100310/jsp/frontpage/story_12199379.jsp (accessed 25 October 2011).

Mazumdar, Jaideep. 2006. 'Voodoo Cricket'. *Outlook*, 14 August Online: http://www.outlookindia.com/article.aspx?232176 (accessed 25 October 2011).

Ministry of Minority Affairs. 2007. *Report of the National Commission for Religious and Linguistic Minorities*. Online: http://minorityaffairs.gov.in/newsite/ncrlm/ncrlm.asp (accessed 25 October 2011).

NDTV. 2010. 'Buddhadeb's Civic Polls Gameplan'. 24 May. Online: http://www.ndtv.com/news/india/buddhadebs-civic-polls-gameplan-27378.php (accessed 25 October 2011).

News One. 2011. 'Top Muslim Clerics Bat for Mamata'. 4 April. Online: http://www.inewsone.com/2011/04/04/top-muslim-clerics-bat-for-mamata/40941 (accessed 25 October 2011).

Nielsen, Kenneth Bo. 2010. 'Contesting India's Development? Industrialisation, Land Acquisition and Protest in West Bengal'. *Forum for Development Studies* 37 (2): 145–70.

______. 2011. 'Congress Factionalism Revisited: West Bengal'. In *Trysts with Democracy: Political Practice in South Asia*, edited by Stig Toft Madsen, Kenneth Bo Nielsen, and Uwe Skoda, 157–92. London: Anthem Press.

Paul, Cithara. 2010. 'Massage for Minorities'. *Telegraph*, 5 December. Online: http://www.telegraphindia.com/1101205/jsp/frontpage/story_13261119.jsp (accessed 25 October 2011).

Popular Front India. 2010. 'Popularfront Campaign for Muslim Reservation Reaches West Bengal'. 11 February. Online: http://popularfrontindia.com/pp/story/popularfront-campaignmuslim-reservation-reaches-west-bengal (accessed 25 October 2011).

Prokerala News. 2010. 'West Bengal Doubles Funds for Muslims, Madrasas Education'. 22 March. Online: http://www.prokerala.com/news/articles/a123166.html (accessed 25 October 2011).

Qasmi, M. B. 2007. Nandigram Turmoil, 'Boiling the Nation'. *Asian Tribune*, 27 November. Online: http://www.asiantribune.com/index.php?q=node/8414 (accessed 25 October 2011).

Rahman, Shaikh Azizur. 2009. India's Left Front Pays the Price of "Arrogance". *The National*, 23 May. Online: http://www.thenational.ae/article/20090524/FOREIGN/705239801/1103/NEWS (accessed 25 October 2011).

Rajalakshmi, T. K. 2011. 'Left in the Cold'. *Frontline* 28 (1): 88–90.

Robinson, Rowena. 2007. 'Indian Muslims: The Varied Dimensions of Marginality'. *Economic and Political Weekly* 42 (10): 839–43.

Roy, Anirban. 2010. 'TMC Mum on Kolkata Mayor'. *India Today*, 4 June. Online: http://indiatoday.intoday.in/site/Story/100141/India/Mamata+mum+on+Kolkata+mayor.html (accessed 25 October 2011).

Ruud, Arild Engelsen. 2003. *Poetics of Village Politics: The Making of West Bengal's Rural Communism*. New Delhi: Oxford University Press.

Ruud, Arild Engelsen. 2011. 'Democracy in Bangladesh: A Village View'. In *Trysts with Democracy: Political Practice in South Asia*, edited by Stig Toft Madsen, Kenneth Bo Nielsen and Uwe Skoda, 45–70. London: Anthem Press.

Samaddar, Ranabir. 2009. 'Prescribed, Tolerated and Forbidden Forms of Claim Making'. In *State of Justice in India, Volume 1: Social Justice and Enlightenment: West Bengal*, edited by Pradip Kumar Bose and Samir Kumar Das, 153–79. New Delhi: Sage.

Sarkar, Sumit, and Tanika Sarkar. 2008. 'A Place Called Nandigram'. In *Nandigram and Beyond*, edited by Gautam Ray, 19–53. Kolkata: Gangchil.

Sengupta, Swati. 2010a. 'Bengal Tops in Minority Scholarships'. *Times of India*, 12 September. Online: http://timesofindia.indiatimes.com/india/Bengal-tops-in-minority-scholarships/articleshow/6538782.cms (accessed 25 October 2011).

_______. 2010b. 'Higher Education Allowance for Muslim Girls'. *Times of India*, 25 October. Online: http://timesofindia.indiatimes.com/city/kolkata-/Higher-education-allowance-for-Muslim-girls/articleshow/6806108.cms (accessed 25 October 2011).

Sifynews. 2010. 'West Bengal Increases OBC Quota for Muslims'. 24 September. Online: http://sify.com/news/west-bengal-increases-obc-quota-for-muslims-news-national-kjywubhgcec.html (accessed 25 October 2011).

Sivaraman, Satya. 2009. 'Nothing's Right for Left'. *Hardnews*, April. Online: http://www.hardnewsmedia.com/2009/03/2781 (accessed 25 October 2011).

Sodhan, Kavita. 2009. 'Mamata Visits Rizwanur's Family on Eid'. *Mynews*, 21 September. Online: http://www.mynews.in/News/Mamata_visits_Rizwanur's_family_on_Eid__N26314.html (accessed 25 October 2011).

Statesman. 2010. 'Why Muslims No Longer Support the Left'. 13 June. Online: http://www.thestatesman.net/index.php?option=com_content&view=article&show=archive&id=330973&catid=39&year=2010&month=6&day=13&Itemid=66 (accessed 25 October 2011).

_______. 2011. 10 'English-Medium Government Madrasas to Come Up Next Year'. 21 February. Online: http://www.thestatesman.net/index.php?option=com_content&view=article&id=359922&catid=73 (accessed 25 October 2011).

Telegraph. 2010a. 'Muslim Quota Support with You-First Cry'. 1 February. Online: http://www.telegraphindia.com/1100202/jsp/nation/story_12053645.jsp (accessed 25 October 2011).

_______. 2010b. 'Mayor Mystery: Take Your Pick'. 4 May. Online: http://www.telegraphindia.com/1100504/jsp/bengal/story_12409540.jsp# (accessed 25 October 2011).

_______. 2010c. 'Trinamul to Assess Impact of Rahul Tour'. 18 September. Online: http://www.telegraphindia.com/1100918/jsp/nation/story_12951810.jsp (accessed 25 October 2011).

Thaindian News. 2010. 'Sovan Chatterjee to Be New Kolkata Mayor'. 6 June. Online: http://www.thaindian.com/newsportal/politics/sovan-chatterjee-to-be-new-kolkata-mayor-lead_100376068.html (accessed 25 October 2011).

Times of India. 2010a. 'Mamata Deliberately Stoking Panic Among Muslims, CPM Tells Chidambaram'. 20 May. Online: http://timesofindia.indiatimes.com/india/Mamata-deliberatelystoking-panic-among-Muslims-CPM-tells-Chidambaram/articleshow/5955071.cms (accessed 25 October 2011).

_______. 2010b. 'Sovan Mayor, but Advisers Hold the Key'. 7 June. Online: http://timesofindia.indiatimes.com/city/kolkata-/Sovan-mayor-but-advisers-hold-the-key/articleshow/6018413.cms (accessed 25 October 2011).

_______. 2010c. 'Mixed Response to State's New Quota Move'. 25 September. Online: http://timesofindia.indiatimes.com/city/kolkata-/Mixed-response-to-states-new-quota-move/articleshow/6623137.cms (accessed 25 October 2011).

_______. 2010d. 'West Bengal: Govt to Initiate More Welfare Measures for Muslims: Buddhadeb'. 2 November. Online: http://timesofindia.indiatimes.com/india/West-Bengal-govt-toinitiate-more-welfare-measures-for-Muslims-Buddhadeb/articleshow/6860728.cms (accessed 25 October 2011).

_______. 2011a. 'Didi Seeks Help of Pirzada of Furfura Sharief for Rly Line'. 18 January. Online: http://timesofindia.indiatimes.com/city/kolkata-/Didi-seeks-help-of-Pirzada-of-Furfura-Sharief-for-rly-line/articleshow/7307897.cms (accessed 25 October 2011).

_______. 2011b. 'Identity Politics to Play a Vital Role During Polls'. 9 March. Online: http://timesofindia.indiatimes.com/city/kolkata-/Identity-politics-to-play-a-vital-role-duringpolls/articleshow/7659868.cms (accessed 25 October 2011).

Ummid. 2010. 'WB Minorities Department Clueless About Muslim Reservation'. 17 February. Online: http://www.ummid.com/news/2010/February/17.02.2010/wb_minority_dptm_clueless_about_muslim_quota.htm (accessed 25 October 2011).

Yadav, J. P. 2010. 'Mamata Sprints for Urdu'. *Telegraph*, 6 August. Online: http://www.telegraphindia.com/1100806/jsp/nation/story_12778787.jsp (accessed 25 October 2011).

Yadav, Yogendra, and Sanjay Kumar. 2006. 'Why the Left Will Win West Bengal Again'. *Hindu*, 16 April. Online: http://www.hinduonnet.com/2006/04/16/stories/2006041609221200.htm (accessed 25 October 2011).

Chapter 6

EXCLUSION AS COMMON DENOMINATOR: INVESTIGATING 'DALIT-HOOD'[1]

Guro W. Samuelsen

Through the mechanisms of competitive electoral politics, caste is being continuously reinvented in contemporary India. The 'deepening' of democracy has come with a fragmentation of politics, producing new political bodies representing newly politicized groups that express new demands in a new language (Yadav 1999). This development has shattered modernist expectations that democracy, industrialization and economic liberalization would lead to a shift from 'traditional' primordial identities to people seeing themselves as citizens whose rights and duties should be negotiated individually, primarily through the ballot. Rather, formulations of rights claims in India have happened increasingly along caste and community lines.

In this chapter, this process of politicization is seen through the idea of 'Dalit-hood'. The activists who figure here are part of an emerging politics of difference, seeking to redefine collectively the status of the group to which they belong. This politics of difference is based on the assumption that 'social exclusion' makes Dalits a unified group. The material I present here is based on six months of fieldwork among Dalit activists in North India in 2009. During this time I spent three months as an intern with the Dalit Cooperation Committee (DCC),[2] a Delhi-based umbrella organization engaging in advocacy, legal aid, mobilizational activities and awareness raising. Divided into four branches focusing on different problem areas, my internship was with the Women's Wing of the DCC. In this urban, middle-class context, the chapter analyses activists' claims to Dalit-hood.

The activists in the DCC consider themselves to be 'Dalit', a term referring to those who were previously called 'Untouchable'.[3] The activists are either born into *jātis* (castes) that are categorized as Scheduled Caste (SC), or they are Christians considered to have converted from so-called 'Untouchable' *jātis*. They are from different parts of India and come from a variety of socioeconomic backgrounds, but are connected through an organizational network. In the words of Eleanor Zelliot (2005, 267), 'dalit implies those who have been broken, ground down by those above them in a deliberate and active way', and the word itself contains 'an inherent denial of pollution, *karma*, and justified caste hierarchy'.[4] Designating both a condition of oppression – historical and contemporary – and resistance to this oppression based on a contestation of its rationale, the term Dalit has political implications. This chapter seeks to engage critically with Dalit-hood through investigating how it is understood by the DCC activists, and how it is applied by them to others. What does it entail, in this context, to 'be Dalit'? How does an ascribed and highly stigmatized identity become a resource for political assertion? And how does this identity politics shape activist efforts to increase social inclusion?

Today, Dalit is both an identity ascribed by birth and an identity acquired through becoming 'aware' (Hardtmann 2009, 50). It is a self-description which has been 'chosen by the group itself and [is] used proudly' (Zelliot 2005, 267), but it is also a label which is applied by scholars and activists to people who have never used it themselves. Hence 'Dalit' is a top-down designation which tends to 'suggest that the huge Untouchable population of India has been swept up into a single radical politics' (Mendelsohn and Vicziany 1998, 4), something which is surely not the case. The actual degree of identification with the term among 'ordinary' SCs is largely unknown. In an interesting commentary, Alan Marriott (2003) notes how SC respondents to the National Family Health Survey in 1998–99 replied to a subordinate question about their caste: 'while harijan [...] was used by 1,351 respondents in 18 different states, and a number of respondents used scheduled caste, not one respondent chose dalit'. Still, in the present scholarly discourse, Dalit has substituted other terms when talking about these groups, as evident, for instance, in the establishment of centres of Dalit studies across India. I argue that the 'natural' existence of this group must be questioned through highlighting the processes through which it is construed. Stressing that Dalit is not a self-evident category, I wish to emphasize that within this politics, people are both claiming and being claimed. While fighting social exclusion, Dalit politics is both *exclusivist* – in the sense that participation hinges on caste membership – and *inclusivist* since all those who are born into the concerned castes are seen as part of this politics. This emphasis should enable sensitivity as to how this label is used in claims to represent, and 'speak for', others.

While the DCC activists are in opposition to what they see as a Brahmanical ideology, manifest in discriminatory notions and practices, their relation to the Dalits for whom they claim to speak is more ambivalent. Claiming to represent all Dalits on the basis of a shared notion of Dalit-hood, they employ various strategies to negotiate the social distance between their own educated, middle-class selves, and the poor and oppressed Dalit of their discourse. While such efforts are also about solidarity, social exclusion is reproduced in activist narratives, and I argue that this exclusion is, paradoxically, constitutive of their identities as activists. This is expressed through a dichotomy between the 'forward' and the 'backward' – a dichotomy which is strengthened by the confluence of notions of development and modernity with popular conceptions of caste.

Claiming subalternity involves telling stories of exclusion, discrimination and hardship. On the other hand, being an activist involves stories of bravery, strength, and opposition. Central to this investigation is the discrepancy between how activists subscribe to a unitary and inclusivist Dalit identity, and how they differentiate themselves from 'ordinary' Dalits. Here, authentic experiences of marginalization and exclusion become a necessity to legitimately represent others. This leads activists to insist on the particularity and exceptionality of the Dalit condition, lending certain static qualities to their efforts to bring about social change. While they explicitly seek to address, confront and overcome social exclusion, I argue that their strategy for inclusion is formed in response to a reified and stereotyped understanding of caste, producing contradictory outcomes.

Dalit-hood

The construction of Dalit-hood takes place through the reiteration of stories based on individual experiences that tend to refer back to historical practices that have come to symbolize Dalit-hood. Simon Charsley (1996) has shown how the notion of 'the Untouchables', first put to use by colonial government officials who were eager to create clear, pan-Indian categories for administrative purposes, generated a profusion of claims for higher status from castes usually considered 'low'.[5] The idea of the 'Untouchables' as a distinct social segment was then taken up by socioreligious and nationalist reformers (Charsley 1996, 5–6). One of these reformers was B. R. Ambedkar, who saw this label as having the potential to unite people of different castes and languages by emphasizing their common experience of being at the receiving end of both caste and class hierarchies. Consequently, he asserted that the 'Untouchables' were 'a separate element in the national life of India' and 'argued fiercely for the fundamental nature of an Untouchable–Hindu divide' (Charsley 1996, 9).

The 'Untouchables' as a clearly demarcated, pan-Indian group never existed independently of this historical politics of naming. In its contemporary usage, Charsley (1996, 19) has argued that the concept 'sets up a category defined as the bottom of a hierarchically ordered society but in practice traps and equates a variety of castes [that are] differently placed economically, socially, culturally and politically.' While caste-based exclusion is not irrelevant in contemporary India, 'it is a factor of empirically varying significance which has been attributed an a priori salience beyond all other considerations by the twentieth-century conceptual development of "the Untouchable"' (Charsley 1996, 19). Similarly, Lloyd and Susanne Rudolph (1967, 133–4) have noted that the legal and administrative term Scheduled Caste 'lends the category "untouchable" a spurious social definitiveness and homogeneity'. The same, I argue, can be said about the term 'Dalit'.

The notion of Dalit-hood springs from a historical understanding wherein certain 'low' caste groups are seen to form a separate element in Indian social, cultural, and economic life, as a result of their exclusion from these spheres of society. That Dalits have traditionally been, and still are, excluded from Hindu mainstream society is the activists' main allegation against 'non-Dalits'. In their understanding, this religiously legitimized exclusion is what has created the Dalits as an identifiable and socially separate group. Human history has produced what is rejected as a natural trait – they reject caste as an expression of natural, inborn traits, but recognize its existence as social reality. In this first part I will present how the notion of Dalit-hood is conveyed by the DCC activist. While the activists speak of their own experiences, their stories play into larger narratives of social exclusion and oppression. Rather than seeing 'untouchability' as a modern expression of inequality or a result of colonial politics (Dirks 2001), the activists see it as ancient practices, anchored in tradition and sanctioned by religion. Situating such practices squarely within the domain of 'the traditional', its abolishment also becomes closely associated with 'the modern'.

When Kamal, an activist in his twenties, was a school-going child in Delhi, he would go to his mother's village in the summer holidays. Following his aunt around the village while she worked, Kamal had inadvertently touched the hearth in a 'caste Hindu' courtyard. When the woman of the house saw this she came rushing out and slapped and abused him. This sudden outbreak of anger made no sense to Kamal – he could not understand what he had done to upset her. His aunt reluctantly explained that the woman had reacted this way because he belonged to a family of scavengers whose task it was to empty the dry latrines in the village. Returning to Delhi, Kamal urged his mother to give up scavenging and solemnly declared that he would 'never lay hands on the broom'. The experience made him intent to rid his family of the stigma derived from this practice.[6]

Kamal's choice of story to describe the beginning of his politicization is an example of how stigmatized practices have come to embody the Dalit condition. Cleaning work, manual scavenging and handling dead people and animals are considered tasks through which Dalits are reproduced, and reproduce themselves, as lesser beings. In particular, the image of scavengers collecting human excreta with their hands and carrying the waste in baskets on their heads is seen as proof of the inhuman condition of the Dalits and the cruelty of the Hindu social system.[7] Decades earlier, Gandhi had recognized the potency of this image and 'selected the Bhangi, a scavenger caste of North India, to represent the problem of untouchability' (Zelliot 2005, 154). The carrying out of such tasks is also seen as a reason why people of other castes regard Dalits as unfit to carry out more 'respectable' work. Consequently, the activists consider abolishing such occupations as central to their objective of Dalit liberation.

Telling me his story, Kamal stressed that he had been treated this way even though his clothes and appearance was 'better' than that of the village children. The violent reaction to a child touching a courtyard hearth was seen as *more* unfair and despicable since that child was clean, school-going, neatly dressed, and on a visit from the big city. Contesting the morality of a traditional hierarchy of purity and pollution, Kamal thus argued for progressive middle-class values of education, cleanliness, urbanity and 'good' appearance. Reminiscent of colonial and later attempts to reform the Dalit population in order to improve their lot, notions of reform and self-improvement are still central to the contemporary Dalit movement.

Seeing the caste system as originally a system of occupational categories, as was done by Gandhi (Zelliot 2005, 154), has been dismissed as an historical explanation for the institution of caste.[8] Some *jātis* were never 'traditionally' associated with any occupation; and among those who were, many never carried out these tasks, while others relied as much on other occupations for their livelihood. In short, the idea that *jātis* are primarily occupational groups has never been a sufficient description of realities. Moreover, transitions in the economy have rendered some traditional occupations obsolete and led to the creative reinvention and renewed appropriation of others (Mendelsohn and

Vicziany 1998, 7–8). For example, Lloyd and Susanne Rudolph (1967, 134) have reported how the traditional leather workers (Chamars) of Rajasthan were eager to dissociate themselves from their customary trade of leather working in 1956; but by 1963, 'because of generous government financial and technical support [...] Chamars were straining to exclude "opportunists" from invading their ancient monopoly'. In the contemporary era, new markets, new occupations and increased social mobility have further weakened whatever correspondence previously existed between *jāti* and occupation. Still, the stereotypical image of 'the Dalit' as one who carries out spectacularly denigrating tasks has come to epitomize the Dalit condition, shaping the way 'Dalit issues' are presented by activists.

The Struggle for Education

Describing what it had been like to grow up a Dalit, a narrative of struggle (*sanghars̩*) was pervasive among the activists. This was manifest in different contexts, but often pertained to the educational sphere. The activists are highly educated, ranging from those who have completed higher secondary education to PhD holders. While none had been kept out of school, poverty and lack of 'awareness' had detrimental effects on their educational progress. Several recounted a lack of family support, and some described their parents as 'backward'. The struggle lay in overcoming these obstacles to achieve the status they now hold as assertive activists and employees of an organization of international repute. In Pushpa's rendering, getting educated relied upon the efforts of her mother who had been one of the few literate women in her village and determined to educate her two daughters:

> Until 10th [grade] I studied in Mausa, and after 10th, when I turned fifteen years, I got married along with my older sister.[9] That happened because my family background was a little [...] One could say it was because of money. There was not a lot of money. The family didn't have any support. My father used to do sewing, he is a tailor. So my dad, when we were small – or until my marriage when I was fifteen – my father used to drink a lot. Whatever he earned he would spend it on drinking. So my mother got me educated. Our village was seven-eight kilometres away [from the school]. We went [there] by foot and came back by foot as well. Because there was a money problem we studied in a government school and didn't have to pay monthly fees. We couldn't study in a private [school] because there the money problem comes up.

After her marriage, Pushpa wanted to continue her studies and luckily found that her in-laws had a 'progressive' mindset despite not being educated themselves. Although they supported her, the young daughter-in-law was not exempted from her duties in the household:

> My in-laws allowed me to study. They supported me fully. So then I did BA, coming from my in-laws I did it [...] After having done all the housework in the morning

> I went to college, and in the evening I came back and did the housework, and in the night I studied.

Compared to the average SC condition of landlessness and poverty, the activists' families were relatively resourceful. A few have parents who belong to the educated Ambedkarite middle class, while most come from modest or poor backgrounds.[10] Nevertheless, all activists had one close relative who had acquired some education, who had secured government employment or other permanent salaried employment, or who owned a small plot of agricultural land.[11] Hence, their social positions may be described as ambivalent: they were born into castes that are seen as untouchable and 'backward', but were at the same time better off than many SC families in their localities. This is in accord with what Mendelsohn and Vicziany (1998, 238–48) found when investigating the backgrounds of SC MLAs and MPs in North India. Even if their economic bases were weak, all elected representatives came from families that had been able, in one way or the other, to acquire some material leverage.

School was, not surprisingly, also the arena for many of the activists' first experiences of discrimination. As the educational sphere is shared by all, they were made aware of their 'difference' through encounters with teachers and other students. Meena, an activist in her early thirties working for the DCC in Bihar, had been made to sit on the floor next to the mat that the other children sat on and to drink from her hands instead of from a glass like the others. The experience of such discrimination obviously informed the process of identity formation among the activists: 'Reinforced through constant practice, this "education" profoundly shapes Dalit consciousness and identity' (Shah et al. 2006, 13). While the exclusion enforced by these practices is highly symbolic, its impact is both psychological and social. A group being symbolically marked as taboo also leads to its social exclusion and material disadvantage (Woodward 1997, 12). Many talked of such experiences:

> I got lower marks, too. The teacher, if there was any sum in mathematics, then if you knew it you had to come to the board and solve it. I was good at studying from the beginning and I worked a lot, too. Our father made us work hard. So when I wanted to go and write the teacher would say no, you stay seated, these people will come, the other students will come. In that way they discriminated. And it was understood by everyone. All the students understood that is why they are not calling Diksha there even though she can solve it. So because of that I got lower marks. (Professor Diksha)

Within the DCC, the continuation of discriminatory practices against children on the grounds of their caste is seen as institutionalized efforts to perpetuate Dalit social exclusion and material deprivation. Having no prerequisites to understand why they were singled out for detrimental treatment, activists described such experiences as confusing and frustrating. The emphasis among the activists on becoming 'aware' and 'empowered' may be read as a response to this exclusion. As will be demonstrated in the final part of this chapter, through reinventing themselves as empowered and assertive, the activists (re) gained the ability to speak out.

Constructing the 'Dalit' and Her Oppressor

Today, the general perception in India is that SC children attend school in large numbers free from the 'grosser forms of humiliation' that were practiced upon them in the past (Mendelsohn and Vicziany 1998, 11). But in the activists' view, despite constitutional provisions protecting their rights, Dalit students in contemporary India cannot, like their non-Dalit peers, expect to be fully accepted and included in educational settings. They stress that this is the case despite the existence of a comprehensive formal support system for the SCs in schools and universities. Indeed, their narrative of struggle should be seen as part of a critique of an Indian majority society paying lip service to Dalit advancement. Common to the educational narratives that were recounted to me is that they convey a notion of struggle, but also, importantly, of progress.

In India, as elsewhere, the meaning of education is wider than simply being a necessity to obtain employment in an increasingly specialized labour market. It also symbolizes progress and modernity. Manuela Ciotti (2010, 120) has argued that education may be seen as 'a living category of progress' in India, and that 'discourses on education as an idiom of knowledge and progress are quintessential to self and community representation' (ibid., 126). This discourse tends to frame the uneducated Dalit as its 'other', something that is also pronounced within the DCC.

> In the development (*vikās*) of Dalit women; now there is no development, they are very backward. In every place they are backward; economically, educationally. In education their place is minuscule and there has been no change in the social view of the people. So they are always the victims of that, they suffer way too many incidents of atrocities and oppression, and they are always the victims of sexual exploitation. And because they have such insecure jobs they always remain dependent on one or the other. (Professor Diksha)

Statements like this were ubiquitous, both in my conversations with the activists and in the printed material produced by the DCC. Ciotti (2010, 9) has argued that entitlements to benefits through the policy of positive discrimination 'has resulted in a "socially schizophrenic condition" of progressing through claims of lagging behind amongst Untouchables and other protected categories'. The result is that '"Backwardness" [has become] an incredibly coveted attribute' (Ciotti 2010, 9). Consequently, while arguing for the urgency of their needs, the activists also partake in the construction of 'the Dalit' as the perennially poor and oppressed subject of a national narrative of progress and development. Diksha's statement should be seen in light of this development discourse wherein Dalits – and Dalit women in particular – are construed as the backward subjects of the modernizing state, seen to be lagging behind and in need of aid and reform. It is my argument that the confluence of an international discourse of development and a dichotomy between the 'forward' and the 'backward', in Indian popular perception inextricably intertwined with caste, leads to the reinforcement of this construction.[12]

Talking of her school days, Meena explained that her results had been good but that her teacher's thinking had been crooked. Since Meena achieved good results, he saw her as a threat to students belonging to his social group ('upper castes'), preventing them from 'going forward'. As is also illustrated in the excerpt below, Meena interpreted discrimination into a competitive frame:

MEENA: In college also, in the one where I did my graduation, [discrimination] was there also. When people came to know; when the professors and students came to know that she is a Dalit woman, then a little feeling of untouchability came there too. I was bright in the studies and got a good number in my university, so for that reason those people were a little down at that time.[13]

GURO: But was it also in college a matter of seating?

MEENA: No, it was in obtaining education, like when I asked for any notes and so on from some upper class professor or if I asked for any help from any upper class students, then they did not give it. They didn't want to give it. She is from a low caste, she is Dalit, don't give it to her. And if she goes forward then we will be behind (*pīche*), like that. There was that feeling.

Here, discrimination is interpreted as a mechanism by which teachers try to protect those of their own (higher) social group from the challenge represented by Dalit students. In this (otherwise Hindi) quote, the activist used the English term 'upper class'. I believe that this is not an expression of a class consciousness, but pertains to difficulties with referring to their discriminators in 'caste' terms, as they belong to all sorts of castes and caste segments. This will be further discussed below. In this statement and other similar ones, 'class' is used interchangeably with *varg*, or community, and designates those who are seen by the activists to hold social and positional power, and who are by default assumed to be both 'upper caste' Hindu and 'upper class' (in the sense of having economic clout).

Meena's interpretation also shows how, when the progress of one caste is measured in relation to that of other castes, the progress of one contributes to the stagnation of the others in a zero sum game. In this way, competition for seats and positions is experienced as a competition between castes. Within this narrative, progress is shaped 'under the form of a "social race" amongst castes' (Ciotti 2010, 119). The collective perception of competition leads to a reinforcement of loyalties that are ultimately based on caste, through the sharpening of notions of 'us' and 'them'. In the interview below, Meena upholds her assumption that those who are helpful towards a Dalit individual are themselves Dalit, despite her experience showing that individuals do not always behave according to this.

MEENA: Yes, and then I got support from some lawyers of my own community, from professors of my own community; they gave me question books and so on. [Thinking] that she is a Dalit woman and we need to help her advance further, she is a good student. So they helped me. Not everyone helped me; those who were from my own community were the ones who gave me help.

GURO: You mean from Dalits?

MEENA: From Dalits, some OBCs, some upper class who were quite intellectual, who were not concerned about untouchability at all; those kinds of people. And where there were bad people I didn't get any help.

Distinguishing between 'upper-class people' and 'people of my own community', it becomes clear that individual behaviour is, not surprisingly, at odds with a world view wherein people are seen as 'good' or 'bad'. Among the Chamars of Manupur, Ciotti (2010, 120) observed that the social race for progress described above was envisioned to be between essentialized *varna* blocks like Brahmans and Shūdras. In the DCC, this race is rather perceived to be between two essentialized 'groups': the Dalits and the oppressive 'other'. This 'other' remains evasive and is interchangeably designated with terms like 'upper class', 'high caste', 'Hindu', 'non-Dalit', 'big people', or simply as 'they'. A similarly dichotomized view of Indian society is also apparent in Ambedkar's writings. I maintain that this emphasis on 'difference' goes against attempts to integrate the 'Untouchables' into Hindu society as in Gandhian visions of reform, as well as against integrative analyses of Indian social organization, most forcefully formulated in Dumont's *Homo Hierarchicus* (1980). 'Difference' is hence an oppositional stance that provides a definite starting point for mobilization through creating clear-cut categories of 'oppressor' and 'oppressed'.

When positionality is reduced to individual experience and linked to grounds for authority, it 'encourages a view of experience which sees it as ontological, singular and fixed' (Moore 1994, 2). This is at best imprecise social analysis, reflecting that the activists are not primarily concerned with trying to work out how discriminatory mechanisms are played out within various spheres of social, cultural and economic life.

Inclusion through Affirmative Action?

Within the DCC, this competitive frame of interpretation was very pronounced when talking about affirmative action. Almost all the activists had benefited from government policies in one way or the other. While some had qualified for reserved seats in institutions of higher education, most had received financial support in the form of small scholarships throughout their schooling. They saw these measures as just and as necessary for the progress of the Dalit community. However, access to privileges formally granted to them by the abstract and benevolent state were often denied them by actual representatives of this state – teachers and other superiors – who failed to live up to the activists' expectations of equal treatment and meritocracy. Such subtle forms of discrimination persist also in institutions and within groups that they consider to be modern and progressive, and from whom they would have expected more:

> In Delhi when we were small I got a scholarship … So what happened was that the teacher made a lot of trouble for me. He made difficulties when handing it out … To get it we had to fill out forms, and then for the form we had to get a stamp from

> a Minister, from someone, from an MLA, from an MP, or from a Councillor. In that way he made difficulties by saying again and again; not like this, go again and do this, do that. [It was] very difficult. Sometimes I felt that it would be better not to get it. We got books and we got clothes, but I mean they were making a lot of trouble. So that is also discrimination. On the time of handing it out the teacher was very angry, irritated, like why [should I] give to them. (Vikram)

Teachers masking their ill will as bureaucratic procedures, the discrimination described here is covert and the denial of rights is explained as teacher antipathy towards Dalits. Kamal, who ran a tuition centre in Delhi, described how one of the children there had been abused by her teacher in the classroom over a trivial wrongdoing:

> There was a girl who had lost one of her library books. So the teacher told her to fetch the book and come [back]. So she said, ok, I lost it, I will pay as much as the book was. She was a child, too. Says the teacher; no, how could you forget the book? That scholarship you are getting, that you people won't forget. Then how could you forget the book? [...] This is straight forward a caste issue. *We* are getting scholarships and that makes *you* angry.

These narratives demonstrate the persistence of prejudices against Dalits, and how teachers and professors attempt to counter what they presumably see as pampering of the SCs through state policies of affirmative action. Hence, the narratives may be seen to turn the Indian debate about affirmative action and its consequences on its head. In this debate, the argument strongly voiced by critics is that reservations are diametrically opposed to meritocracy. Claiming that the establishment of quotas and reserved seats seriously lower the quality of professionals, of the services and of the bureaucracy, and that skewed competition corrupts educational institutions, they argue that reservations is an impediment to the overall development of the country. In debates on affirmative action, 'merit has become an ideology justifying continued upper caste monopoly. "Merit" is contrasted not with "incompetence", but with "reservation"' (Omvedt 2004). Describing the ways in which Dalits are denied their rights within the educational system, activists demonstrate how continuing prejudices and group loyalty tend to override 'merit' in these interactions, laying bare the status-quoist aspect of anti-reservation arguments. While reservations are a state strategy for inclusion of socially excluded groups, its implementation is hampered by entrenched powers who perceive the threat to their privileges. Also, increased social segmentation seems to be one of its effects.

Becoming an Activist

In continuation of the narrative of struggle, the activists also shared a narrative of progress and opposition, describing how they had become 'empowered' and 'aware':

> There is a Vina Das in Patna, she is a professor. She is a Dalit woman, from the Chamār *jāti*. When I used to go to Vina Das she would always teach me about

> Bābāsāheb. He is this, he did this, he did that. Listening to her I felt like, *bāp*, I really don't know anything! So much has happened and I don't even know that people of my community have done such a lot – that people of my community are doing such great things! From that Vina Das I learnt quite a lot. [She was] the one who made me very aware about our constitution, about our consciousness that Bābāsāheb made, all that. So I became aware and to further his movement I went and took it up, that I will work for my own people. (Meena)

'Becoming an activist' is described as coming out of ignorance to achieve awareness and an assertive Dalit consciousness. Meena became aware through getting to know the true history of her community, which induced pride and became the source of a new ideological conviction. Such narratives are common among the DCC activists and are often centred on the life and thought of Ambedkar. His emphatically rational and modern critique of Hindu social institutions is a central theme in contemporary Dalit assertion, and as has been noted by Beltz (2004, 248), among his followers Ambedkar is seen as 'the Authoritative Reference'.

In these narratives, personal change is understood as moving from a state of being 'backward' to a state of being 'forward', something which has normative implications for their views of what the Dalit community needs as a whole. As observed by Ciotti (2010, 120), 'the spread of education has triggered a reflexivity process […] Contemporary [N] orth India has witnessed the phenomenon of low-caste reinterpretation of the past, to make it suitable to these castes' new selves'. Hence becoming an 'empowered' activist also entails notions of progress that are intimately linked to upward social mobility, something that will be further explored in the final part of the chapter.

Professor Diksha had grown up in Maharashtra as one out of eleven siblings. While her mother was illiterate, her father had been a police officer and a devoted follower of Ambedkar. Her father had a strong belief in the virtue of education and with the aid of government scholarships aimed at SC students, all his children eventually became graduates. In the 1950s and 1960s, overt discrimination against SCs was customary in Maharashtrian schools, and Diksha was in the sixth or seventh grade when she opposed this for the first time:

> There was Sharda's idol (*mūrti*) […] Sharda *pūjā* (worship) […] and there was Ganapati *pūjā*. Those were the two occasions when they installed idols in the school hall and all the children went there and prayed and offered flowers. And I made very nice flower garlands, very beautiful. So once I had made a garland. They used to tell us to make a garland and bring it [to school]. And when I had made a garland and brought it then the teacher would get me and say that I will put it. You shouldn't put it and place your hand on the idol. So one day I became very angry. I said that you are telling me to make the garland and then you don't allow me to put it on the idol of Ganapati, but I will put it. Then [the teacher] said that you can't do it, you will pollute the idol (*bhraṣṭ karnā*).[14] But I didn't listen to anyone's protests and I went; in front of everyone I went and hung the garland [on the idol] and remained standing there. I was thinking that today some teacher will beat me, but that day

> they all kept quiet. Nobody said anything in response to my opposition. Because if anyone had said anything I would have gone and told my father that those people insulted me in such and such way and then he would have seized them and they would have been punished. And the discrimination was forbidden by law as well, so they all kept quiet.

After finishing her BA, Pushpa had been appointed head teacher in a girl's school in Jaisalmer district, far away from where she lived in her in-law's village. Leaving her daughter with her mother and her husband with his family, she went across Rajasthan to work. The school she was to manage had eight female teachers, out of which one was a Dalit and the rest belonged to non-Dalit castes. Being unaccustomed to caste discrimination, Pushpa had not asked the teachers about their caste and neither had they asked her:

> [At the school] only the non-Dalit women made food and *cāy-pānī*; that [task] was kept for those who belonged to the Rajput caste. At the time when the untouchability practice happened to that teacher, they said to me, madam, don't tell her to come into our kitchen. I said why not? Then they said that she is Dalit, she is from the Meghwal caste [...] so you shouldn't touch her, because how can we eat if she has touched it? I said ok, that's why. I didn't tell them which caste I belong to.[15] Then the next day I told the teacher; I said Mehnaji, you give *roṭīs* to the girls.[16] Because when we were serving food everyone had a duty; which teacher will have the duty of serving food today, who will make them [the children] keep quiet today, who will lead the prayer today. In that way everyone's duty would ambulate [...] So I told her [Mehna] that you serve the food, you please give *roṭīs* to the children. So at first – she knew those things because she was from that area – she didn't obey me, saying no, madam, I won't give them. I said why won't you serve it? I am telling you to serve food to the girls. Because I was seeing these things I knew what was on her mind. Then on my command she started serving, and then the one who was making food in the kitchen, a Rajput woman, she came out and seized her hand. Seizing her hand she said you don't serve food. Then she said to me, madam, why are you telling her to? She is from a low caste; those people are an inferior caste! If her hand has touched it then how can we and the children eat? How can we eat the food? Then suddenly I got very angry and I seized her hand and pulled her out from the courtyard. Making her stand on the street I said that there is no place here for you and I locked the main gate. From then on I didn't allow her to enter there. In that way I did opposition. I did not accept those kinds of people there at all.

Both these narratives revolve around archetypical kinds of discrimination against Dalits: that of avoiding contact with food and drinks to be consumed by people belonging to castes that consider themselves ritually purer; and that of denying Dalits access to temples, gods and goddesses that are worshipped by these same castes. In both instances, the teachers' acts invoke belief in physical pollution, and hence have to be understood in light of a painful and humiliating collective memory. Both Diksha and Pushpa read their experiences into the narrative of Dalit oppression and exclusion, and their reactions are seen as directed against the reproducers of such beliefs.

While they describe their reactions as emotional and spontaneous, the narratives also disclose enabling factors. Both women had unusual measures of security and support; Professor Diksha's father was a politically conscious police officer, and Pushpa was in a position of authority as head teacher of the school. Besides the power and status derived from this, another aspect of Pushpa's situation also enabled her decisive handling of the episode. After having been thrown out of her workplace, the Rajput teacher had approached the Project Officer (PO) in charge of the schools in the area. The PO, who was also a Rajput, had called on Pushpa and asked her why she had thrown the teacher out. Replying that he should rather ask her what the teacher had done, Pushpa reasserted that she would not allow this teacher back into the school. Provoked by this, the PO had threatened to transfer her to an area in Jaisalmer district which is considered very 'backward':

> He tried to frighten me, saying that if you keep opposing these things I will send you to Ramghat. So then I became even angrier. I said that I have already come all the way from my home district to Jaisalmer, so for me that [Ramghat] is not very far. I can go to Ramghat and work, that is no problem. You won't be able to scare me.

Faced with this answer, the PO realized that his strategy of instilling fear through threatening to uproot her had no effect. Having already left her daughter and husband behind to go out and work, Pushpa was in a relatively autonomous position. Being married but living apart from her in-laws created a space which offered good measures of both freedom and support, a space from within which Pushpa was free to 'do opposition'. Emphasizing the enabling factors in these narratives, I do not see a lack of agency, but a *relational* notion of agency. As Ciotti (2009, 113) has argued with regard to female low-caste politicians in Uttar Pradesh, it is often the 'supposedly "oppressive" household boundaries rather than alternative outer spaces that, under a series of enabling circumstances, initiate women's political activities'. Indeed, the narratives show the importance of family support to enable assertion, confirming that the political agency of women activists is shaped by their husbands and families.

A third feature that I wish to emphasize is the 'staged' and provoking aspects of these narratives. Pushpa consciously provoked the Rajput teacher to commit what is actually a law breach under the SC/ST (Prevention of Atrocities) Act 1989. Rather than simply confronting her on the basis of her utterances, Pushpa commanded the 'Untouchable' teacher to hand out *roṭīs*, fully aware of the reaction this would probably provoke. Letting the episode play out this way allowed her to forcefully demonstrate her intolerance for this behaviour in front of the other teachers and the children, asserting her authority as head teacher. For some activists, displaying their assertiveness through provocative language was a part of their style. In relation to a rape case she was following through the judicial system, Ritu had gone to the village of the victim. There,

> [The upper caste peers of the accused] were saying that this is a matter of the village and a compromise should be made in the village itself. When they were urging her

> to compromise I said only one thing that if it was your daughter or wife in her place and this had happened to her, then would you compromise? If you are willing to do this then go and fetch my husband and give your wife to him. And then you compromise. I will also compromise. Immediately they became angry and ran off. (Ritu)

The public and spectacular aspects of these narratives show that activist actions are not merely intended to punish wrongdoers and protect victims of discrimination, but to make an example of habitual transgressors in order to deter others from committing similar wrongs. Backed by a comprehensive legal framework and the formal support of the state apparatus, such actions serve to highlight continuing injustice despite the alleged official adherence to equality, nondiscrimination and the abolition of untouchability. The element of provocation illustrates that activists do not see themselves simply as benevolent protectors of their communities. While providing aid to individual victims of discrimination or violence, it is just as important to hold the local police accountable, to make them register FIRs (First Information Reports) at the police station,[17] to get cases registered under the Scheduled Caste/Scheduled Tribe (Prevention of Atrocities) Act 1989 rather than under the general Indian Penal Code, and to expose officials who do not carry out their duties according to rules and regulations. Hence, while activist self-representations include a notion of being a 'saviour' of the Dalits, conferring justice upon the destitute masses, they also have a political agenda. This consists in demanding change through holding individual representatives of the local state accountable and through publicizing irregularities and power abuse by staging protests and alerting the media so as to discourage others from doing the same.

Through telling such stories the activists inscribe themselves into a proud tradition of Dalit assertion. The idiom presented here is reminiscent of Ambedkar's burning of the *Manusmriti* (Rodrigues 2002, 10), as well as of BSP leader and former Chief Minister Mayawati's policy of 'Dalitizing' public space in Uttar Pradesh. It is a characteristic of modern Dalit assertion in general, as if they had read Michael Moffatt's description of the 'Consensus at the Bottom of Caste' (1979) – where the 'Untouchables' are seen as loyally accepting their marginal roles in village society – and agreed upon proving him wrong. Invoking a shared idiom of resistance also serves to legitimize the activists as part of the Dalit struggle and to demonstrate their dedication to the cause. In the last section I will show how their right to represent the Dalits was constructed upon such experiential legitimacy.

Social Exclusion and Activist Legitimacy

During my first day at the DCC office, one of the activists asked me rhetorically, 'where is your pocket?' I was dressed in a *pañjābī* suit with loose *pajāma* trousers and a long *kurtī*, and had no pocket. Shobna explained that Indian women's wear, like the *suit* and the *sāṛī*, do not have pockets where money can be kept, symbolizing Indian women's economic dependence on men. In particular, Dalit women's economic dependency on their fathers, husbands and employers is seen to make them extremely vulnerable to exploitation. Shobna's question was one that the activists would regularly pose to Dalit women when addressing them in gatherings arranged by the DCC. The idea is to initiate discussions through which the women will be made aware of the inequalities inherent in gendered power structures. Shobna then showed me the pocket in her own FabIndia-*kurtī* and said smilingly, 'but we are "empowered" women! We have pockets, we have our own money'.

Surely, this is a representation of Indian women as oppressed; although men are seen as the natural breadwinner and the economic head of the family in India, poor and rural women also commonly have some money at their disposal, kept in the blouse or in the *pallū* of the *sāṛī*. What the representation above does is hence to conjure up an image of Dalit women as being in need of the help of the activists. Moreover, activist self-representations are contrasted with descriptions of Dalit women as poor, oppressed and deprived of agency.

The activists in the DCC are educated, have 'respectable' jobs and most live in Delhi or other major cities. Many have travelled widely across the country, they read newspapers and crack jokes about national politics, and they have a good knowledge of the functioning of the state. In addition to their work with formal laws, rules and regulations, the activists are acutely aware of challenges related to the actual functioning of the Indian state apparatus. Its deficiencies in terms of corruption, discriminatory practices, and below-par implementation of government schemes are issues that they regularly attempt to address. Indeed, the very efficiency of their activism is premised on both formal knowledge and informal abilities to 'make things happen'. They know how to navigate the bureaucracy, to get the police to register an FIR, and to get the attention of the local media. These abilities are particularly empowering in a society where the gap between the common man's knowledge and the intricacies of the functioning of the state is so great as to seem unbridgeable for those who do not possess the required resources. While there is nothing specifically 'Dalit' about this gap, in this context I contend that the gap is sustained by the way the reified 'poor Dalit' emerges from activist discourse. Activists whose families live in rural areas recount that it is difficult to explain to them exactly what they do for a living. Being unfamiliar with words like 'advocacy' and 'networking', their rural kin is seen as being able to understand such modern concepts only to a limited extent. Ritu, who handled the alleged rape case above, had heard a female relative telling someone that 'she (Ritu) gives justice to Dalit women'. Such stories were conveyed with considerable amusement.

> I was speaking in a meeting in a village, there was a rally going on, and then suddenly I, what do you say; there is dominant caste, right? And I couldn't remember what that is called in Hindi. So the moment I said dominant I realised that they won't understand it, and their understanding [of this] had to be profound. And then I was thinking that if they are going to understand I will have to ask someone what you call "dominant caste" in Hindi? What you say is "upper cas[...]" – "upper" is also English [laughs]. *Ucc* caste eh [...] *jāti*. High caste (*ucc jāti*)! That is what you say. I said those who are understood to be a higher caste (*baṛī jāti*) than you, I gave an example, and then they understood. So there are a lot of language problems sometimes for us who are connected to the ground level. (Pushpa)

To encounter language problems when speaking in one's mother tongue indicates the extent of social removal that results from upward mobility. Education, professional training, urbanization and economic betterment produce a distance between the activists and the people they engage with. Having a different language, which is otherwise thought to poignantly express the social location of the speaker, as in the argument that Dalit women must necessarily talk differently (Guru 1995), here comes to symbolize the distance between the activist and the grassroots.

While Pushpa directly acknowledged this remove, the activists would often emphasize their proximity to the ground level by being a 'real grassroots activist'. This highly valued notion was related to a sacrificial ideal that could also be discerned in their reports from the field. Oral and written reports from their work in rural areas tell of long days and physical strain, of travelling in crammed buses on dusty roads, of walking under the scorching sun and of working late and getting up early without taking time to eat properly during the day. Employees on the national level complained that it was difficult to use these accounts in reports to funding agencies because of a tendency to record personal hardship and sacrifice rather than the conduct of meetings, the names of meeting participants and what had been discussed and agreed upon.

In the same vein of community service and sacrifice, several activists had chosen to work in low-status locations during fieldwork and while they were studying. One senior activist told me that she had chosen a specialization considered to be of low prestige even though she was among the top students in her class. This typically entailed involvement with rural populations or with the poorest sections in city slums. Describing how her co-students had gone to lengths to avoid working in poor and 'dirty' locations, Shobna explained that she was not concerned with poverty and unhygienic conditions, illustrating that working for the Dalit cause is also about taking on a moral responsibility. Presenting their work in this way 'evokes principles of selflessness and sacrifice' (Ciotti 2012, 1). And when describing their work for the Women's Wing, similar self-representations surface:

> If I go to the village the women there are sitting down on the ground, in the dirt. So when I go there to them and sit I am not looking at that time if my clothes are becoming dirty, how I am sitting and things like that. With anyone, of whatever kind they are, when I am with them I can behave like they do. (Pushpa)

Being able to talk to 'everyone' implies the ability to adapt to settings that are materially and socially different from one's own. Generally, activists emphasize their ability to build and maintain close relations with the people they work among, unaffected by outer appearances. The competence to manoeuvre successfully across domains is seen as grounded in their specific social positions as the educated and able representatives of the lowest rungs of society. This in-between position enables them to move between the 'modern' and the 'traditional', the urban and the rural, the 'forward' and the 'backward', and to convey meanings across these divisions. In that sense, these abilities are related to the activists' ambivalent social positions. Similarly, Craig Jeffrey, Patricia Jeffrey, and Roger Jeffrey (2008, 68) have described how young lower-caste men in Uttar Pradesh emphasized 'the adaptability of the educated', which was the ability to 'shape their behaviour according to the nature of social situations'. Evoking notions of authenticity and proximity is also a way to minimize the class and educational gap between themselves and the 'common Dalit'. In my interpretation, the emphasis on sacrifice is also part of the legitimization of their status as having the prerogative to speak for the Dalits. Correspondingly, they criticize the political establishment and mainstream development organizations for being unrepresentative and unable to understand Dalit issues.

When the purpose is to describe their relation to their 'subjects', Dalit activists emphasize proximity and solidarity, underplaying the substantial difference which is manifest in these interactions. In other contexts, they acknowledge and underline these very differences, demonstrating their own abilities and knowledge. These coexisting notions of in-/exclusion through solidarity and difference express some of the difficulties inherent in an anticaste mobilization wherein caste membership is a central benchmark for participation in the movement.

Conclusion

As we have seen, the notion of Dalit-hood has emancipatory potential through providing an alternative interpretative framework for experiences of social exclusion, creating space for a fundamental critique of Hindu social organization. Still, the label contains inherent limitations. Since the definition of who is a 'Dalit' is ultimately based on *jati* belonging, this might seem contradictory within a movement whose self-professed goal is to abolish caste. I argue that the anticaste rhetoric of the activists is, in this sense, embedded in an idea of caste-as-community, where castes are seen as 'natural' groups and believed to share certain features. This does not necessarily imply that they think of caste as inherited 'substance' (Kolenda 1978, 71–74); but it reflects a belief in a common history, in shared needs of the present, and in a *collective* future destiny. The narratives presented here show how notions of untouchability are implicitly reproduced in an essentializing and inclusivist activist discourse. There are historical reasons for their insistence on Dalit-hood as a prerequisite for group belonging. As Kothari writes:

> Provoked by the phenomenon of co-optation over such a long period, there has emerged a tendency among the *dalits* to insist on 'autonomous', exclusivist identity and membership, striking a discordant attitude towards movements and intellectuals and political activists that are committed to them but belong to other castes. (Kothari 1997, 456)

This insistence also requires individuals to identify as Dalit as a premise for their inclusion, a requirement which may not always be easily harmonized with the strong ambitions of upward mobility among ordinary SCs today. As Rao (2006) has written about the 'Depressed Classes' politics of nineteenth-century Maharashtra, their identity was one to be 'transcended, not reified, but this could only happen by identifying themselves as a stigmatized community'. While a Dalit identity is increasingly becoming something that can be presented with pride, it never stops representing deep-seated stigma, producing subjects that are vulnerable to mechanisms of social exclusion.

I have argued that Dalit activist self-representation is dependent on its dichotomy with the discursive image of the Dalit. Activist identities as empowered and aware are constructed with reference to how they perceive poor Dalits to be unaware and lacking empowerment. I see this as a problem of representation. Speaking on behalf of the 'oppressed masses', the activists construct their own self-image against a reified and stereotyped Dalit. The effect is that they create a homogeneous representation which compounds social differentiation within the Dalit category. This serves to reproduce and keep alive the image of 'the Dalit' as a perennially poor and oppressed figure. While sympathetic to the emancipatory intentions of the Dalit movement, it is necessary to 'question the analytical value of such hierarchies of suffering' (Shirman 2004, 5305–6).

The very existence of these activists is to some extent an outcome of state policies of affirmative action, and they live and work in social spaces that were previously largely off limits to people of their descent. The DCC activists set out not merely to change popular perceptions about the Dalits as a group, but also to reform the Dalit community. As their community is 'backward', it is in need of reform. This discursive 'backwardness' does not just entail poverty and oppression, but also lack of 'awareness'. In this way the activists create a singular victimized image of the Dalit and make this image stand for all those who are denoted by this ambiguous label. I have further argued that activists' self-images were construed in opposition to this particular image of the backward Dalit, and that their activist identities relied on the dynamics of this contrast. They emphasize this difference – a difference rooted in education, 'empowerment' and knowledge – which is seen to confer upon them a higher social status, and thereby reproduce exclusionary practices that define people in or out of such categories.

Also, 'Dalit-hood' cannot be reduced to shared interests or dedication; it is also about an inherited social position. As argued by Dipankar Gupta (2004, xix-xx), 'castes cannot change intrinsically as long as they are fundamentally founded on identities that draw their sustenance from a rhetoric of natural differences [...] the more things change the more they are the same'. Hence while derogatory qualities and meanings attached to their caste belongings are opposed and denied, caste as a primary social unit is reproduced through employing caste solidarity and emphasizing caste concerns in activist efforts to unite and mobilize the Dalit population.

Notes

1 This chapter is based on parts of my MA thesis titled 'The Remaking of Caste Identity: Dalit Activists in New Delhi', submitted to the University of Oslo in June 2011. The thesis is available at: http://www.duo.uio.no/sok/work.html?WORKID=121384. For support and supervision during the thesis work, I would like to thank my supervisor, Arild E. Ruud, and the rest of the South Asia group at the University of Oslo. From my thesis reviewers, Ute Hüsken and Manuela Ciotti, I received greatly helpful comments and criticism. Also, I wish to thank the editors for their useful criticism and their help with developing thesis material into a book chapter. The responsibility for any shortcomings in the chapter is mine alone.

2 All names have been changed to protect the anonymity of the activists, including the name of the organization. The exception is place names, which have been altered only where they may compromise anonymity.

3 Similarly placed caste groups also exist elsewhere in South Asia, and the terms 'Dalit', 'Untouchable', and 'Scheduled Caste' are similarly used to designate these groups in Pakistan, Nepal, and Bangladesh.

4 Italics in the original.

5 An example of what was later coined 'Sanskritisation' by sociologist M. N. Srinivas (2009).

6 I speak Hindi and did not use an interpreter during my fieldwork. Some of the activists spoke English, but many did not, and the *lingua franca* at the office was Hindi, liberally sprinkled with English terms. The interviews that I cite throughout the chapter were recorded, and I alone am responsible for their translation.

7 The number of people working as manual scavengers in India is disputed. While the Indian state had identified 115 thousand scavengers to benefit from a government rehabilitation scheme in 2007, the official figure was reported at 676 thousand in 2010 (*Indo-Asian News Service* 2010). The largest organization working for the abrogation of this practice, the Safai Karamchari Andolan, suggests that there were 1.3 million manual scavengers in India in 2005 (Desai 2009). For an account of various state governments' denial of the continuation of manual scavenging, see Zaidi (2006).

8 Gandhi wrote in *Harijan*, his newspaper, that 'one born a scavenger must earn his livelihood by being a scavenger, and then do whatever else he likes' (Zelliot 2005, 154). While opposing the evils of 'untouchability' and discrimination on the basis of caste, Gandhi maintained that Indian society should be organized according to the *varna* scheme, with its assignment of traditional duties on the basis of birth.

9 The name of Pushpa's home district has been replaced with the fictitious Mausa district.

10 The Dalit movement is sometimes referred to as the Ambedkarite movement after B. R. Ambedkar, the 'Untouchable' leader and chairman of the Drafting Committee of the Indian Constitution. Ambedkar's writings on caste, untouchability and Hinduism are central in Dalit discourses across the country, and his image, in the shape of a statue (Jaoul 2006) or a button (Hardtmann 2009) has become the most salient identity marker proclaiming allegiance to the Dalit movement(s). The 'Ambedkarite middle class' hence indicates that activists' parents were followers of Ambedkar, and that they were educationally and occupationally somewhat better off.

11 While government employment is highly coveted, most of the activists' family members who had obtained this were employed in Class IV, the menial grade which includes sweepers.

12 See also Ciotti (2010, 49) and Frøystad (2005).

13 The ranked results of students in Indian colleges and universities are often published in the newspapers, featuring photographs of their top achievers.

14 *Bhraṣṭ karnā* may also be translated as to violate, to debase, or to corrupt (McGregor 1993).

15 Pushpa herself belongs to the Meghwal *jāti*.

16 Flat, unleavened *roṭīs* are an essential part of most meals in the wheat-growing regions of North India.

17 An FIR (First Information Report) is a written document produced by the police when they receive information about an offence which is cognizable to the jurisdiction of a court. Only when an FIR has been registered will the police begin the investigation of a case. The FIR is also a point where accusations made by Dalits or other marginal groups against local vested interests are often effectively impeded.

References

Beltz, Johannes. 2004. 'Contesting Caste, Hierarchy, and Hinduism: Buddhist Discursive Practices in Maharashtra'. In *Reconstructing the World: B.R. Ambedkar and Buddhism in India*, edited by Surendra Jondhale and Johannes Beltz. New Delhi: Oxford University Press.

Charsley, Simon. 1996. '"Untouchable": What is in a Name?' *Journal of the Royal Anthropological Institute* 2 (1): 1–23.

Ciotti, Manuela. 2009. 'The Conditions of Politics: Low-Caste Women's Political Agency in Contemporary North Indian Society'. *Feminist Review* 91: 113–34.

______. 2010. *Retro-Modern India: Forging the Low-Caste Self.* New Delhi: Routledge.

______. 2012. 'Resurrecting Seva (Social Service): Dalit and Low-Caste Women Party Activists as Producers and Consumers of Political Culture and Practice in Urban North India'. *Journal of Asian Studies* 71 (1): 149–70.

Cohn, Bernard S. 1987. 'The Census, Social Structure and Objectification in South Asia'. In *An Anthropologist among the Historians and Other Essays.* Delhi: Oxford University Press.

Desai, Darshan. 2009. 'Inhuman Bondage: 1.3 Million Manual Scavengers Exist in India Despite Ban'. *Indo-Asian News Service*, 27 July. Online: http://www.thaindian.com/newsportal/health/inhuman-bondage-13-million-manual-scavengers-exist-in-india-despite-ban_100223461.html (accessed 21 November 2011).

Dumont, Louis. 1980. *Homo Hierarchicus: The Caste System and Its Implications.* Chicago and London: University of Chicago Press.

Dirks, Nicholas B. 2001. *Castes of Mind: Colonialism and the Making of Modern India.* Princeton: Princeton University Press.

Frøystad, Kathinka. 2005. *Blended Boundaries: Caste, Class, and Shifting Faces of 'Hinduness' in a North Indian City.* New Delhi: Oxford University Press.

Gupta, Dipankar, ed. 2004. *Caste in Question: Identity or Hierarchy?* New Delhi: Sage.

Guru, Gopal. 1995. 'Dalit Women Talk Differently'. *Economic and Political Weekly* 30 (41–2): 2548–50.

Hardtmann, Eva-Marie. 2009. *The Dalit Movement in India: Local Practices, Global Connections.* New Delhi: Oxford University Press.

Indo-Asian News Service. 2010. 'Will Work to Eradicate Manual Scavenging by Year-End'. 5 February. Online: http://www.thaindian.com/newsportal/uncategorized/will-work-to-eradicate-manual-scavenging-by-year-end_100315316.html (accessed 21 November 2011).

Jaffrelot, Christophe. 2003. *India's Silent Revolution: The Rise of the Lower Castes in North India.* London: Hurst & Company.

Jaoul, Nicolas. 2006. 'Learning the Use of Symbolic Means: Dalits, Ambedkar Statues and the State in Uttar Pradesh'. *Contributions to Indian Sociology* 40 (2): 175–207.

Jeffrey, Craig, Patricia Jeffery and Roger Jeffery. 2008. *Degrees Without Freedom? Education, Masculinities, and Unemployment in North India.* Stanford: Stanford University Press.

Kolenda, Pauline. 1978. *Caste in Contemporary India: Beyond Organic Solidarity.* Prospect Heights: Waveland Press.

Kothari, Rajni. 1997. 'Rise of the Dalits and the Renewed Debate on Caste'. In *State and Politics in India,* edited by Partha Chatterjee, 439–58. New Delhi: Oxford University Press.

Marriott, Alan. 2003. 'Dalit or Harijan? Self-Naming by Scheduled Caste Interviewees'. *Economic and Political Weekly* 38 (36): 3751–2.

McGregor, R. S., ed. 1993. *The Oxford Hindi-English Dictionary.* New Delhi: Oxford University Press.

Mendelsohn, Oliver, and Marika Vicziany. 1998. *The Untouchables: Subordination, Poverty and the State in Modern India.* Cambridge: Cambridge University Press.

Moffatt, Michael. 1979. 'Harijan Religion: Consensus at the Bottom of Caste'. *American Ethnologist* 6 (2): 244–60.

Moore, Henrietta L. 1994. *A Passion for Difference: Essays in Anthropology and Gender.* Cambridge: Polity Press.

Omvedt, Gail. 2004. 'Untouchables in the World of Information Technology'. *Contemporary Review* 284: 286–8.

Ortner, Sherry. 1991. 'Narrativity in History, Culture, and Lives'. Working Paper 66, Program in the Comparative Study of Social Transformations. Ann Arbor: University of Michigan.

Rao, Anupama. 2006. 'Representing Dalit Selfhood'. *Seminar* 558.

Rodrigues, Valerian, ed. 2002. *The Essential Writings of B. R. Ambedkar*. New Delhi: Oxford University Press.

Rudolph, Lloyd I., and Susanne Hoeber Rudolph. 1967. *The Modernity of Tradition: Political Development in India*. Chicago and London: University of Chicago Press.

Shah, Ghanshyam, Harsh Mander, Sukhadeo Thorat, Satish Deshpande, and Amita Baviskar. 2006. *Untouchability in Rural India*. New Delhi: Sage.

Shirman, Rachel, 2004, 'World of Dalit Women'. *Economic and Political Weekly* 39 (50): 11–17.

Srinivas, M. N. 2009. *Social Change in Modern India*. New Delhi: Orient BlackSwan.

Woodward, Kathryn, ed. 1997. *Identity and Difference*. London: Sage.

Yadav, Yogendra. 1999. 'Electoral Politics in the Time of Change: India's Third Electoral System 1989–99'. *Economic and Political Weekly* 34 (34–5): 2393–9.

Zaidi, Annie. 2006. 'India's Shame'. *Frontline* 23 (18).

Zelliot, Eleanor. 2005. *From Untouchable to Dalit: Essays on the Ambedkar Movement*. New Delhi: Manohar.

Chapter 7

INCLUSION OF THE EXCLUDED GROUPS THROUGH PANCHAYATI RAJ: ELECTORAL DEMOCRACY IN UTTAR PRADESH

Satendra Kumar

This chapter examines to what extent the new panchayati raj, through the 73rd amendment to the Indian constitution in 1993, has led to greater inclusion of hitherto excluded social groups in the institutions of local government and decision-making processes. In June 1994 the government of Uttar Pradesh (UP), the largest state of the Indian republic, amended the UP Panchayat Act of 1947 to extend the recently implemented 27 per cent quota for the Other Backward Classes (OBCs) in administration and education to panchayati raj institutions (PRI).[1] At the same time, the UP government also made the reservation of seats for the Scheduled Castes (SC) (in proportion to their demographic profile) and women (33 per cent) mandatory at all levels of the panchayati raj system in accordance with the 73rd amendment. Besides devolving governmental power to the village level, this amendment also aimed at ensuring the participation of hitherto excluded castes and social groups in decision making.

In this chapter I examine the results of these policies. I am specifically concerned with two simultaneously occurring processes: on the one hand, I examine how these policies have facilitated the inclusion of hitherto excluded social groups. This had led to a marked change in the relations of domination and subordination between the upper castes and the OBCs both in UP and North India more broadly. On the other hand, I analyse how this 'politics of inclusion' has also produced new patterns of political *exclusion.* I pursue this second line of investigation to argue that the introduction of reservation aimed at including excluded groups has in fact ended up creating new kinds of exclusions. I focus my analysis on Khanpur, a multi-caste village in Meerut district.[2] I analyse here the workings of the eighth village panchayat (1999–2005) – which overlapped with my fieldwork in 2004 – and the ninth village panchayat election, which I documented during a short period of fieldwork in 2005. I use the study of the two panchayats, and the varied experiences of different OBCs with participating in village democracy, as a window to understand the actual workings of the policy of reservation in which the state tries to homogenize the socially, politically and economically heterogeneous OBC caste groups. Caste groups from different socioeconomic and political backgrounds have been put together under the category of OBCs by the Indian state in order to improve their social, economic and educational positions. The chapter seeks to understand how the policy of reservations has brought about changing dynamics of power relations among the various castes of the OBCs.

Writings on electoral democracy and other aspects of political life emphasize the gradual deepening of democracy in India over the last 50 years (Yadav 2000). Democracy has worked as a platform for the lower castes to launch their struggles for social justice. Yet, the existing literature largely focuses on democratic politics at the macro level. In contrast, a study of electoral democracy at the village level may reveal a significantly more complex picture since the participation of different caste groups in PRIs is closely related to existing inequalities and the role these castes have in state sponsored programmes of political inclusion. There is thus a need to focus our attention on the meanings and modes of engagement with democracy by caste groups with considerable difference in their sociocultural and religious backgrounds (Ruud 2003; Spencer 2007; Banerjee 2008). Such an undertaking necessarily includes an analysis of the ways politics operates on the ground.

Utilizing their domination in Khanpur's village panchayat, the landowning upper OBCs (notably the Gujjars and Ahirs/Yadavs) have managed to exclude many of the lower OBCs both with regard to decision-making processes and the distribution of available resources. The modalities through which the upper OBCs express and reinforce their domination include supra-village networks, landholdings,[3] caste associations and participation in electoral democracy through party politics. Money and muscle are equally used to exclude other caste groups. The chapter thus demonstrates that only by disaggregating the homogenizing category of OBC can one identify how mechanisms of inclusion and exclusion continue to operate. Ironically, by placing very diverse castes into an inclusive and overarching 'OBC category', the state's reservation system ends up perpetuating (some of) the inequalities that the category was originally meant to redress. Reservations have given some lower caste groups access to power, but the hierarchies within these groups, based on caste, size of population, land and wealth, have reasserted themselves through new political affiliations, alliances and antagonisms. Despite radical changes in the rural power structure of western UP, lower, artisan, service and other OBCs remain marginal in local politics.

Caste and Democratic Politics in UP

In order to understand the nature of exclusion in the Khanpur village panchayat, it is important to understand the recent political history of UP and the major role that caste has had in shaping its political landscape over the last thirty years. The state of UP, which is considered one of the socioeconomically most 'backward' states, occupies a central place in national politics as it supplies one-sixth of the members to the Lok Sabha. The politics of UP can be divided into three phases. In the first phase, which lasted from Independence to the late 1960s, the Congress Party dominated the political arena of

UP by forging a formidable coalition of Brahmins, Muslims and SC. Its leadership was generally monopolized by the higher castes who had control over blocs, village panchayats and cooperative institutions (Brass 1965). In the second phase land reforms and the Green revolution, along with the policy of positive discrimination, brought prosperity to the middle castes such as Ahirs, Jats, Kurmis and Gujjars, and prepared them to challenge Congress domination.

In the third phase, beginning in the early 1990s, UP's political landscape has been characterized by the rise of 'lower castes' in opposition to the higher castes. This phase is associated with the rise of the Samajwadi Party (SP) and the Bahujan Samaj Party (BSP), who have mobilized the lower strata of society against the higher castes under the slogans of social justice, equality and demands for a greater share of political power. The Chamars and the BSP, under the leadership of the late Kanshi Ram and now Mayawati, have been the most active protagonists in the so-called Dalit politics in UP. Since 1995, the BSP has held power at the state level four times and in 2007 it formed a majority government on its own. The BSP's aim has been to capture state power for the benefit of 'the oppressed majority', and it has prioritized opposing caste oppression (Lerche 1999; Singh 1992). The BSP has placed Chamars in key positions within the bureaucracy and increased the speed and rigor with which crimes against SCs (and Chamars in particular) are investigated. The BSP is also trying to win positions in local institutions such as panchayats, municipalities and cooperatives. In rural areas the local panchayat institutions – the key channels through which goods and services are delivered – have become contested arenas in which the poor and dominant alike articulate their interests and claims. The next section provides an historical development of the panchayats in UP.

History and Structure of the Panchayat in UP

The panchayat system in its traditional form has a long history in UP. The state was the first to introduce panchayat legislation (UP Panchayat Raj Act of 1947) after Independence and took the lead in the Community Development Programme (Hatim 1976). The UP Panchayat Raj Act of 1947, drafted at the end of the colonial period as a replacement for the inconsequential 1920 UP Village Panchayat Act, intended 'to instil in the people the spirit of self-reliance and common endeavour to ameliorate their conditions without depending too much on federal and state government' (Government of UP 1994, 1). The Act aimed to set up a *gaon* panchayat (also called a gram panchayat) in every village alongside *panchayati adalats* (*nyaya* panchayats) with jurisdiction in judicial matters over a dozen villages. The government hoped that 'these panchayats once established, will not only revitalise corporate life in the rural areas but will also prove efficient instruments for carrying into effect the Rural Development Schemes of the Government' (Government of UP 1948, 5; for the history, see also Sharib 1944; Purwar 1960; Hatim 1976).

This Act has been repeatedly amended. The latest amendments of 1994 have brought the provisions in line with the Constitutional Amendment Act of 1993, to grant more powers to panchayats and organize them into a three-tier system. The three-tier system is composed of the gram panchayat at the village level, the *kshetra samiti* at the block level (*khand*) and the *zilla parishad*, or district panchayat, at the district level. The latter two *samitis* (councils) allow for some integration with lower as well as higher elected bodies. Apart from directly elected members, membership in these two bodies comprises chairpersons of the lower councils and local members of the Legislative Assembly and Parliament. The UP system includes two more councils covering two distinct and yet overlapping geographical areas. The *nyaya* panchayat, comprising mainly the deputed members of the gram panchayat, covers an area that extends over several villages but is smaller than the block.[4] The other institution which has been an integral part of the UP system (similar to other states in India), at least on paper, is the *gram sabha* (village meeting). Twice a year, the entire village population is expected to meet and make recommendations and suggestions on development programmes, finances, community welfare programmes and identification of beneficiaries of government programmes.

The panchayat is composed of the *pradhan*, deputy *pradhan* and ordinary ward members. The panchayat – which comprises a village or a group of villages with a population of around a thousand – is divided into a number of territorial constituencies or wards from which the members are elected. The constituencies are rotated in order to comply with the provisions of reservations based on gender and caste (Lieten and Srivastava 1999). The gram panchayat is chaired by the *pradhan* or, in his or her absence, by the deputy *pradhan*. While the ward members elect the latter, the *pradhan* is elected directly by the electorate.

Over the years the powers and duties of the gram panchayats have grown considerably. The 1994 UP Amendment Act gave the panchayat a wide-ranging set of responsibilities in the agrarian economy, including agricultural extension, land consolidation, land reforms, soil conservation, water management, animal husbandry, social forestry and fisheries. In addition, duties related to the provision of rural housing, education, electricity, electrification, village roads, sanitation, social welfare, the public distribution system and poverty alleviation programmes have been entrusted to the panchayats. The panchayats are expected to constitute a number of committees to assist them in the execution of their duties, such as the Vikas Samiti (agriculture, rural industry and development schemes), the Shiksha Samiti (education), and the Samata Samiti (welfare of women, children, SCs/STs and backward classes, and protection of these groups from 'social injustice and exploitation in any form').

In order to finance the various schemes, the panchayats, apart from the limited amount of grants received from the higher levels of administration, have considerable powers to impose taxes and acquire property. Taxes can be levied on land, animals, vehicles, entertainment establishments and market transactions. Additionally, imposing surcharges on cleaning, street lighting, irrigation and other facilities, which the panchayat may provide, can also generate income.

Social and Political Structure in Khanpur

Khanpur is a revenue village in the district of Meerut. It is located about 100 km northeast of Delhi in Western UP. In generic terms, Khanpur is part of a larger Gujjar belt, which is called 'Gujrot' in local parlance. Between 2004 and 2005, the village had a population of 2,823 people living in 447 households. People from 15 different castes live in three *mohallas* – Gujjar, Ahir and Chamar – which have overlapping boundaries. These castes can be divided into the upper castes, the OBCs and the SCs. The Chamars comprise the largest group, followed by the Sainis, the Gujjars and the Ahirs. Gujjars and Ahirs, who are ranked next to each other in terms of ritual status, constitute the dominant castes of the village.[5] These two caste groups combined constitute 19 per cent of the households in the village and own about 42 per cent of the agricultural land. A couple of Brahmin households used to serve as their ritual priests, but the majority of the Brahmin households were landowning farmers. Currently, none of the Brahmins work as ritual priests and the people of Khanpur use the services of a priest from the neighbouring village. The Chamars and the Valmikis have their own priests. Gujjars and Ahirs generally dominate the everyday affairs of the village and panchayat in terms of decision making and controlling resources.

Khanpur had its first statutory panchayat in 1949 under the UP Panchayat Raj Act of 1947. Prior to 1949, Khanpur had two kinds of panchayats: one was a village panchayat with a fluid council of elders; the other kind was informal caste panchayats, one for each caste. The two panchayats differed significantly in their constitution and function. For example, the village panchayat dealt with the issues concerning the whole village, whereas the caste panchayats dealt mainly with caste issues such as marriage and divorce, or intracaste disputes. This council of caste elders would also keep an eye on the day-to-day socio-judicial affairs of their caste members. The new statutory panchayat created in 1949 was different in nature and scope from both the previous panchayat systems, as its members were elected and served a fixed term. Under the Panchayat Raj Amendment Act of 1994, as per the roster system, the *pradhan*'s seat was reserved for an SC candidate in 1995 and an OBC candidate in 1999. The SC person elected as *pradhan* in 1995 was a Chamar, and in 1999 the *pradhan* elected belonged to the Gujjar caste.

The Khanpur village panchayat is divided into thirteen wards. In the village panchayat election, besides the *pradhan*, a block development councillor (BDC) is also elected. Ward members elect the deputy *pradhan* or *up-pradhan*. In some cases, a ward is coterminous with a particular caste. For instance, ward 3 is practically coterminous with the Dhimvar's street. And yet, the village panchayat does not have representatives for each caste. BDCs elect a block *pramukh* (block head) from among themselves. For the third-tier district panchayat, members are elected at the same time as the village panchayat elections are held. Members of the district panchayat elect the district panchayat president.

In 2004, of the thirteen members of the village panchayat, two were Gujjars, two Ahirs, one Saini, one Dhimvar, one Fakir and six Chamars/Jatavs (SC). One of the six Chamar members was the deputy *pradhan*. There were four women ward members and one BDC was a Gaderiya woman. The *pradhan* was a Gujjar. Thus, three groups emerge as the main political players in the village: the Gujjars, Ahirs and Chamars. The Gujjars and Ahirs head the main factions in the village. In panchayat politics and elections, factions and *guts* (blocs) play very important roles. These factions and *guts* overlap with castes and clans. Faction and village leaders also have networks outside village across castes and villages. The following sections provide the details of the structures and workings of factions and *guts*, and caste associations and networks respectively.

Factions, *Guts* and *Mohallas*

Politics and men's social life in Khanpur revolves around factionalism, which is known as *partibazi* in popular village parlance. The village's two main factions, the Gujjar faction and the Ahir faction, are headed by Ramsharan Gujjar and Gopal Ahir respectively. Factions are vertical alliances between landowning cultivators (upper OBCs), tenant and contract cultivators (lower OBCs), artisan–service castes (artisan–service OBCs), small and marginal farmers (other OBCs), and landless labourers and the SCs. The landowning cultivators belong to the dominant and ritually higher upper OBCs such as Ahirs and Gujjars. The other four (tenant and contract cultivators, artisan–service, marginal cultivators, and landless labourers) comprise ritually and economically lower castes such as Dhimvars, Sainis, Gaderiyas (lower OBCs), Kumhars, Lohars, Badhais, Nais, Dhobis (artisan–service OBCs), Fakirs (other OBCs) and Chamars and Valmikis (SCs). The faction is a fluid group in terms of membership. However, members of a family lead a faction with their extended kin. Two opposing extended families (Gujjar and Ahir) formed the axes of factionalism in Khanpur. Historically, there was little relation between factional alliances and caste. While landowning families belonging to the dominant castes were always the leaders of the respective factions, an individual's choice of which faction to support had little to do with his caste. For example, the Ahirs on the whole split their alliances between the two factions, as do the Gujjars. Thus, what I call the Gujjar faction comprises not only a section of the Gujjars, but also a considerable section of Ahirs, the majority of Brahmins and Gaderiyas, half of the Dhimvars, some families of the Fakirs, Dhobis, Nais and Lohars, and the Chamars of Thakedarwalle. Similarly, the Ahir faction is composed of a big section of Ahirs, the majority of Sainis, the Chamars of Badwalle, all the Kumhars, some Dhimvar, Gaderiya and Badhai families, and some Lohar, Nai and Brahmin families.

Another important fluid group of people that one encounters in Khanpur is at the *mohalla* level and is called a *gut* or bloc. A *gut* consists of a couple of influential people in a *mohalla*. Each *mohalla* may have more than one *gut* but one of them is dominant and plays a crucial role in *mohalla* politics. Generally, each *gut* aligns itself with one of the factions in the village. Most of the time *guts* take the initiative to decide matters of importance, such as who will run for the panchayat election, or which *biradari* (caste) should get ward membership in the panchayat elections. *Guts* are very active in the context of everyday and electoral politics. Faction and *gut* memberships are not stable structures like panchayats and co-operatives. *Guts* are formed and re-formed by the initiatives of individuals. They are often temporary in nature and tend to disappear when they have served their purpose. Factions and *guts* are both crucial elements of village politics even though vertical factional politics is moving towards horizontal caste politics, as I discuss below.

The fluid social groups in the form of *guts* and factions consist of individuals of various capacities and influences. In addition, the Gujjars and Ahirs continue to play the role of *jajmans* in terms of patronage. In the recent past historical *jajmani* (patron–client) relationships had been the basis for vertical alliance in the village politics. This base has been weakened over a period of time. Today artisan–service castes such as the

Table 7.1. Caste groups in Khanpur.

Caste Group	Religion	Households	Population
UPPER CASTES			
Brahmin (priest)	Hindu	13	76
Bania (trader)	Hindu	01	5
Total		**14**	**81**
OBCs			
Gujjar (cattle herder)	Hindu	45	276
Ahir/Yadav (milkman)	Hindu	40	252
Saini (veg. grower)	Hindu	76	478
Gaderiya (shepherd)	Hindu	31	216
Dhimvar (water nut grower)	Hindu	29	194
Lohar (blacksmith)	Muslim	07	53
Badhai (carpenter)	Muslim	05	42
Kumhar (potter)	Hindu	05	33
Nai (barber)	Muslim	14	102
Dhobi (washerman)	Muslim	04	29
Fakir (mendicant)	Muslim	23	171
Total		**279**	**1,846**
SCs			
Jatav/Dalit/Chamar	Ex-untouchables	147	866
Bhangi/Valmiki	Ex-untouchables	07	30
Total		**154**	**896**
Grand Total		**447**	**2,823**

Source: Field data.

Lohars, Badhais, Kumhars, Dhobis and Valmikis do not work for their former *jajmans*. The disintegration of the traditional relations of the *jajmani* system and the emergence of off-farm employment opportunities are redefining relationships between former *jajmans* and artisan–service castes. The landless labourers now have more space to negotiate their wages and more freedom to work outside the village. The numerical strength of the Chamars and the economic rise of the Gaderiyas and Sainis have also put up challenges to the domination of the Ahirs and Gujjars. In contrast, the Brahmins and Banias have, given their small numerical size and their occupational shift from agriculture to urban jobs, been excluded over a period of time in formal panchayat politics. Table 7.1 provides a profile of the number of households and population of each caste in Khanpur in 2004.

An important recent development is that the Chamars have emerged as a decisive group.[6] The Chamars live in two *mohallas*: Badwalle and Thakedarwalle, and have two *guts* respectively. The majority of the Badwalle Chamars are small and middle cultivators, while the majority of the Thakedarwalle Chamars are labourers who work either as farm wage or contract labourers at canals. A section of the Thakedarwalle Chamars still depends on the farms of the Gujjar farmers for a livelihood, and this section of the Chamars supports the Gujjar faction in political matters from time to time.

Factionalism is an expression of the political struggle for power and prestige among various castes in general, and particularly among dominant castes. In Khanpur, factions also compete for the resources of the panchayat that are channelled by the developmental state. Panchayat resources have thus become a key arena for political competition among various castes. The competition for resources among different caste groups has escalated since village politics became part of wider political networks and structures.

Caste Leaders, Caste Associations and Networks

Each caste has one or more men who are considered leaders, or *netas*, by the caste members. They lead the caste in political matters and help members form alliances with other castes. Broader political- and caste-based networks may extend well beyond the boundaries of the village where different political equations and dynamics are at work. The emergence of new political parties in the 1980s and 1990s at the national and regional levels has had a particular impact on the politics in Khanpur and its neighbourhood. These 'new' political parties have made their presence felt at the local level and have politicized local identities in new ways. In this process of local politicization, caste and kin have played a crucial role. People are increasingly mobilizing along caste lines in the regional politics of in western UP, and this is also influencing village politics (as I discuss later) which is gradually moving from a bipolar factional system based on broad multi-caste alliances, to one of multipolar competition between more narrowly (in caste terms) formed factions. For example, the Gujjars have people like Ramsharan, Sevaram and Mahkar as their leaders, who are very well connected with other Gujjar leaders in the region through kin, clan and marital relations. These Gujjar leaders, who have links that stretch beyond the village via caste associations and political parties, bring wider regional caste issues into village politics. Thus, in the village there are several caste leaders who play the role of connecting their fellow caste members to associations based outside the village (often in urban centres). There are also caste leaders who are affiliated with various political parties. For instance, Ramsharan attends the Congress Party meetings regularly in Meerut town, while a Chamar ex-*pradhan* runs a BSP office in the village. The other castes also have some kind of caste leaders who represent their castes within and outside the village, although these leaders are neither supreme nor uncontroversial. Only the Valmikis, Kumhars, Lohars, Dhobis and Nais do not have any such caste leader, or *neta*, in the village.

It is against this backdrop that I examine the election, composition and functioning of the panchayat at Khanpur. Prior to 1994, Khanpur's panchayat had all the ingredients needed to deliver the goods of a village democracy. But the history of the village indicates that these 'goods' never materialized.

The 1999 Village Panchayat Elections

In the eighth panchayat election held in 1999, three candidates (Ramsharan Gujjar, Puran Saini and Rajjak Badhai) contested for the post of *pradhan*, which was reserved for an OBC. Ramsharan Gujjar was supported by the Gujjar faction and a big section of the Chamars, including the Thakedarwalle *gut*. A few Chamars supported Puran, who is a Saini and a lower OBC. Rajjak, a Badhai of the artisan–service OBCs, received support from a section of Ahirs. Ramsharan Gujjar won this three-cornered fight garnering the votes of the majority of Gujjars (except some who supported the Ahir faction), Gaderiyas, Dhimvars and most of the Chamars.

When this election was first announced, influential persons from the Gujjar and Ahir factions began working out their strategies to select their candidates. Both the Gujjar and Ahir factions, along with the Sainis, Gaderiyas and Dhimvars, were concerned that unless they united behind a consensus candidate, the Chamars, given their greater numbers, would be successful in electing their choice of candidate as *pradhan*. Being the dominant group by virtue of their relatively large landholdings and organizational power as well as their numbers in the region, the Gujjars held a series of meetings to decide who should contest for the post of *pradhan*.

The first meeting was held in the sitting room of Sevaram whose grandfather had been the head of the village prior to independence. The meeting was the first step towards reaching a consensus among the Gujjars to put a 'good candidate' from their own caste. In the second meeting, the Gujjars and Gaderiyas sat together to decide on a joint candidate. It was influential persons among the Gujjars – including Sevaram, the ex-*pradhan* Mahkar and his cousin's brother – who requested that influential men among the Gaderiyas attend the meeting. In a well-thought-out-strategy, Gujjar leaders proposed a Gaderiya as candidate for the post of *pradhan*. He declined, saying he could not afford to spend a large amount of money on an election campaign. Consequently, the meeting was adjourned until the next day, and with the consent of the Gaderiyas, an elderly and respected Gujjar named Bhulle was appointed to suggest an alternative candidate. The following night, Ramsharan approached Bhulle and requested that Bhulle should propose his name the next day. Bhulle ostensibly agreed to do so.

The next day when the meeting was held, Sevaram first inquired whether the Dhimvars wanted to put up their own candidate, and if not, whether they would support the Gujjars. The Dhimvars declined putting up a candidate of their own because none of them could, or would, shoulder the financial burden of running an election campaign. Bhulle then proposed Ramsharan's name. Ramsharan's candidature was endorsed by members of the three castes present, who agreed that the post of *pradhan* should go to the Gujjars' *mohalla* this time. The Gujjars had thus succeeded in manoeuvring the lower OBCs in their favour so that in this particular case, the reservations for OBCs ended up benefitting the already powerful groups at the expense of the more marginal OBC communities. In the following sections I show how the dynamics of reservations for SCs similarly ended up benefitting the already influential Chamars caste, but not Valmikis who, like the Chamars, are also SCs.

Politics of Alliance and Reciprocity

In order to gain the full support of the Gaderiyas and Dhimvars during the 1999 election, the Gujjar faction suggested a deal to the Gaderiyas: if the latter supported Ramsharan for the post of *pradhan*, the Gujjars would support the Gaderiya's candidate for the BDC in exchange. A section of the Gaderiyas agreed to the deal and went on to field their own candidate for the BDC, which was reserved for women.

While the Gujjars were thus building an alliance with the Gaderiyas and Dhimvars, other castes such as the Chamars had been busy exploring the possibilities of fielding their own candidate for the *pradhan* post. In 1988 and again in 1995, a Chamar from Badwalle had become the *pradhan* on a reserved seat. These were the first occasions when the Chamars had refused to align with either the Gujjar or the Ahir faction and had united to field their own candidate instead. The Chamar candidate had won partly because he had received the support of a section of the Badhia (an artisan OBC) led by Rajjak. In 1999 the Chamars decided to reciprocate. The Badwalle *gut* called a joint meeting which was attended by all *guts* of the Chamars, who unanimously decided to field Rajjak as the 'chosen' candidate of the Chamars and Muslims. The Ahir faction also declared its support to Rajjak. The deal between Rajjak and the Badwalle Chamars would mean that the post of deputy *pradhan* would eventually go to the Chamars. It is noteworthy, however, that while a Chamar had become the *pradhan* in 1995, no Valmiki ever got a chance to stand as a candidate. The Valmikis remained excluded from the formal village politics. They had neither the necessary numbers nor the resources to enter into electoral alliances. In village politics, alliances are formed on reciprocity, which is part of the village and patron–client culture.

Identities of Caste and Religion in Village Politics

Other castes were eager to enter the fray in 1999 as well. After having been relegated and marginalized in village politics over a period of time, the Sainis decided to field a candidate of their own to counter the growing influence of the Chamars. The political rise of BSP in UP had made Chamars more assertive, even aggressive, in Khanpur, and they had started to harass the Sainis, including Saini women. The Sainis' decision to field a candidate was perhaps a defence mechanism. A group of elders and youths alike proposed the name of Puran Saini. From experiences in the previous elections, the Sainis had learnt that other castes hardly ever supported the Sainis' candidate for the post of *pradhan*. The Gujjars and Ahirs would, despite their perpetual factionalism and political rivalry, unite in order to prevent a lower caste candidate (including a Saini, Gaderiya or Chamar) from holding the post of village *pradhan*. The Sainis had watched the Chamars' political ascendancy very closely, as they lived side by side with them in the village. The general opinion among the Sainis was that their candidate for the 1999 *pradhan* election should be powerful and have resources for contesting elections. Puran Saini invited Tara Chand, a Saini leader from the Congress party, to speak at a meeting, where he encouraged all the Sainis to support Puran's candidature. In his address Tara Chand told the Sainis,

> We should learn from the Chamars who are organized and participating in politics. They are voting en bloc for the Bahujan Samaj Party (BSP), which is in return

> helping them in many ways. But we neither have any political party nor a powerful leadership whom we support and vote for. We should participate in democratic politics more and more to make our identity known.[7]

The Sainis responded to this request and almost the whole Saini community, and particularly the young people, would eventually vote for Puran Saini.

Two days before the election, many rumours criticizing Rajjak (the Muslim and Chamar-supported Badhai candidate) began to circulate in the village. The Gujjars claimed that Rajjak would set up a slaughterhouse if he won the elections, and that a loudspeaker would be placed on the mosque. The slaughterhouse is a common stigmatizing imagery used against Muslims during political campaigns and elections in western UP. The Gujjar campaigners also revived the locally famous story of Yusuf Ali's murder. Yusuf Ali was the former *zamindar* of the village. He was killed by Gujjar dacoits during the infamous communal riots of 1942 which spread across North India. The Gujjars of Khanpur and neighbouring villages called it 'the victory of the Gujjars over the Muslims' and spoke of it as the restoration of Gujjar rule to stress how the Gujjars had wrested this village from the clutches of its erstwhile Muslim rulers: 'How can a Muslim be the *pradhan* of the village where the majority of inhabitants are Hindus? How would a Hindu tell his relatives outside the village that he is living in a village headed by a Muslim?' the Gujjar campaigners asked rhetorically. The campaign against Rajjak continued for two days, and the specific imagery pertaining to Muslim rule in India and Muslim *zamindars* in the village and the region were repeatedly evoked and retold. The result was that the election ended up being contested primarily on the emotive and explosive issue of Hindu–Muslim relations. Despite the mobilization against Gujjars, the majority of the Chamar vote went to Ramsharan Gujjar. A small section of the Chamars voted for Puran Saini in the name of *mohalla* unity, and only some Chamars voted for Rajjak, who secured mostly Muslim votes. The Gujjars' campaign rhetoric and their invocation of historical narratives thus worked very well in their favour.

Longstanding local factionalism in Khanpur came to a halt in this election as several new factors came into play. Important among these was the issue of communalism. When a section of the Gujjar and Ahir elite of the village sensed that they may well start losing out to lower OBCs (such as the Sainis, Lohars or Badhais) they strategically adopted a communal discourse to create divisions among the lower castes (Baviskar and Mathew 2009). The imagery of the Hindu nation-state as being destroyed by Muslim 'invaders' frames this political script. It is noteworthy that the communal Bharatiya Janata Party (BJP) won the parliamentary seat from Meerut–Mawana in the 1990s three times in a row. The BJP with significant success sought to reconcile caste differences by propagating a larger and 'casteless' Hindu identity embedded in local Arya Samaj discourses. And in each campaign the BJP made 'the slaughterhouse' an issue. The slaughterhouse of Meerut city has been a big political issue in the Lok Sabha and Nagar Nigam (Municipal Corporation) election campaigns in rural and urban localities, and the local Hindi media gave it special attention. In this case both regional and national political imageries were appropriated effectively into village politics. Muslims who voted for Rajjak Badhai did so more or less on identity lines. All the Gujjars, along with the Gaderiyas, Dhimvars and the majority of the Chamars voted for Ramsharan Gujjar. Interestingly, this time the Gujjars overcame their longstanding internal factionalism and voted en bloc for Ramsharan.

The village panchayat election of 1999 was largely influenced by national and regional political parties (Congress, BJP, SP and BSP). Some of these parties have an office in Khanpur itself, and all of them have many ardent followers in the village. These parties also shaped caste and religious consciousness in the village by connecting local issues to wider sociopolitical forces and issues: 'No village panchayat election in Khanpur was ever contested in this manner before; now Hindu–Muslim identities were placed before the people,' Rajjak Badhai emphasized. According to him,

> Caste and old clan rivalry in the form of factions had dominated the village panchayat elections in the recent past. But Hindu–Muslim identities were not used. However, this time old stories of Muslim domination and hegemony were aired, rumoured, and images of past Muslim *zamindars* were projected in a distorted manner by the Gujjars to win the election. They created fear through a slogan which said that if Rajjak wins the election he will get a slaughterhouse constructed in the village.

As we can see form Rajjak's statement, factional politics is increasingly taking a back seat to the ongoing constructions of politicized communal identities.

The Power of Wealth, Muscle and Crime

There is a widely shared assumption among Khanpur's villagers that they should elect as panchayat *pradhan* a person who has money, resources and politico-bureaucratic links outside the village. Entertaining people with sweets, meat and liquor is considered the norm. If someone is not able to provide such things, the villagers talk behind his or her back, and sometimes rebuke him or her up front, saying things like 'Why is she contesting an election if she does not have money to spend and entertain people with food?' That is why, when elections take place, people of a particular caste or *mohalla* will typically seek candidates who are well off and well connected, rather than someone with a reputation for being honest and educated. However, money is not all that matters. The combination of numbers (the size of the candidate's caste in a particular locality), wealth and the institutions of caste and kinship also play important roles in the selection of the candidate. According to one of my Gujjar respondents, Ramsharan spent around Rs 1.5 lakh in 1999, the largest amount spent by any candidate. This worked in his favour. To illustrate the influence of money and wealth in the 1999 election, I show below how one Gaderiya patriarch used his wealth to have his chosen candidate run for the BDC post.

The Gaderiyas, as per the deal with the Gujjars described above, put up *their* candidate for the BDC election. The seat was reserved for women. Sarjit, an influential Gaderiya man, decided to lend a woman Rs 5,000 to contest the election. With this backing the woman went on to get elected. When I asked her about her being elected she explained:

> I do not know anything. We – my husband and I – were asked to contest in this election by Sarjit. My husband did everything on my behalf. My job was only to

> give my thumb impression. I respect Sarjit Baba; so whatever he asked we did. Sarjit helped us financially to contest this election. After the election my life has not changed at all. After election now no one asks me what I am doing and how I live in the village. Sarjit got his money back after selling my vote to block *pramukh*.

The elected BDCs in turn elect one of their own for the post of block *pramukh*. In 1999 the only candidate was Samay Kaur, who had held the post during the previous term as well. When she was elected the last time, no one had dared to contest against her. Yet, while Samay Kaur formally holds power, it is commonly accepted that her son Billu, whose criminal activities are well known in Meerut District, runs everything in her name. In 1999 a schoolteacher in Tigari (a village near Khanpur) had decided to file a nomination to contest against Samay Kaur. He was shot dead the next day, and people suspected that Billu killed him. After that, no one tried to contest against Samay Kaur, and according to the district polling data, she was elected unopposed. According to Sarjit, Billu had, on the day before the block *pramukh* election, dispatched a car to pick Sarjit up along with the BDC and her husband. The three of them were taken to a hotel where several other men and women from different villages were present. After a couple of hours, more BDCs were brought in. Later, they were all taken to Pahadpur where the polling station for the block *pramukh* was located. All BDCs were well taken care of. Once polling was over, the BDCs were sent back to their villages. Sarjit described the situation in the following words:

> We did not want to cast our vote for Samay Kaur [but we had to]. Billu is very notorious for his unlawful activities. No one dares contest against him or his mother. We were left without a choice. Jats and Gujjars dominate this area. Both communities are landowners and they have their political leaders in power and are very well connected with government officers. Billu is a Jat and Jats are the most powerful community in this region. We have to live with them. So we cannot afford to make them our enemy.

Sarjit's account brings out the Gaderiyas' experience with the PRI and shows how political democracy in Khanpur is being experienced differently by different caste groups (Jodhka 2006). At the village level the Gaderiyas (and other lower castes) are excluded by Gujjars and Ahirs, and at the block and district levels they are marginalized by Jats and other upper castes who can rely on multiple sources of capital, money, muscle and larger political networks based on caste and kin (Jeffrey 2001, 2010). In the not too distant past, these upwardly mobile OBCs – the Jats, Gujjars and Ahirs – had themselves used their economic resources and numerical strength to wrest political power from the upper castes both in Khanpur and throughout western UP. Now these upper OBCs use the same means to obstruct any further inclusion of the lower OBCs.

Conclusion: Inclusion of the Excluded Groups

The introduction of the new panchayat raj has certainly accelerated the processes of inclusion of certain hitherto socioeconomically and politically excluded groups. It has made formerly 'invisible people' like women and SCs visible at village public spaces.

The emergence of a new and assertive rural public, irrespective of caste and sex, as a result of panchayat institutions is a definite trend today (Krishna 2002; Ciotti 2010). In Khanpur, the village panchayat had been dominated by upper castes ever since the first election took place, but power was soon taken over by the upper OBCs who rose to power partly due to broader economic and political processes unleashed in India's postcolonial democracy. However, the new provisions to include marginalized groups into the local political system and government benefited the dominant and more resourceful caste groups such the Gujjars, Ahirs and Jats, who continue to corner the larger benefits of decentralization and development across UP (Michelutti 2008; Jeffrey 2010). Despite the official view of OBCs as a homogeneous category, internal caste stratification amongst OBCs reasserts itself, as the upper OBCs, even though numerically smaller, retain their hegemony through means fair and foul. Tellingly, lower, artisan–service and other OBCs have not managed to make their political representation proportional to their population and they continue to be outmanoeuvred by the upper OBCs. A structurally similar process of 'internal exclusion' can be observed within the SC category. The Chamars have successfully become part of the new power structures, while many other SCs who lack social and political resources – such as the Valmikis – have not.

Socially, economically and ritually, caste has always produced hierarchy and inequality. However, when conjoined with democracy and its promise of universal franchise, caste can paradoxically become a vehicle of egalitarianism and dignity (Kothari 1970; Rudolph and Rudolph 1987; Béteille 1996; Weiner 2001; Gupta 2004). Lower castes are not leaving behind their caste identities, but rather actively deconstruct reinventing their own caste histories to constitute themselves as easily mobilized social categories, and using their strength of numbers to their electoral advantage and to fighting prejudice and domination. Fifty years ago Srinivas (1962) argued that caste was moving towards a 'horizontal consolidation'. Such horizontal mobilization and organization of caste played an important role in Khanpur in doing away with factional politics based on vertical of patron–client relationships that had for long perpetuated the dominance of the Gujjars and Ahirs. Instead, a new politics based on ideologies of social justice and demands for proportional representation and redistribution made the various castes increasingly conscious of the power that resides in numerical strength, as we have seen to be the case with Khanpur's Chamars. The traditional *partibazi* based on clan rivalry and *jajmani* relationship is similarly and slowly losing its relevance in Khanpur politics. Caste identity is gaining strength as caste associations and political parties have been able to connect villagers to the politics of the larger region, the state and the nation. In this new context of caste politics, the Gujjars and Ahirs seek to maintain their domination through new strategies, for instance, by using panchayat offices to extend the benefits of various welfare schemes to their supporters and sympathizers, and by building supra-village networks. The also use money and muscle power to subvert the proper functioning of democracy, or they use agricultural and off-farm income to bribe voters, polling officers and the police in order to win village panchayat elections.

Development programmes have given a new dimension to the relationship between old patrons and clients. People from the lower OBCs (Sainis, Gaderiyas, Dhimvars), artisan–service OBCs (Lohars, Badhais, Kumhars, Nais and Dhobis) and other OBCs such as the Fakirs, try to fulfil their personal interests by strategically rallying around the leaders of the dominant OBC castes, the Gujjars and Ahirs. Artisan–service OBCs and other OBCs in particular, have neither the numerical strength that is required in democratic politics, nor do they posses the economic and educational resources needed. The artisan–service and other OBCs thus remain politically and socially marginalized in village, regional and national politics. In Khanpur, no candidate from the lower artisan–service and other OBCs has ever been elected as village *pradhan*. Still, these excluded OBCs do try to exert pressure on village politics through membership in political parties and by attending meetings and rallies organized by their caste leaders in towns, cities and adjoining the village. They also seek to extend only issue- and interest-based support to local leaders rather than professing permanent loyalty. This shift in the relationship between patrons and clients has been described as a move from 'clientalism' to 'brokerage' (Gupta 1998; Jeffrey 2000). In this regard, the old style village politics that was based on two or three fluid political factions is no longer applicable as electoral democracy has created multiple power centres in the village. As amply demonstrated here, a caste-based politics may far from always expand power and influence to the numerically smaller and economically weaker sections of the population; but given the continued and highly competitive mobilization of castes and communities in UP, castes that are excluded today may emerge as influential political actors tomorrow.

Notes

1 In 1990, the Janata Dal Prime Minister V. P. Singh implemented 27 per cent reservations in federal educational institutions and jobs for the OBCs. This was in addition to the 22.5 per cent reservations that had existed since the 1950s for the SCs and STs. The OBCs include the low-to-middle-ranking poor pastoral-peasant and labourer castes throughout India, and are estimated to comprise 40 to 51 per cent of the Indian population.

2 In order to protect the identity of the village and its people, I use pseudonyms throughout this chapter.

3 The political economy of agriculture is closely linked with caste, thereby conditioning social and economic relations.

4 Its functions are judicial in nature. It can take cognisance of minor criminal or revenue cases.

5 Srinivas (1962, 10–11) advanced the concept of 'dominant caste.' According to him, a dominant caste has six attributes: possession of a sizeable amount of the arable land locally available; strength of numbers; a high place in the local hierarchy; Western education; jobs in government administration; and sources of income.

6 In the past the Chamars had been divided in several small *guts* and were more easily manipulated in favour of either Gujjars or Ahirs. Since 1988 Chamars have started asserting themselves as distinct community.

7 I received a tape-recorded copy of this speech.

References

Banerjee, Mukulika. 2008. 'Democracy, Sacred and Everyday: An Ethnographic Case from India'. In *Democracy: Anthropological Approaches*, edited by Julia Paley, 63–95. Santa Fe: School for Advanced Research Press.

Baviskar, B. S. and George Mathew, eds. 2009. *Inclusion and Exclusion in Local Governance: Field Studies from Rural India*. New Delhi: Sage.

Béteille, Andre. 1996. 'Caste in Contemporary India'. In *Caste Today*, edited by Chris J. Fuller. New Delhi: Oxford University Press.

Brass, Paul R. 1965. *Factional Politics in an Indian State: The Congress Party in Uttar Pradesh.* Berkeley and Los Angeles: University of California Press.

Ciotti, Manuela. 2010. *Retro-Modern India: Forging the Low-Caste Self.* New Delhi: Routledge.

Government of UP. 1948. *Local Self-Government in the United Provinces.* Lucknow: Government Press.

______. 1994. *Panchayati Raj Act 1994.* Lucknow: Government Press.

Gupta, Akhil. 1998. *Postcolonial Developments: Agriculture in the Making of Modern India.* New Delhi: Oxford University Press.

Gupta, Dipankar. 2004. 'Introduction: The Certitudes of Caste: When Identity Trumps Hierarchy'. In *Caste in Question: Identity or Hierarchy?* edited by Dipankar Gupta. New Delhi: Sage.

Hatim, Shahida. 1976. *Panchayati Raj in India, with Special References to Uttar Pradesh.* Aligarh: AMU.

Jeffrey, Craig. 2000. 'Democracy without Representation: the Power and Political Strategies of a Rural Elite in North India'. *Political Geography* 19 (2): 1013–36.

______. 2001. 'A Fist is Stronger than Five Fingers: Caste and Dominance in Rural North India'. *Transactions of the Institute of British Geographers* 25: 1–30.

______. 2010. *Timepass: Youth, Class, and the Politics of Waiting in India.* Stanford: Stanford University Press.

Jodhka, Surinder Singh. 2006. 'Caste and Democracy: Assertion and Identity among the Dalits of Rural Punjab'. *Sociological Bulletin* 55 (1): 4–23.

Kothari, Rajni, ed. 1970. *Caste in Indian Politics.* Delhi: Orient Longman.

Krishna, Anirudh. 2002. *Active Social Capital: Tracing the Roots of Development and Democracy.* New York: Columbia University Press.

Lerche, Jens. 1999. 'Politics of the Poor: Agricultural Labourers and Political Transformations in Uttar Pradesh'. In *Rural Labour Relations in India*, edited by T. J. Byres, Karin Kapadia, and Jens Lerche, 182–241. London: Frank Cass.

Lieten, G. K. and Ravi Srivastava. 1999. *Unequal Partners: Power Relations, Devolution and Development in Uttar Pradesh.* New Delhi: Sage.

Michelutti, Lucia. 2008. The Vernacularisation of Democracy: Politics, Caste and Religion in India. New Delhi: Routledge.

Purwar, V. 1960. *Panchayats in Uttar Pradesh.* Lucknow: Universal Book Depot.

Rudolph, Lloyd I., and Susanne H. Rudolph. 1987. *In Pursuit of Lakshmi: The Political Economy of the Indian State.* Delhi: Orient Longman.

Ruud, Arild Engelsen. 2003. *Poetics of Village Politics: The Making of West Bengal's Rural Communism.* New Delhi: Oxford University Press.

Sharib, Z. H. 1944. *Rural Government in United Provinces.* Bombay: Local Self Government Institute.

Singh, J. 1992. *Capitalism and Dependence: Agrarian Politics in Western Uttar Pradesh, 1951–1991.* Delhi: Manohar.

Spencer, Jonathan. 2007. *Anthropology, Politics, and the State: Democracy and Violence in South Asia.* New Delhi: Cambridge University Press.

Srinivas, M. N., ed. 1962. *Caste in Modern India and Other Essays.* Bombay: Media Promoters & Publishers.

Weiner, Myron. 2001. 'The Struggle for Equality: Caste in Indian Politics'. In *The Success of India's Democracy*, edited by Atul Kohli, 193–225. Cambridge: Cambridge University Press.

Yadav, Yogendra. 2000. 'Understanding the Second Democratic Upsurge: Trends of Bahujan Participation in Electoral Politics in the 1990s'. In *Transforming India: Social and Political Dynamics of Democracy*, edited by Zoya Hasan, Francine R. Frankel, Rajeev Bhargava and Balveer Arora, 120–45. Delhi: Oxford University Press.

Chapter 8

MAKING SIKKIM MORE INCLUSIVE: AN INSIDER'S VIEW OF THE ROLE OF COMMITTEES AND COMMISSIONS

Tanka B. Subba

A large number of tribes in India were brought into the Hindu fold, of course, in very different and often uneven ways, over the past several centuries. Some of them, like the Meiteis and Ahoms in India's Northeast, were accepted as Kshatriyas while others like Rajbansis in North Bengal were accorded the status of Shudras in the *varna* order. There may be several reasons for such variations in what Nirmal Kumar Bose (1941), a doyen of Indian anthropology, called the 'Hindu method of tribal absorption', but if a tribe being absorbed has an inferior status vis-à-vis a dominant Hindu majority community, the former seems to have little or no chance of being accepted as a cultural equal, as was the case of Rajbansis vis-à-vis the dominant Bengali Hindus. Ahoms and Meiteis, on the other hand, did not face any dominant majority community as the Rajbansis did, and were instead themselves locally 'dominant'.

Sikkim, an erstwhile Himalayan kingdom ruled by the Namgyals from 1641 until its so-called 'merger' with the Union of India in 1975, was so located with Tibet on its north, Nepal on its west, Bhutan on its east and the Darjeeling district of West Bengal on its south, that it never experienced the 'kshatriyaization' movement of the seventeenth and eighteenth centuries that swept the valleys of Northeast India. Sikkim may have been left out also because it clearly did not then have Hindu population which would be prone to such a movement; its population was, until the end of nineteenth century, either Buddhists or Animists. But certainly prior to 1975, the concepts of Scheduled Castes (SC) and Scheduled Tribes (ST) were not unknown to the people of Sikkim due to their geographical and social proximity with the people of Darjeeling but these categories came alive in Sikkim only after the 'merger' in 1975. The same castes were recognized as SCs and the same tribes as STs in Sikkim as those recognized so in the late 1950s in the hills of Darjeeling in the state of West Bengal.

The purpose of this chapter is to critically evaluate the role of the committees and commissions that the government of Sikkim created during the last five years to make itself socially and politically more inclusive. Such a need arose because some of the former Most Backward Classes (MBCs) were demanding their inclusion in the list of STs since the early 1990s and during the past four years; even the advanced groups like Bahuns, Chhetris and Newars, who are categorized as Other Backward Classes (OBC) in Sikkim, are making the same demand. But a critical evaluation of the role of committees and commissions is perhaps necessary here for the following reasons. One, the recommendation of a state to the central government for inclusion of certain caste or ethnic group in the list of STs, SCs, or OBCs is based on the report of such committees or commissions appointed by state governments. Hence, it is the first procedural step towards the process of social inclusion. Two, the state government appoints such a body and specifies the terms of reference and facilitates its functioning. It is, however, up to the state government to accept or reject the report partially or totally. Three, while such a body is often headed by an anthropologist or a sociologist, he is not always the most qualified person to perform that role, but which he rarely declines because of the sense of importance and purpose he feels about it. The pecuniary benefits of serving on such bodies cannot be ignored either. But at the end of the day, he often comes out with a report that lacks clarity of vision and purpose, as is evident from the Roy Burman Commission report being put under close scrutiny in this chapter.

The background of some ethnic groups demanding inclusion in the list of STs can be traced back to what is known as the *Janajati* movement of the 1990s (see Subba 1999). This movement was characterized by a feverish attempt of some Hinduized Nepali communities to return to their pre-caste and pre-Hindu social practices, languages, and religions. Most of them had their own languages, which were Tibeto-Burman, and their own religions (Animism and Buddhism), but who together constituted the Nepali society outside Nepal, accepted the Indo-Aryan Nepali language as their lingua franca, and Hindu religion as their religion during the past two centuries or so. The main goal of this movement was to 'dehinduize' them in order to hopefully make it easier for them to be listed as STs. The common perception of the people in the state is such that they consider one of the surest ways to get jobs is to be listed as STs. The expectations of some such communities have gone up especially after the inclusion of Limbu and Tamang in the list of STs in Sikkim and West Bengal in January 2003. However, despite the constitution of a committee in 2005 (the Sinha Committee) and a commission in 2006 (the Roy Burman Commission) to facilitate their inclusion, no new caste or ethnic group has been added to the list of STs to date.

For the castes and ethnic groups of Sikkim today, inclusion in the list of STs seems to be the only goal which, at a glance, looks like a reversal of their social orientation, which it perhaps is, but it is also an especial kind of reversal, for they do not want to be included in the list of SCs or OBCs. But the reasons for not wanting to be included in the list of SCs or OBCs are not the same. For instance, the main reason why the seven ethnic groups demanding ST status (Rai, Gurung, Magar, Yakkha, Jogi, Bhujel and Sunuwar) do not want to be included in the list of OBCs is the 'creamy layer clause' dangling like Damocles' sword.[1] They also avoid the OBC category because this is dominated, at least in Sikkim, by rather advanced castes like Bahun, Chhetri and Newar, and competing with them is very difficult for most other Nepali castes and ethnic groups living there. On the other hand, they do not want to be together with other SCs because this means a 'fall' in their caste status. At present, they may be Shudras, but they are not untouchables; but as SCs, they would be clubbed together with untouchables. Thus, a large number of Hinduized Nepali castes and ethnic groups are seeking a change in their identity from caste to tribe, though the normal transition is from tribe to caste (cf. Subba 2006). A reverse transition is not easy because it involves a lot of undoing and shedding of the cultural baggage that was already part of their everyday lives. The STs now, with the inclusion of Limbus and Tamangs, constitute a total population of 218,387 or 37.5 per cent of the total population. If the state government has its way, facilitated by the report of the Sinha committee, the percentage of ST population will be 61.1 per cent and it could well be 100 per cent if the recommendation of the Roy Burman Commission is implemented.

In the particular context of Sikkim, recognition as ST offers many opportunities. First, it will protect the lands belonging to such a category from being alienated to nontribal people. Second, the ST status may also be followed by seat reservation in the state assembly. Third, it may guarantee certain rights under the Indigenous and Tribal Peoples' Convention of 1989 (No. 169). Although India is yet to ratify it, this convention promises, among other things, collective rights to such people 'to exercise control over their ways of life and economic development' and to ensure their participation in 'the formulation, implementation and evaluation of plans and programmes of national and regional development that may affect them directly' (Tomei 2005, 4).

Here, Amartya Sen's conception of favourable and unfavourable exclusions (Sen 2000, 28–9) seems useful because, on the one hand, the ethnic groups in Sikkim are favourably excluding themselves from being demarcated as SCs or OBCs or even MBCs, they, on the other hand, are being unfavourably excluded by not being demarcated as STs. Thus, the real issue is not inclusion or exclusion per se, but the terms of inclusion or exclusion as played out by the processes of social interaction mediated through committees and commissions.

An Ethnographic Context of Sikkim

The original inhabitants of Sikkim were Lepchas, Limbus and Magars, although many British administrators have written, and Indian writers have blindly repeated, that only Lepchas are original inhabitants of Sikkim. This error must have crept into its history perhaps owing to the fact that Lepchas inhabited the area through which the Indo-Tibetan trade routes passed and hence were known to the British and others engaged in the trade with Tibet. And since the early history of Sikkim was written by the British administrators and travellers, they had the monopoly of representing the history of this kingdom in the way they represented the history of the Orientals. The Limbus and Magars, who lived in the inaccessible areas of the present-day West and South districts of Sikkim since as early as the Lepchas perhaps lived in its North and East districts, were thus not known to the outside world as original or even early inhabitants of Sikkim. The early habitation of the Limbus and Magars is however clearly established by Maharaja Tashi Namgyal and Maharani Yeshi Drolma (1908) in their manuscript translated as *The History of Sikkim*.

But apart from Magars and Limbus, who are identified as Nepali ethnic groups today, there is no evidence of early settlement of any other castes or ethnic groups in Sikkim. One of the earliest other Nepali groups to settle in Sikkim was Newar. The rulers of Sikkim brought them to Sikkim because they had the technology of minting coins and making pagoda-type houses, which were rather popular in Sikkim. A few of them later became members of Sikkimese aristocracy as well, but their number has never been large enough (21,713 from 2005 to 2006), which indicates that not many of them migrated to Sikkim. Considering the fact that the Rais in Sikkim constitute the single largest community (77,954 from 2005 to 2006) constituting 13 per cent of the total population of the state, it is suspected that they migrated to Sikkim rather early, although it is very much possible that they migrated in much larger number than others because of their traditional habitat in east Nepal being close to Sikkim and they lost most of their lands to the high caste Nepalese migrants from the western part of Nepal. Most Nepalis in Sikkim migrated from Nepal in the second half of the nineteenth century due to various pull factors unleashed by British rulers and active encouragement by a few local feudal lords. The Marwaris and Biharis from the plains of India also migrated to Sikkim around the same time to take advantage of the lucrative Indo-Tibetan trade and other business opportunities.

By the end of the nineteenth century the Nepalis were already in the majority, but they experienced, till the1940s, what Amartya Sen calls 'active exclusion' (Sen 2000, 14), such as higher land tax for them compared to the rate for the other two communities (Lepchas and Bhutias), forced labour called *kalo bhari, kuruwa, bethi* and *jharlangi* to carry goods across the border with Tibet or provide free labour for construction of roads and bridges within Sikkim, and the powers of the local feudal lords to beat or jail them for any defiance or dereliction. The life of Nepalis, except some Newars, in Sikkim was that of serfs under a feudal system, which changed for the better only after they launched a peasant movement in the early 1940s, which according to its leader C. D. Rai, was inspired by the freedom movement in India. But the success of this movement made the Bhutia rulers cautious and they worked out, rather dubiously, a 'parity system' in 1951 to contain the rising democratic aspirations of the Nepalis. Under the system, there would be equal number of reserved seats between Lepcha and Bhutia, two Buddhist tribes of Sikkim, on the one hand and the Nepalis, who are mostly Hindus or Hinduized Animists, on the other. The first general election of the State Council of Sikkim was based on this parity system with six seats each, which was increased by one each in the next election of 1958. In 1967 four more reserved seats were added: one for General, one for Limbus, one for Sangha, or monastery, and one for SCs. But the ordinance issued in 1979 by the government of India, four years after Sikkim's merger, changed the entire scenario, as it reserved 12 seats for Lepchas and Bhutias, one for *Sangha* and only two for SCs. The remaining 17 seats of the state assembly were declared as General, which was taken as a breach of trust not only by the Limbus, whose lone seat in the assembly was de-reserved, but also the Nepalis who had participated in the democratic movement, among others, for the overthrow of hereditary monarchy, which led to its merger with India in 1975.

To use the words of Naila Kabeer, the ordinance of 1979 at once created 'privileged inclusion' for Lepchas and Bhutias, *Sangha* and the SCs, whereas for Limbus and other Nepalis it was a '"hard-core" exclusion' (Kabeer 2000, 11).

Although the distribution of assembly seats remains the same to date, except the first chief minister, who was of Lepcha origin, all subsequent chief ministers have been Nepalis, which indeed shows their political dominance in the state, which is due to their numerical strength of about 74 per cent of the total population of the state. All Nepalis are protected in Sikkim either as STs and SCs of the Central list and OBCs or MBCs of the state list. But it is not clear why only two MBCs – Limbu and Tamang – were included in the list of STs in 2003. Indeed, these two communities had lot of similarities with other MBCs. The caste strictures were lax about them, as they paid little heed to what many high castes would consider as sources of pollution, such as eating pork and beef or drinking alcohol. The label *matwali*, or 'those who drink', was often used to represent all of them together, although some of them, under the influence of various religions, did not drink or eat meat. They were also generally perceived to be more backward than Bahuns, Chhetris, Newars, Bhutias, Marwaris and Biharis. They were stereotyped as quick to get angry and not able to think through their head. In short, they were depicted as 'tribes', or *janajati*. It was in the backdrop of such perceptions, followed by their demands to be included in the list of STs, that the Sinha Committee was constituted by the government of Sikkim in February 2005.

The Sinha Committee

On 23 February 2005 the government of Sikkim issued a notification announcing the constitution of a committee under the chairmanship of Professor A. C. Sinha, a retired professor of sociology from North-Eastern Hill University, Shillong, with the mandate 'to prepare an ethnographic report on Gurung, [Kirat Khambu] Rai, Ma[n]gar, Dewan, Jogi, Bhujel and Sun[u]war ethnic communities residing in the State of Sikkim.' The committee had as its members one anthropologist from North Bengal University specializing in the study of Muslims of North Bengal, one other anthropologist from North-Eastern Hill University (present author), whose doctoral research was on caste and class relations in Sikkim and Darjeeling, and one historian from Manipur University specializing in the history of ancient Kiratas. Hence, only the chairman and the present author had a close acquaintance with the society, culture, history and politics of Sikkim. But neither the chairman nor the other members of the committee had any clue as to how they were chosen and by whom. It was later learned from one North Bengal University professor from Sikkim that someone from his state had asked him who could be invited from his university to be a member of what is referred to here as the Sinha Committee. He was, however, not consulted about whom to invite from North-Eastern Hill University or Manipur University.

The committee was to submit its report within 100 days from the date of notification. However, the notifications reached some members very late and the committee could not start functioning before 2 April 2005. They all arrived in Gangtok on 1 April. They were warmly welcomed with Buddhist scarves and flower garlands by the representatives of ethnic groups under consideration for inclusion in the list of STs in Sikkim. On the next day, they discussed the terms of reference, worked out the aspects to be covered in the report and which member would take care of which aspect. The committee members also heard the representatives and received the ethnographic reports they had prepared on behalf of their ethnic organizations. Most of those reports were prepared by persons with no experience in writing ethnographic reports. The committee decided to meet again in Gangtok on 26–28 May 2005 for the purpose of discussing the draft report, its finalization and submission. On this occasion, the representatives of various ethnic groups submitted revised/additional/supplementary reports that the members of the committee did go through before finalizing their report.

Thus, this report embodies the results of research carried out by the members of the committee over a long period of time as well as what Foucault (1980) calls the 'subjugated knowledge' of the communities in question. In addition, the members of the committee did library work and the chairman himself conducted extensive field visits to confirm some of the information provided in the ethnographic reports prepared and submitted by the concerned ethnic organizations to the committee at the time of its first meeting in Gangtok. The committee members also examined relevant government documents related to the provisions governing SCs, STs and OBCs, although the committee had no such obligation. Further, the committee desired to meet some intellectuals of Sikkim to know their views on the subject, which was helpful in concretizing some of the ideas of the committee members.

It may be recalled here that Pawan Chamling had revolted against the former chief minister, Nar Bahadur Bhandari, on the issue of non-implementation of the Mandal Commission report that related to the inclusion of the OBCs for affirmative action in Sikkim. The ethnic groups brought under the commission's recommendation were Rai, Limbu, Yakkha, Tamang, Magar, Gurung, Sunuwar, Bhujel and Jogi, who occupied the stratum below the twice-born castes like Bahun and Chhetri, but above the untouchables like Kami, Sarki and Damai. When Nar Bahadur Bhandari refused to accept the demand of some members of the state legislative assembly to implement the Mandal Commission report, some of the representatives of the above ethnic groups led by the chief minister left the party (Sikkim Sangram Parishad) and formed a new party called the Sikkim Democratic Front. The Sikkim Legislative Assembly finally, on 19 May 1994, decided to consider 'Sikkimese of Nepali origin' as 'socially and educationally backward classes' or OBC. Consequently, the ethnic groups like Bhujel, Gurung, Limbu, Magar, Rai, Sunuwar and Tamang were declared as OBCs in Sikkim on 2 June 1994. But by then it was too late, as Bhandari was soon voted out of office.

In partial modification of earlier orders by Notification No.2/WD of 2 June 1994 and Notification No. 236/SW/251(3)/WD of 15 June 2000, the state government declared the following ethnic groups as 'Most Backward Classes': Bhujel, Dewan (Yakkha), Gurung, Jogi, Rai, Magar, Sunuwar and Thami, and the following as 'Other Backward Classes': Bahun, Chhetri, Newar and Sanyasi (see Sikkim Government Gazette Extraordinary No. 308 dated Gangtok, Friday 19 September 2003). While there was no category called

MBCs in the central government list, even the OBCs of Sikkim were not included in the central list of OBCs.

Although it was not a part of the terms of reference for the Sinha Committee to recommend any ethnic group(s) listed in June 2000 under MBCs, the members were well aware of what the government of Sikkim and people belonging to the concerned ethnic groups expected of it. It was very clear in the ethnographic reports submitted by the representatives of the communities listed above. So, the committee considered the following criteria for its ethnographic report: origin and history, population and settlement, rites of passage, kinship and social organization, traditional economy, language and literature, material culture, folk-traditions, and religion.

The ethnographic reports on seven ethnic groups listed in the notification showed that all but one (Jogi) had the foundation of Animism or Bonism (a pre-Buddhist form of religion found in the Himalayas), and a superstructure of Hinduism or Buddhism or a combination of the two. They were basically nature worshippers through the medium of shamans. Their culture was mostly folk and oral. They offered flowers, water, grains of new crops, and blood of birds and animals to various deities presiding over rivers, houses, crops, forests and mountains. They also had their own languages, which some of them had lost during the past two centuries or so. Some others were so dispersed or were so few numerically that it was not possible for them to keep their languages alive. Furthermore, they all shared a certain sense of deprivation vis-à-vis the Buddhist Lepchas and Bhutias in Sikkim, who were patronized by the theocratic and hereditary Namgyal rulers for centuries, and they continued to receive special privileges as STs after Sikkim became the 22nd state of India in 1975. The Nepali ethnic groups first demanded OBC status, which was granted in 1994, but after 2003 their demand for ST status became perceptibly vigorous. The sense of exclusion among those who were yet to be listed as STs was rather vivid in the ethnographic reports submitted to the Sinha Committee. Hence, the committee decided to include the following recommendations in its executive report to facilitate the state government in taking necessary steps towards fulfilment of their aspirations:

1. If any caste is to be considered for the status of ST in future, the ones identified in the present report as 'Kiratas' (Rai, Yakkha, Sunuwar) make the most suitable case because the Kiratas are mentioned in the ancient texts like the Ramayana, Mahabharata, and the Upanishads as Mongoloid people living in the eastern Himalayas.
2. The next eligible group of castes is referred to in the report as 'analogous to the Kiratas' (Magar, Gurung, and Bhujel) for consideration of the status of ST because they are both physically and culturally similar to those who are categorized as 'Kiratas'.
3. Jogis are found best suited for inclusion under OBC rather than ST category because they were mendicants by profession and moved from village to village blowing conch shells at night and collecting alms the next day.

Unfortunately, the government of Sikkim reportedly sent the Sinha Committee report directly to the government of India for its consideration of granting the ST status as per the above recommendations without first considering and approving it in its assembly.

The unofficial advice of the chairman to the state government to first constitute a small committee of experts to study the report and place its recommendations in the state assembly for its consideration of approval before recommending the same to the central government was apparently ignored. Nor did the state government make the content of the report public to elicit their responses to the recommendations of the committee. Instead, the state government constituted a commission chaired by one of the most senior anthropologists in the country, Professor B. K. Roy Burman. How the state government identified him for heading the commission and how it identified the other members of the commission is however a matter of much speculation. The nomination of the speaker of the state assembly as a member of this commission was also a matter of great surprise, because that would make the discussion of the commission's report in the state assembly redundant.

The Roy Burman Commission[2]

The Roy Burman Commission was officially called the Commission for Review of Social and Environmental Sector Policies, Plans and Programmes (CRESP). The initial terms of reference for this commission was to examine the current statutory status of all the communities in Sikkim and make appropriate recommendations, but on the insistence of its chairman, the revised terms of reference included (1) Review of the constitutional status of castes and communities in Sikkim in historical, cultural–ecological and political–economic contexts and making appropriate recommendations, (2) Review of the policies, plans and programmes in respect of the Scheduled Castes, Scheduled Tribes, OBCs and other categories of population and (3) Review of Strengthening State Plans for Human Development (SSPHD) for recommending measures for improvement of the quality of life of all sections of the population of Sikkim. The chairman further insisted that the commission be set up under the Commission of Inquiry Act so that necessary documents may be obtained from any source within the country. His conditions for acceptance of the post were accepted by the state government and the commission started functioning from 1 December 2005,[3] just six months after the Sinha Committee submitted its report.

About one year later, on 27 December 2006, the commission was requested to look into the following supplementary terms of reference:

1. Protection of 12 seats reserved for the Bhutia and Lepcha communities in Sikkim Legislative Assembly.
2. Reservation of seats for Limbu and Tamang communities in Sikkim Legislative Assembly consequent upon the inclusion of these communities in the list of Scheduled Tribes.
3. While Bahun, Chhetri and Newar communities have already been declared as OBCs under a state government notification, they may be recommended for notification as OBCs in the central government list.
4. Recommendation of remaining ethnic communities like Rai, Gurung, Magar, Sunuwar, Thami and Bhujel to be declared as Scheduled Tribes in Sikkim.
5. Recognition of Lepcha as the 'most primitive tribe'.

6. Increase in the total number of seats in the State Legislative Assembly.
7. Setting up of a Central University in Sikkim.

The final report of 484 pages was submitted on 30 September 2008 and the printed version of the same was released on 26 February 2009.

This report contains a lengthy introduction (28 pages), physiography and sacred space and time (15 pages), political economy of migration and sex ratio in Sikkim (4 pages), ethno-cultural profile (72 pages), socioeconomic indicators (142 pages), ethnic identities, ethno-history and ethnic processes (8 pages), political and administrative processes (20 pages), dialectics of reverse inequality in Sikkim (13 pages), review of environmental and social sector policies, plans and programmes as prelude to promotional activity for the human development agenda (4 pages), recapitulation, amplification and recommendation (16 pages), bibliography (5 pages) and annexures (140+ pages). Following is presented a critique of the main recommendations of this commission.

One, the commission has recommended that 'unified indigenous Sikkimese', meaning Lepchas, Bhutias and Nepalis, are to be categorized 'as a secondary tribe with its social orbit coinciding with the territory of Sikkim', but does not care to explain anywhere in the report what it means by 'a secondary tribe'. The report says that 'the unified Sikkimese social entity can also be called a territorial tribe' (page 320, paragraphs 11 to 13), thereby introducing another concept called 'territorial tribe', again without explaining it. Further, the report uses the expressions 'indigenous Sikkimese' as well as 'unified indigenous Sikkimese' without explaining the difference between the two, if any, although it appears that it has used the latter expression to include the Nepalis as well. Furthermore, it wrongly assumes that the various castes and ethnic groups of Sikkim are monolithic in terms of primordial characteristics like language, culture and religion, or in terms of their association, perception and articulation of the membership criteria. By painting all the castes and ethnic groups of Sikkim in one colour and labelling them as secondary or territorial tribes, the commission has created a lot of conceptual conflagration.

Two, regarding some supplementary terms of reference, the report recommends continuation of the 12 seats reserved for Bhutias and Lepchas on historical grounds, but does not recommend the same for Limbu and Tamang on grounds of 'changed circumstances'. What those changed circumstances were is, however, left unexplained. It considers the demand for inclusion of the state's OBCs under central list as redundant because it 'recommends the entire indigenous peoples of Sikkim to be notified as Scheduled Tribes', and on the same ground, considers as redundant the specific demands of Rai, Gurung, Magar, Sunuwar, Thami, Newar and Bhujel for inclusion in the list of STs.

Three, the report says that any recommendation to include the 'unified indigenous Sikkimese' in the ST list should be preceded by an assessment of its likely impact within the state, and within the country and neighbouring countries. This is a welcome idea, because decisions taken in one part of the country can have unintended consequences on other parts of the country and even neighbouring countries. But, incidentally, no such assessment was made before making its recommendations to declare all 'unified indigenous Sikkimese' as STs. It is, of course, not easy to make such assessment objectively.

But there should have been at least some clarification about what would happen to those 'unified indigenous Sikkimese' who are already listed as SCs, STs, OBCs and MBCs. Would they enjoy multiple constitutional privileges or forego their current constitutional status? The question is relevant because only seven out of eighteen ethnic groups in Sikkim had originally demanded ST status. Was it ethical on the part of the commission to recommend a constitutional status that they had not asked for till the coming of the commission itself? Was it also ethical to ignore the apprehensions of Lepcha and Bhutias, or Limbus and Tamangs about the possible consequences of such a decision on them?

Four, it is also claimed in the report that two political parties – Bharatiya Janata Party (BJP) and Sikkim Himali Rajya Parishad Party – have favoured the idea that all the indigenous people of Sikkim should be listed as ST (page xvi, paragraphs 1.2 and 2.0). Notwithstanding the fact that these two political parties have virtually no existence in Sikkim in the sense that they have not been able to send a single representative to the state assembly to date, what BJP has demanded is inclusion of all indigenous communities of Sikkim under ST or SC, and not just ST, as the report gives the impression. Even the other political party did not favour the idea of ST status for all indigenous Sikkimese people, as mentioned in the report; what the other party has favoured is that Article 371F(g), which says that 'the Governor of Sikkim shall have special responsibility for peace and for an equitable arrangement for ensuring the social and economic advancement of different sections of the population of Sikkim [...]' may be implemented, and makes no mention of OBC, ST or SC status for the people of the state.

Five, it is also difficult to guess what made Roy Burman accept the word 'indigenous' after arguing in several of his publications during 1990s against the concept (e.g. Roy Burman 1992; 1995; 1997) on the ground that the concept has been pushed in India by international agencies like the United Nations, World Bank and International Monetary Fund, and is not applicable to India. Be that as it may, it is next to impossible to identify today who is 'indigenous Sikkimese' and who is not even in the specific context of Sikkim, because both Bhutias and Nepalis have quite recent migrants from Tibet and Nepal respectively, the border between Tibet and Nepal being rather porous and the Indo-Nepal border being still open. But the huge literature on indigeneity clearly shows that aboriginality, or 'first citizenship', is only one of the three major criteria of indigeneity, the other two being marginality and self-identification (Karlsson and Subba 2006). With the endless tussle among the UN working groups, participating nations and activists over the criteria of indigeneity, it is not likely that some amicable criteria will emerge any time soon.

Six, the report devotes more than 140 pages to the presentation of data on socioeconomic parameters, but the analysis of the same has nothing to do with the recommendation. For instance, according to its own findings, the Bhutia tribe is a fit case for descheduling. However, the report does not recommend descheduling of the Bhutias because according to the commission, the benefits from descheduling them may not automatically flow to the backward tribes but instead may make such descheduled tribes politically weaker and vulnerable.

Seven, the commissions' greatest flaw, perhaps, was not to hold public hearing and give opportunity to the people of diverse ethnic backgrounds to express their views, apprehensions, and so forth, on the terms of reference given to it. Hence, there was no democratic space given to the people before deciding anything about them.

Eight, the report says that final recommendations on the inclusion of all 'indigenous Sikkimese' in the list of STs cannot be made 'without examining the financial carrying capacity' of the state (pages 329–30, paragraph 24). This is a valid point, because without financial resources, political inclusion has no meaning. Where the money will come from needed to be asked, but the question was unfortunately left unanswered by the Roy Burman Commission that raised it. After having raised the issue, the Roy Burman Commission should have carried out a financial carrying-capacity study of the state. It should at least not have claimed that the state does not have the financial wherewithal for implementing its recommendation without carrying out such a study. Actually, the question of financial implication is insignificant in Sikkim, because actually only seven ethnic groups wanted an ST status till the Roy Burman Commission came into being. Of them, two have just about three thousand individuals and two others have just about five hundred persons only in the whole state. Among the remaining three groups, Magar has about 15 thousand, Gurung about 34 thousand and Rai about 78 thousand. But the argument about financial implications becomes deceptively powerful when all the castes and ethnic groups of Sikkim are included in the list of STs. There is particularly no rationale for extending the status of ST to the socially and economically forward groups like Bahuns, Chhetris and Newars of Sikkim just because they have also demanded the commission to list them as STs. Such demands should have been scrutinized on the basis of the data collected by the commission, but unfortunately that did not happen.

Nine, while the commission recommends all 'indigenous Sikkimese' to be extended the status of ST, it recommends a 40-member state legislative assembly (from the present 32) with the following arrangement of reserved seats: Lepcha and Bhutia (12), Scheduled Tribe (20), Scheduled Caste (2), General (4), *Sangha* (2). The above distribution of reserved seats does not make any sense if all indigenous Sikkimese are to be included in the list of STs as recommended by the commission.

Finally, the report is full of typographical errors about names of local places and communities, which indicates that the local members of the commission did not read the report before putting their signatures on it. The chairman, who apparently wrote the most critical chapters of the report by himself, has very little acquaintance with Sikkimese history, society and culture, although his knowledge of the Indian society generally is legendary and he is rightly referred to as 'Walking Encyclopaedia'.

As expected, the Lepchas and Bhutias of Sikkim have already filed complaints against the recommendations of the report, which is going to be placed in the state assembly for consideration and approval of some of the recommendations of the commission, which have far-reaching ramifications for a small Himalayan state like Sikkim. Besides, the above critique clearly shows that the commission's recommendations are not based on sound logic, solid ethnography or people's participation. Therefore, these recommendations need further debate both at intellectual and popular levels before they may be considered by the state's legislative assembly. Any hasty decision in this regard may have catastrophic consequences on the people of Sikkim.

Conclusion

No matter how poorly prepared, the Roy Burman Commission report has raised the expectations of a large number of the people of Sikkim, because the commission's recommendations are taken far more seriously than the report of a committee like the one appointed in 2005. But the process of inclusion of all the indigenous communities of Sikkim in the list of STs is not going to be easy even if the state government accepts the recommendations of the commission. The central government, without whose acceptance the commission's recommendations have no meaning, has no consistent policy of its own in this regard, nor do the federal states follow any uniform criteria for recommending a certain ethnic group for inclusion in the list by the central government. For instance, when Sherpas and Tamangs were included in the list of STs, there is no logic why the Buddhist Gurungs were excluded. Again, when Limbus were included in the list, there was no reason why Rais, Yakkhas and Sunuwars were not. After all, the current interest of development analysts and policy makers is not in inequality per se, but in what is called 'horizontal inequality', or inequality between ethnic groups, which if left unattended for too long, can be a potential cause of civil conflicts (Stewart 2002; Ostby 2004).

It is indeed difficult to say what clicks about the process of enlisting certain ethnic groups as STs, for there are no uniform criteria followed in the country for including them in the list of STs. There are Brahmins listed as ST in Himachal Pradesh, and there are several examples of the same community being listed as ST in one state and SC or OBC in another. Anthropologists themselves would not agree on any two criteria for identification of communities for possible inclusion in the list of STs. Nor is it easily justifiable to argue in favour of uniform criteria like 'primitiveness' and 'backwardness' or 'homogenous culture' for the purpose of affirmative action, because the tribal situation in the country is highly heterogeneous, both internally and externally, in respect of social structure, political organization, demography, economy, income, religious beliefs and practices, customs and laws, and so on. Hence, any criteria would be problematic in a vast country like India.

It is such a situation that creates space for ad hocism, political expediency and intense negotiations to get the constitutional recognition that a particular community wishes for. The constitution of the committees or commissions headed by some anthropologists (or not) is often an eyewash, nor are the reports submitted by them always sound enough to be taken note of by the state or central government. Quite justifiably, the political party in power has its own agenda behind supporting the case of one or the other community for inclusion in the list of STs. There is little that anthropologists can do except facilitate what the government wants or critique the manner in which inclusion of one and exclusion of the other community is finally given the official seal of approval by the central government with gazette notifications. Their long tradition of working on tribes is ignored, which they often rue, but it is perhaps they who first need to fill the huge gap between ethnography and policy making, or between micro studies and macro perspectives. All this may require repositioning of the discipline and readjusting its methodological tools that may be strongly opposed from within the discipline.

But they must do this if they do not wish to be excluded from policy making and from being counted.

Notes

1 'Creamy layer' is an expression first used by Sattanathan Commission in 1971 to refer to relatively wealthier and educated members of Other Backward Classes, who are not eligible for reservations or quotas in government services or other affirmative programmes of the government.

2 'Commission' is a legal term, covered under certain constitutional provisions. Once a commission's recommendations are accepted, the government is legally bound to implement them. In case they are not, one may challenge the government for noncompliance in a court of law. Thus, it has a judicial connotation. On the other hand, a 'committee' is a working arrangement to apportion the work to be studied by some expert members. It is more of an administrative and executive nature rather than judicial.

3 The constitution of the Roy Burman Commission was slightly different. The chairman was former Deputy Registrar General of the Census of India, 1961 with a brief stint as a professor in Visva-Bharati University, West Bengal. The Speaker of Sikkim Legislative Assembly and two cabinet ministers of Sikkim government were members, followed by the president of the Indian Anthropological Society (AnSI) and the former director of the Anthropological Survey of India, former coordinator of Tribal Studies Panel of the Indian Council of Social Science Research, New Delhi, and three Indian Administrative Service (IAS) officers of whom one was earlier secretary to the Sinha Committee.

References

Bose, Nirmal Kumar. 1941. 'The Hindu Method of Tribal Absorption'. *Science and Culture* 7: 188–94.

Foucault, Michel. 1980. *Power/Knowledge: Selected Interviews and Other Writings 1972–1977*, edited by Colin Gordon. New York: Random House.

Kabeer, Naila. 2000. 'Social Exclusion, Poverty and Discrimination: Towards an Analytical Framework'. *IDS Bulletin* 31 (4).

Luhmann, Niklas. (1983) 1993. *Legitimation durch Verfahren*. Frankfurt/M: Suhrkamp.

Karlsson, Beppe G. and Tanka B. Subba, eds. 2006. *Indigeneity in India*. London: Kegan Paul Ltd.

Namgyal, T. and Yeshi Drolma. 1908. 'History of Sikkim'. Typescript, 48pp.

Ostby, Gudrun. 2004. 'Do Horizontal Inequalities Matter for Civil Conflict?' Paper presented at the PAC Winter Meeting in Barcelona, Spain, 10–11 December.

Roy Burman, B. K. 1992. 'Indigenous and Tribal Peoples, Global Hegemonies and Government of India'. *Mainstream*, 5 September.

______. 1995. '"Indigenous" and "Tribal" Peoples and the UN and International Agencies'. Rajiv Gandhi Institute for Contemporary Studies, Paper No. 27.

______. 1997. 'Tribal and Indigenous People – A Global Overview'. *The Eastern Anthropologist* 50 (1): 17–25.

______. 2008. *Report of the Commission for Review of Environmental and Social Sector Policies, Plans and Programmes (CRESP)*. Gangtok: Department of Information and Public Relations, Government of Sikkim.

Sen, Amartya. 2000. 'Social Exclusion: Concept, Application and Scrutiny'. Social Development Papers No. 1, Office of Environment and Social Development, Asian Development Bank, Manila.

Sinha, A. C. 2005. 'Ethnographic Report on Selected Communities of Sikkim'. Typescript, 89pp.

Stewart, Frances. 2002. 'Horizontal Inequalities: A Neglected Dimension of Development'. QEH Workshop Paper Series No. 81.

Subba, Tanka B. 1999. *Politics of Culture: A Study of Three Kirata Communities in the Eastern Himalayas.* Hyderabad: Orient Longman Ltd.

______. 2006. 'From Caste to Tribe: An Autobiographical Essay'. Plenary Lecture delivered at the 2nd Inter-Congress of the Indian National Confederacy and Academy of Anthropologists, organized by the Anthropological Association, Mysore, India, 21–23 February.

Tomei, Manuela. 2005. *Indigenous and Tribal Peoples: An Ethnic Audit of Selected Poverty Reduction Strategy Papers.* Geneva: International Labour Office.

Chapter 9

ENCOUNTERING 'INCLUSION' AND EXCLUSION IN POSTINDUSTRIAL MUMBAI: A STUDY OF MUSLIM EX-MILLWORKERS' OCCUPATIONAL CHOICES

Sumeet Mhaskar

Since the early 1990s India's move towards economic reforms and marketization has contributed to its 'rise' on the global economic landscape.[1] This 'rise' of India is attributed to the adoption of liberalization policies, which are also expected to eliminate discrimination based on caste, religion and gender. Since economic liberalization enhances competition among firms, scholars have argued that more emphasis will be placed on 'efficiency and skill' while recruiting a worker rather 'than the caste of the worker and his loyalty to the firm' (Panini 1996, 60). This claim is not new. Modernization theorists have long argued that industrialization and urbanization, and the associated ideas of modernity, such as the rationalities of the state, big businesses and planned development will reduce the influence of social institutions such as caste, religion and language (e.g. Srinivas 1969, 270).

In contrast to this view, recent studies have demonstrated that social institutions such as caste and religion continue to play a significant role in the economy, especially in deciding the life chances of individuals (e.g. Thorat and Newman 2010a; Harriss-White 2003). Thorat and Newman's (2010b, 23) study on economic discrimination in the formal urban labour market offers evidence of continued discriminatory barriers for highly qualified Dalits and Muslims. These empirical findings suggest that economic liberalization is not contributing to the dissolution of social institutions such as caste, religion and gender in the labour process. While both views discussed above refer to the formal labour market, little is known about the informal economy where most of the Indian workforce is located.[2] Moreover, even less is known about the manifold forms of exclusion associated with caste, gender and religion in the informal economy. Among these social institutions, this chapter looks at minority religious identity, with a particular focus on Muslim ex-millworkers' occupational choices in contemporary Mumbai. A caveat is necessary here as caste-specific variation within the Muslim community has been a subject of intense debate in recent years.[3] Hence, it would have been interesting to analyse, comparatively, occupational choices for Muslim caste groups such as *Ashrafs* (high caste Muslims), *Ajlafs* (backward caste Muslims) and *Arzals* (Muslim ex-untouchables). However, since the majority of my sample are *Ashraf* Muslims it is not possible to do a broader comparison. Nonetheless, this chapter hopes to shed light on the general situation of Muslims. This may provide leads for future research.

The chapter seeks to investigate the following questions: What trends are emerging in terms of the survival and coping strategies employed by Muslim ex-millworkers vis-à-vis non-Muslim ex-millworkers? How are Muslims, as a marginalized community, coping with the challenges posed by changes in the political economy? Broadly speaking, what is happening to religion as a social institution in the context of neoliberal urban socioeconomic transformation and how far are the existing inequalities and hierarchies buttressed? To answers these questions, this chapter will rely on qualitative and quantitative data collected between August 2008 and August 2009 and from December 2010 to January 2011. As for the qualitative data, 80 in-depth interviews were conducted among Mumbai's ex-millworkers who lost their jobs since the late 1990s. Semi-structured interviews were also conducted with all major trade union leaders and government officials. In addition, informal discussions were carried out with political activists, social workers and various other actors engaged in varied ways with the issues of Mumbai millworkers. In survey data terms, information was collected on 924 ex-millworkers' households who have stayed back in Mumbai, and 113 households of ex-millworkers that have migrated back to their villages.

The chapter is structured in the following way: In the opening section I outline the case of Mumbai city and Muslims with particular reference to the cotton textile industry. After this, I examine Muslim ex-millworkers' occupational choices in relation to non-Muslim ex-millworkers. I argue that the feeling of *karahiyat* (Urdu word meaning aversion, nausea, disgust, dislike, disdain, detest, loathing, abhorrence, disagreeableness and hideousness) and suspicion, in terms of terrorism and mafia activities, contributes towards the discrimination of Muslims in the labour market. I also argue that the rise of Hindu extremist and nativist politics, led by the Shiv Sena and the Bharatiya Janata Party (BJP),[4] who have been ruling Mumbai's civic bodies for the last few decades, are further causing vulnerabilities among Muslims. Finally, I argue that lack of political patronage deters Muslims from carrying out certain kinds of small businesses. Muslims are thus pushed towards occupations which are both of low social status and provide meagre economic earnings. Thus, as seen through Amartya Sen's (2000, 28–29) concepts, Muslims in Mumbai face unfavourable exclusion and unfavourable inclusion. The former suggests that Muslims 'are being *kept out* (or at least left out)' while the latter indicates that they 'are being included – maybe even forced to be included – on deeply unfavourable terms' (ibid., 28–2,9, emphasis in the original). The factors influencing Muslims' contemporary situation range from the local to the international. In the conclusion I return to the questions posed in this section.

Mumbai

Mumbai, India's commercial and finance capital and the capital of Maharashtra State, serves as an interesting case to examine the issue of communal discrimination in an urban context. According to the 2011 census (provisional), Greater Mumbai is the largest metropolis in India with a population of 18.4 million people, and Muslims account for about 19 per cent of the city's population. Mumbai was one of the first Indian cities to undergo the raft of economic, technological and social changes associated with the growth of capitalism. Mumbai accounts for about 40 per cent (USD 15 billion) of the total share of Maharashtra's economy. Greater Mumbai alone contributes about USD 10 billion to the state's economy. The city also contributes around 33 per cent of all India income tax collections, 60 per cent of all India customs duty collections, 20 per cent of all a India central excise tax collections and 40 per cent of the country's foreign trade and significant quantum of corporate taxes (Municipal Corporation of Greater Mumbai 2005).

The dynamics of social institutions such as caste, religion and language, the practice of 'untouchability', communal conflicts/riots and the politics of identity have all played a significant role in shaping Mumbai city. These factors have affected social, political and economic processes, which in turn have affected social institutions. The urban industry was for long seen as a crucial site for understanding the above processes in the city. As such, the textile industry in Mumbai has historically attracted scholars' attention across disciplines (Chandavarkar 1994; 1998; Wersch 1992; Morris 1965; Adarkar, Menon, and Chandavarkar 2004). Since the last two decades Girangaon ('village of [textile] mills' in the Marathi language),[5] Mumbai's working-class district, is in the throes of major transformations, economically, socially, politically and spatially. This chapter will delve into these dynamics by looking at the case of Muslim ex-mill workers' occupational choices.

The politico-economic developments that have been unfolding in the city over the past two decades will constitute a watershed in the city's history, and inaugurate a new beginning. In the last two decades, Mumbai has experienced industrial decline, similar to other cities in the west (see D'Monte 2002). All the 58 textile mills (32 privately owned, 25 by the National Textile Corporation and one by Maharashtra State Textile Corporation) in Girangaon have been closed down retrenching more than a hundred thousan workers.[6] This closure of mills had a direct implication for the industries that were dependent on the textile industry, such as engineering, dyeing and chemicals, marketing and transport. Furthermore, it also affected small businesses in a significant way.

Mumbai has gradually transformed from an industrial economy into a service sector economy. The service sector includes banking, insurance, Business Process Outsourcing (BPO) and Information Technology enabled services. The number of establishments in financing, insurance, real estates and business services increased from 31,501 establishments to 79,255, with employment increasing from 303,557 to 753,624 during the period 1980–1998 (Ghorpade 2005, 44). In terms of its employment share, the service sector contributed 19.6 per cent in 1983, 'which increased to 25 per cent in 1993, while the finance share was 7.6 per cent in the 1983 and it rose to 11.5 per cent in 1993' (Bhowmik and More 2001, 4823). Mumbai has thus witnessed both the creation of new employment opportunities in the service sector (and a growing new middle class), as well as layoffs in the manufacturing sector. This transformation is affecting both socioeconomic relations and identity politics.

In the early 1980s, the city witnessed an historic 18 month strike involving more than 250 thousand textile millworkers (see Wersch 1992). The textile workforce was once considered among 'the best paid industrial workers in India' (Breman 2004, 155). By the late 1970s, however, millworkers' wages, living standards and working conditions, in comparison to the workers in the newly established industries such as engineering, chemicals and especially pharmaceuticals, had fallen considerably (Chandavarkar 2009, 179). The issue of wage rise and workers' discontent with the officially recognized trade union Rashtriya Mill Mazdoor Sangh (RMMS) were important causes for the 1982–83 strike. Although the strike was eventually put down by the mill owners, with active support of the State apparatus and the RMMS, it has been distinguished for never being officially called off (D'Monte 2002, 81). The mill owners took advantage of the 18-month strike to shut down their mills citing the 'losses' they incurred during this period and the 'sickness' that had begun to ail this industry (Krishnan 2000, 4–8). Darryl D'Monte (2002, 174–86) has pointed to the nexus between organized crime syndicates, the state, political parties, the mill owners and real estate developers in the process of closure of mills and the sale of mill land.

It should also be noted that very few attempts were made by the mill owners to modernize the infrastructure of the mills, even when they had made huge profits, as well as when the government launched various schemes to revive the mills (Krishnan 2000, 5–6). On the contrary, the mill owners pursued short-term gains by diverting their profits to other industries and shifting cloth production to powerlooms in places such as Bhiwandi, which is located in the outskirts of Mumbai city. The growth of powerlooms in the Bhiwandi region is noteworthy. From 86,000 powerlooms during 1980–82 it increased to 250,000 by 1985–87. It further increased upwards to 300 thousand to 400 thousand by 1996, and by 2006 there were 450,000 powerlooms (Roy 1998, 900; Singh 2006). While these figures provide us with a picture of the registered powerlooms, the number goes much higher if one takes into account the unregistered/illegal units.

The mill owners, having outsourced the cloth production to powerlooms, saw it more profitable to sell the mill land in the real estate market (D'Monte 2002, 10; Krishnan 2000, 6). Therefore, the mill owners began demanding permission to sell the surplus land for revival and modernization of mills. However, the restrictions on land use placed limitations on such demands. In 1991 the state introduced Development Control Regulation (DCR) 58, which allowed, for the first time, the sale of surplus mill land for the purpose of the *revival* or *modernization* of the textile mills (D'Monte 2002, 124). While the mill owners did sell the 'surplus' land, and made huge profits from it, there were no attempts to revive or modernize the mills (Krishnan 2000; D'Monte 2002). In fact, most of the manufacturing units in the textile industry were sold at scrap rates to the powerloom owners (Roy 1998, 901).

By 2001 the mill owners further managed to persuade the state to amend the DCR 58 to be able to sell the entire mill land and use it for nonindustrial purposes (Kanga 2006, 30). This paved the way for the closure of textile mills, as the mill owners were now able to sell the mill land and use it for commercial and residential purposes. These developments contributed to the informalization of the textile workforce. This significantly brought down the percentage of formal sector workers, which had already reduced from

65 per cent in 1961 to 35 per cent in 1991. As is well known, the jobs in the informal sector are marked by flexible labour arrangements where the workers receive low wages, work long hours, have scarce labour regulations, have no legal protection and most, importantly, lack most forms of social protection (Bhowmik and More 2001, 4822).

Since the 1990s, changes in India's political economy also affected Mumbai in a significant way. Mumbai was now expected to adapt itself to the role of the 'world class city' where international businesses could locate themselves and link the Indian economy with the global economy (Weinstein 2008, 33). As a result, the state placed more emphasis on the 'environment friendly' industries such as banking, insurance and information technology-enabled services. Thus, under the pretext of establishing 'environment friendly' industries, the state contributed to the dispersal of the manufacturing units from the city. This affected the retrenched textile millworkers in a major way, as the service sector economy demanded altogether different skills and knowledge. This economic transformation also affected the textile workers' neighbourhoods that are undergoing gentrification. In fact, the restructuring of spaces once occupied by the textile industry and working-class neighbourhoods is central to Mumbai's transformation into a 'world class' city. These complex dimensions play a significant role in shaping the sociopolitical and economic process that led to the textile mills closure and the subsequent emergence of the postindustrial economy.

Muslims and Mumbai's Textile Industry

During the mid-nineteenth and early twentieth centuries, industrialization took place in the major cities in the Indian subcontinent. Different social groups migrated within the framework of caste, kinship and village connections to work in these cities (for Mumbai, see Chandavarkar 1994). The migration of Muslim labourers, especially the *julaha-ansaris* (Muslim weaver's caste), from North India to the Mumbai textile mills goes back to the mid-nineteenth century. With the decline of courtly patronage in northern India, particularly in the aftermath of the 1857 revolt, *julaha-ansari* weavers migrated to various parts of the country. A large group came to Mumbai city and were mainly concentrated in areas such as Nagpada, Mominpura, Madanpura and Kamathipura (Hansen 2001, 160; Kulkarni 2004, 120). Their numbers grew rapidly with the construction of railways (Kidambi 2007, 120). *Julaha-ansaris* are *Ajlaf* Muslims.

Social institutions such as caste and religion were reproduced in the cities as a result of the strategies employed by capital for recruitment, labour supply and labour control (Chandavarkar 1994, 10). Caste and religion was also used by the workers to obtain and secure control over scarce jobs. Among various social groups, hereditary weaving castes such as the *julaha-ansari* Muslims were successful in claiming weaving occupations in the textile mills. Also, as Chandavarkar notes, *julaha-ansaris* 'appropriated important areas of control over their own labour'. Not only were the *julaha-ansari* weavers in a position to refuse to work in the night shifts, their 'average earnings were reputed to exceed those of their Hindu counterparts' (Chandavarkar 1994, 320).

As with most mill workers, a large group of Muslim weavers lived in proximity to their workplace. Although the overall number of Muslims in the textile mill's weaving section was not very high,[7] they were quite dominant in the mills located in central Mumbai (ibid., 226). For instance, in the weaving department of the Indian manufacturing mill, 'almost everyone was Muslim' (Newman 1981, 42). In the Hindustan Mills, one of the Maratha caste respondents informed me that the proportion of Muslims was so high that the textile mill almost stopped functioning during *namaz* (prayer) timings. In addition, there were large concentrations of handloom weaving (later on powerlooms) workshops in the Madanpura region (Kidambi 2007, 33).

Besides *julaha-ansari* weavers, *Ashraf* and *Arzal* Muslims also worked in the textile mills. Although Muslims were dominant in the weaving department there were textile mills that discriminated against them. As an example, the Century Textile Mills had an unwritten policy of not employing Muslims. In fact, a Dalit ex-millworker respondent from the same mill claimed that the management only dealt with Muslims when they had very little choice. Such was the case with scrap metal collection, occupations commonly known to be exclusive to Muslims.

Since workers relied on caste, kinship and village networks to obtain and protect their jobs, rivalries over jobs acquired a communal edge. Tellingly, the working class districts became centres for most of the conflicts or riots that broke out between Hindus and Muslims. The communal riots were, at least in part, triggered by the mill owners' recruitment of Muslim workers as strikebreakers (Bhattacharya 1981). This was the case during the 1928–29 strikes. By employing Muslim workers as strikebreakers, employers were able to manipulate the communal factor to bring the strikes to an end. This also helped the employers and the state to keep the working classes fragmented along communal lines.

Expulsion of the Muslim Workforce

From the 1940s onward, the textile industry was challenged by technological innovations and competition from other textile sectors. This resulted, in some cases, in a gradual reduction of the workforce in the textile mills (Hansen 2001, 162). As jobs became scarcer, 'older conflicts and prejudices between the various communities were revived' (ibid., 163). Interestingly, the prejudice expressed by high-caste Hindus against Dalits, to prevent them from working in the weaving shed (Chandavarkar 1994, 226–7), was articulated against Muslims since the 1960s.[8] As Hansen (2001, 163) notes:

> One of these conflicts [between Hindus and Muslims] had to do with the threading of the large looms in the weaving shed, an operation that was often done by *ansaris* and required that they wet the cotton thread with their mouths. Non-Muslim workers would then regard the cloth as polluted and would refuse to touch.

It is important to note here that, historically, caste Hindus have been 'less apprehensive of such contact with Muslim weavers' (Chandavarkar 1994, 227). How did this change come about, and why were Muslims unable to hold on to their jobs in the later period? As a hereditary weaver's caste, *julaha-ansaris* have successfully bargained for their conditions of work. However, since the 1960s, employers were keen on rationalizing the workforce.

Besides, since the 1970s and particularly during the 1982–83 strike, mill owners had begun subcontracting their work to the powerlooms in Bhiwandi. The arrival of automatic weaving machines in a few textile mills also challenged *julaha-ansaris'* claim for skilled work. The anti-Muslim environment, therefore, helped the employers to reduce the Muslim workforce.

Another crucial factor that contributed to the marginalization of Muslims was the split in the communist-led Girni Kamgar Union (Mill Workers' Union) in the late 1960s. This split among the communists resulted in the fragmentation of the opposition to the RMMS. The communists were, therefore, unable to stall the expulsion of Muslims. In many cases RMMS officials were also active *Shiv Sainiks* (Shiv Sena Activists) in their neighbourhoods. Even the ones who supported the communists inside the textile mills were in some cases Shiv Sena supporters.[9] These factors together worked against Muslim mill workers and led to their dismissal. Since the mid-1970s, the situation further intensified with the growing influence of the Bharatiya Kamgar Sena (BKS), the Shiv Sena's trade union (Bhowmik 1998, 152; Hansen 2001, 163). The BKS was 'opposed [to] the idea of class conflict and sought to broker the peace between mill owners and workers' (Prakash 2010, 254). As a result, the employers favoured BKS, as they could get rid of the militant communist unions. The Congress-ruled state, too, supported the Shiv Sena and the BKS, as the latter helped in reducing the communist dominance in the working-class districts (Gupta 1982, 82–3).

While the Shiv Sena began as a nativist political movement and party in the 1960s, arguing for a preferential treatment for the 'sons of the soil' (see Gupta 1982; Katzenstein 1973), it took an explicitly Hindutva turn in 1984 (Hansen 2001, 76). In 1984 an active participation of *Shiv Sainiks* was seen in the communal pogroms that took place in the Bhiwandi region (Hansen 2001, 77). Again, *Shiv Sainiks* played a prominent role as perpetrators during the 1992–93 anti-Muslim pogroms in Mumbai, which erupted in the wake of the Babri Masjid demolition by Hindu extremists (ibid., 121–59). During the anti-Muslim pogroms, *Shiv Sainiks* became more aggressive, and on occasion violent, towards the Muslim millworkers. In many factories, members of the Shiv Sena union threatened Muslim workers, and where the latter protested, physical force was used. Even in the Mazgaon Docks, where the Shiv Sena union was not dominant, workers owing allegiance to the Sena were threatening Muslim workers.

Owing to the disturbed circumstances of the city and the insecurity felt by Muslim workers, they were often unable to report for work for long periods and consequently, in many cases, they faced dismissal. After the pogrom, as Muslim workers began to return for work, the management refused to take them back on the pretext that there would be disturbances again. In many cases, Muslims lost their jobs.

Since the early 1990s, successive events in Mumbai have contributed to the general climate of suspicion and fear towards Muslims. These include bomb blasts in 1993 after the anti-Muslim pogrom, bomb blasts in two taxis in 2003, the explosion of seven bombs in local trains in 2006 and finally, a terrorist attack in 2008. Extra-local political developments have similarly increased the vulnerability of Muslims. In 1996, the Shiv Sena–BJP-led government came to power in Maharashtra against the backdrop of the 1992–93 communal pogrom. At the national level, the National Democratic Alliance government, led by the BJP, came to power in 1999. In the adjoining state of Gujarat, the incumbent chief minister, Narendra Modi of the BJP, rode to power against the backdrop of communal pogroms in both 2002 and 2007. At the international level, the 9/11 attack on the Twin Towers by Al-Qaeda meant that Islam increasingly came to be equated with terrorism. This is inter alia documented in the Sachar Committee's report (see Nielsen, this volume, for a brief background). The report notes how Muslims are being looked upon with a greater degree of suspicion by non-Muslims as well as state institutions (Prime Minister's High Level Committee 2006, 11). This general context of growing anti-Muslim sentiments complicated matters for Muslims, especially with regard to employment and self-employment.

In the last few years, there has been a re-emergence of nativist politics in Mumbai through the Maharashtra Navanirman Sena (MNS). Like the Shiv Sena, the MNS, too, champions the cause of the 'sons of the soil' and argues for preferential treatment for Marathi speakers in matters of employment and self-employment. While the MNS claims to protect the rights of the 'locals', and as such carried out attacks on North Indian 'outsiders', Muslims are evidently not included in the category 'local'. It is against this backdrop that the next section examines the occupational choices of Muslim ex-millworkers in postindustrial Mumbai.

Muslim Ex-millworkers in Postindustrial Mumbai

The postindustrial economy in Mumbai is, as mentioned, dominated by the service sector. This transformation of Mumbai into a service sector economy has posed a challenge for ex-millworkers as this economy requires a workforce with altogether different skills and knowledge. The retrenched mill workers, whether skilled or unskilled, therefore have to rely on the informal sector for their livelihood. Yet, as noted, social institutions such as caste and religion add another dimension to individual occupational chances. I therefore examine the findings from survey data and the narratives of ex-millworkers to see whether being a Muslim minority affected occupational choices.

The survey covered 924 ex-millworkers who lost their jobs and remained in the city. Of these, 577 (approximately 60 per cent) took up some kind of work after the closure of the mills. About 40 per cent of the ex-millworkers were incorporated in the security, courier and shops occupational category.[10] While non-Muslims are represented in substantial numbers in this particular occupational group, this is not the case with Muslim ex-millworkers. For instance, 45 per cent of the high-caste Hindus, 39 per cent of the Other Backward Caste (OBC) Hindus, 46 per cent of the Dalits, but merely 15 per cent of the Muslims are engaged in this occupational group. In contrast, approximately 45 per cent of Muslims are located in industry, repair and processing occupations.[11] This includes wage labour as well as Muslims who are self-employed. These findings resonate with the macro level evidence presented in the report of the Prime Minister's High Level Committee (2006, 99).

A few Muslim ex-millworkers mentioned the possibility of working as security guards. However, the working conditions, especially the 12-hour work shift, deterred them from taking those jobs. Such responses were not uncommon even from non-Muslim ex-millworkers. I argue that the feeling of *karahiyat* and suspicion, in terms of terrorism and mafia activities, towards Muslims place barriers for employment and self-employment opportunities. The most common response to my question as to why Muslims are not hired was that employers do not want to get into 'any trouble'. 'Trouble' here refers to fears that Muslim employees might be associated with a terrorist organization or the mafia. Muslims are, thus left with little option but to rely on those employment opportunities in which their community is already dominant or which high caste Hindus would not avail. Tellingly, Muslims did not perceive barriers in occupations which were casual in nature and involved heavy manual work. These findings resonate with Cholia's (1941) study on the dock labourers in Mumbai. In Cholia's study the majority of Muslim men were employed 'on water or [on] board a vessel', which the Hindus did not prefer 'on account of religious susceptibilities'. However, what deterred the Hindus most was the 'hard life at sea', where diet was irregular (ibid., 128).

In the case of self-employment, approximately 31 per cent of the ex-millworkers in my survey reported to have been 'self-employed' after the closure of textile mills. As mentioned, Muslims are mainly engaged in the industry, repair and processing occupational category. With the decline of the textile mill jobs since the 1970s, Muslims diversified to various occupations such as taxi driving or selling daily-needs products and plastics items. As the survey data indicates, none of the Muslims (and none of the Dalits) reported to have engaged in fast food businesses. This occupation is dominated by OBC Hindus followed by high caste Hindus. There are at least two explanations for this: the first is the patronizing of the business by non-Muslims; the second is access to local political patronage. I argue that Muslims do not engage in the fast food business because of the feeling of *karahiyat* among non-Muslims, which might result in them not frequenting businesses run by Muslims.

However, the most significant aspect in my view is (the lack of) access to political patronage. Most of the fast food businesses (and other hawking businesses) that take place in Mumbai are done without any license from the Municipal Corporation: Since 1978, no new licenses have been issued by the Municipal Corporation (Anjaria 2006, 2140). Consequently, of the total number of street vendors in Mumbai, which amounts to around 200 thousand, only 14 thousand have a proper license to carry out their business (Bhowmik 2001, 9). Having a license was not an issue until 1998 as the Municipal Corporation, under the *pauti* (receipt) system, charged INR 5 to 10 from the nonlicensed hawker – a charge for the 'unauthorized occupation cum refusal removal charges' (Anjaria 2006, 2140). By paying this daily charge, the hawkers could carry out their business. In 1998, however, the *pauti* system was discontinued due to interventions by the judiciary (ibid., 2141).[12] Since then, nonlicensed street vendors, in order to carry out their business, have to pay rents to one or various authorities (police, municipal officials, local political units and in some cases, the Mafia).

Since the Shiv Sena and the BJP have been ruling the civic bodies for the last few decades, it explains why OBC and high-caste Hindus are dominant in small businesses. Two of my respondents (Maratha and OBC Hindu) had to face municipal raids while selling fast food items, which resulted in the confiscation of their products. Both of them went to their respective local municipal councillors and explained their situation. In both cases, the local municipal councillor intervened, and afterwards they ceased to have problems when carrying out their business.

Since political patronage is extended to individuals and groups with electoral calculations in mind, it is likely that non-Shiv Sena supporters would find it difficult to carry out such business in a Shiv Sena dominated neighbourhood. Shiv Sena would generally ensure that Muslims are not allowed to carry out any such business undisturbed. But in areas dominated by Muslims, the Shiv Sena may extend patronage to its Muslims supporters. This helps explain why, despite Shiv Sena's anti-Muslim image, Muslim vendors in the area of Nehru Nagar in Kurla campaigned actively for the Shiv Sena candidates and also participated in their victory processions.

Muslim ex-millworkers, who were engaged in businesses such as waste paper or scrap metal collection, did not face discrimination. A crucial factor here is that these occupations have a lower social status and earnings are meagre. Those engaged in selling vegetables and fruits either carried out the business where they resided or in the areas where they have historically been doing business. In the case of taxi driving, Muslims have been associated with this occupation for a long time and therefore did not perceive discrimination. This is also the case with bicycle repairing, stove repairing and motor mechanic work.

Thus, the picture that emerges from the survey data informs us that, by and large, Muslims are concentrated in the industry, repair and processing occupations, and are represented in lesser numbers in occupations such as a security guards, courier and shops. The feeling of *karahiyat* and suspicion towards Muslims reduces their chances of employment by non-Muslims. Access to political patronage also plays an active role in the kinds of businesses Muslims can get involved in.

Encountering Inclusion and Exclusion

The survey results presented above tell us the occupations where ex-millworkers ended up. However, they do not elucidate the barriers against employment and self-employment faced by these workers. I examined these barriers through in-depth interviews. Ex-millworkers from high-caste and OBC–Hindu backgrounds did not perceive discrimination in the labour market on the basis of caste and religion. In the case of Dalits, while they did not *perceive* discrimination, they remained on the margins in self-employed occupations (Mhaskar 2012). Only Muslim ex-millworkers commented on their experiences of discrimination.

As an example, Ahmed,[13] an *Ashraf* Muslim ex-millworker from Uttar Pradesh, did not manage to obtain any job after the closure of the mills. He therefore, with the help of community fellows, drove a taxi for five years. Ahmed then ventured into the *paan* business.[14] Ahmed told me that it was not easy to carry out this business as 'preparing a *paan* also requires lot of skills'. Ahmed's community fellows helped him with learning the skills he needed so that he eventually managed to run the business. Likewise, Habib, also an *Ashraf* Muslim ex-millworker from Uttar Pradesh, worked on the Bhiwandi powerlooms for six months, only to return to Mumbai because of the nonavailability of work. In Mumbai, Habib's relatives helped him to start bag-repairing work, trained him in the skills required, and assisted him in obtaining a license to do business. Neither Ahmed nor Habib perceived discrimination when they drove taxis, worked the powerlooms, or started bag repairing businesses. As mentioned, these occupations are dominated by Muslims, who generally have a good network to support new entrants from their community.

Similar is the case of Razak, a *julaha-ansari* ex-millworker from Uttar Pradesh who worked as a taxi driver after the closure of the mills. Razak had begun taxi driving during the 1982–83 strike and continued to work on a supplementary basis. Razak did not perceive discrimination while driving the taxi, but he stopped working after he developed a hearing problem. Like Razak, Abdul, another *julaha-ansari* ex-millworker worked on the Bhiwandi powerlooms after the mill closure. However, Abdul left due to work pressure and low wages. Abdul came to Mumbai to sell undergarments on the street. In carrying out the latter work Abdul did not perceive discrimination, given that the work has lower social status and earnings are meagre.

Manzar, an *Ashraf* Muslim ex-millworker from Swan Mills, hails from Uttar Pradesh and his appearance, in terms of his dress – *topi* (cap) and beard – are markers of stereotypical perceptions of a Muslim. Whichever non-Muslim employer Manzar went to, he felt *karahiyat* in their behaviour. Eventually Manzar decided to collect scrap metal and sell plastic items. Here Manzar did not perceive discrimination, as this work is dominated by Muslims and because the occupation is perceived as being of low social status and economic returns are meagre.

Another example is Rehan, an *Ashraf* Muslim ex millworker from Uttar Pradesh. Once one of Rehan's fellow ex-millworkers (a Hindu Maharashtrian) informed him about a vacancy in a shop. When Rehan went to the shop, he was told that there was no such vacancy. Later Rehan found out – through the same friend – that his Muslim identity acted as a barrier. Rehan stated he had faced two or three similar experiences. Eventually, Rehan settled for work that was casual in nature and physically demanding.

Usman is a Marathi-speaking *Ashraf* Muslim ex-millworker from Satara district in Maharashtra. Usman is one of the youngest (42 years old) ex-millworkers I interviewed, and he has acquired a higher level of education compared to other ex-millworkers. He had obtained a bachelors degree in economics from D. G. Ruparel College, one of the most reputed colleges in Mumbai University. Despite his qualifications, he was unable to obtain a good job and ultimately decided to take up his father's position in the textile mill. For the first year after he lost the mill job, he worked as a wireman helper and simultaneously took a computer hardware course. However, his new qualifications as a hardware technician did not help him to find any work. Even when he offered to work for free he did not find any work and was only offered an unskilled job at one of the hardware firms.

While working at the hardware firm, Usman used his spare time to learn more about the technicalities involved in hardware work. On one occasion, he was deputed to pick up a computer, which was to be fixed at the shop, from a customer's house. Although he was sent to just carry the computer to the workshop, he casually enquired about the problem and fixed it at the customer's place. After this incident, he was employed as a hardware technician. This job helped Usman to move to different companies that paid better salaries. This narrative suggests that lack of skills is not the only criteria by which ex-millworkers were excluded from the service sector economy. Usman's Muslim identity acted as a barrier, at least for a certain period of time, in obtaining a job in the service sector economy.

Very few Muslim ex-millworkers have managed to escape discrimination by migrating to countries in the Middle East. However, this option was not available to most Muslim ex-millworkers. Rehmat mentioned that despite obtaining a passport, he did not mange to migrate because of the initial finances required.

The above narratives tell us that prejudice against Muslims, due to feelings of *karahiyat* combined with suspicion in terms of terrorism and mafia activities, create barriers in the labour market. The onslaught of Hindu extremist and nativist forces makes Muslims even more vulnerable. Even the ones who managed to acquire new skills, such as the hardware technician, had difficulties in obtaining a job. This means that most Muslim ex-millworkers who ventured out to obtain a job or carry out a business where Muslims were not dominant, did perceive discrimination. And because they were discriminated against, they were pushed to those occupations where Muslims were already dominant, or to occupations that had a low social status and where earnings were low. The data presented in this chapter tells us that the Muslim community as a whole is likely to perceive and experience discrimination. However, what the data does not tell us is the situation of *Ajlaf* and *Arzal* Muslims, who tend to face double discrimination: first, because they are Muslims, and second, because of their lower caste status (Wankhede 2010, 180). This means that the occupational choices for *Ajlaf* and *Arzal* Muslims might be even more limited due to this double discrimination. Of the two, *Arzal* Muslims may face the most severely limited choices because of their concentration in socially stigmatized occupations such as scavenging and butchering.

Conclusion

In this chapter, I have examined the relationship between minority religious identity and economic discrimination in the city of Mumbai, focusing particularly on Muslims. The findings from the survey data, as well as the narratives presented here, indicate a trend toward exclusion of Muslims in matters of employment and self-employment. While non-Muslims are concentrated in substantial numbers in security guard, courier and shops occupational categories, the proportion of Muslims in these occupations is comparatively low. Muslims tend to be concentrated in industry, processing and repair occupations. The barriers in the labour market force Muslims to take up those occupations where Muslims already dominate, or which the high-caste Hindus will not take up because it has a perceived low social status and economic earnings are meagre. The other option available for Muslims is to take up heavy manual work where wages are low and the nature of work is casual.

On the basis of the evidence presented above, I have argued that the feeling of *karahiyat* and suspicion create barriers for Muslims' participation in the informal economy. The rise of Hindu extremist and nativist forces, such as the BJP and Shiv Sena, have further increased vulnerability for Muslims. Besides, international events such as 9/11 have added fuel to the propaganda carried out by the Hindu extremists. This, I argue, implies that Muslims in contemporary Mumbai face a combination of unfavourable exclusion and unfavourable inclusion. As the evidence suggests, one can argue that economic liberalization in India is not contributing to the dissolution of social institutions. If anything, social institutions may have been strengthened.

Notes

1 This chapter has benefited from discussions at the following conferences and seminars where I have presented an earlier draft of this paper: Department of Society and Globalisation, Roskilde University; CISCA, Aarhus University; Department of Sociology, Harvard University and South Asia D.Phil. Colloquium, University of Oxford. Conversations with Subodh More, Prabodhan Pol, Harish Wankhede and Yashpal Jogdand were useful sources of information in writing this paper. I would also like to thank the editors of this volume for their suggestions on the earlier draft of this chapter. I especially thank Priscilla Solano for thoroughly proofreading and editing this paper as well as helping me in polishing my arguments. All errors are mine.

2 According to the National Sample Survey of Employment and Unemployment carried out in 2004–2005, the Indian workforce constitutes about 457 million workers. Of the total workforce, more than 92 per cent work in the informal sector. Breman's (2004) study on the Ahmedabad textile mill closures examines the occupational choices of the ex-millworkers and documents the discrimination faced by Dalit and Muslim ex-millworkers. However, it does not examine the various occupations different caste groups have been engaged in, in relation to these two groups.

3 Although Islamic religious scriptures do not recommend any kind of hierarchy based on caste, Indian Muslims follow caste-based divisions similar to Hindus. Indian Muslims can be 'divided into two major ethnic groups: those who claimed to be descendants of Muslim immigrants, Syeds, Sheikhs, Mughals, and Pathans, often collectively known as *ashraf*, and those of indigenous origin whose ancestors had to converted to Islam. The latter may be subdivided into three distinct groups: converts from high-caste Hindus such as Muslim Rajputs, converts from clean occupational castes such as Julahas and Qassabs, and converts from unclean occupations castes such as Bhangis and Chamars' (Robinson 1974, 24).

4 Shiv Sena literally means the 'Army of Shiva', derived from the name of Shivaji, the legendary warrior king of seventeenth century western India and founder of the Maratha empire (Katzenstein 1973, 387).

5 The term Girangaon was coined by Vithal Varerkar in his classic novel *Dhavta Dhota*, written in 1933 in Marathi (Varerkar [1933] 1972).

6 Century Mills was the last one to close down in the year 2006. At present, only two textile mills (Tata Mills and Poddar Mills) owned and managed by the National Textile Corporation (NTC), Government of India, are functioning partially. In these mills the workers are employed (or re-employed after retrenchment) on a contractual basis. On 16 November 2007, *DNA: Daily News and Analysis* reported that the NTC had entered into a joint venture with a private corporation called Pantaloons. However, when this work was about to begin on 21 January 2010, a *Hindustan Times* correspondent reported that the mill was set on fire. This has raised doubts as to whether the state is willing to restart any mill given the massive real estate value of the mill land.

7 As per the survey conducted by the Bombay Mill Owners Association (Gokhale 1957, 116), of the total workforce Muslim men constituted 5 per cent and women 1 per cent respectively.

8 Caste Hindus, especially the Marathas, objected to the employment of Dalits in the weaving department on the grounds 'that the yarn sometimes had to be sucked on to the shuttle from bobbins' (Chandavarkar 1994, 226–27). This issue brought the Communists in conflict which Ambedkar as the latter critiqued the former for not addressing this issue.

9 As BKS leader Datta Salve noted, 'We did not like what we saw. The workers were shouting *Lal Baluta Zindabad* (long live the Red Flag) in the factories but were Shiv Sainiks outside' (Gupta 1982, 82).

10 While I have adopted the occupational categorization according to Patel's (1988) study on Ahmedabad millworkers, which is cited in Breman (2004, 195–200), I have created new

occupational groups. I have classified eight occupations as self-employed in traditional caste based businesses. They include leatherwork, carpenter, barber, goldsmith, handloom, washerman, fishing and religious preachers. Following this, I have created a new occupational category: self-employed in fast food, tea and juice, which is included in the trade category in Patel's study. The other two occupational categories that I have created are wage labour in cleaning and manual work, and wage labour in clerical, supervision and marketing.

11 The occupations in industry, repair and processing include bicycle, stove and watch repairing, motor mechanics, motor winding, electricians, plumbing, bag frame making and screen printing.

12 In the mid-1980s the Supreme Court in its judgment on the Delhi hawkers' case suggested to regulate hawking by creating hawking and non-hawking zones. Until the mid-1990s, however, few efforts were made by the BMC as it continued with the *pauti* system. Later, in 1998, a petition was filed by the Citizens' Forum for the Protection of Public Spaces (CFPPS) (later to change its name to CitiSpace) in the Bombay High Court, claiming that the BMC was taking no action on the 1985 Supreme Court ruling. The petitioners cited the *pauti* system as an illegal practise carried out by the BMC, which the High Court ordered to discontinue (Anjaria 2006, 2141).

13 For the purpose of anonymity, I have changed the names of all respondents mentioned in this chapter.

14 *Paan* is betel leaf that is wrapped with areca nut, lime, spices or sometimes with tobacco.

References

Adarkar, Neera, Meena Menon and Rajnarayan Chandavarkar. 2004. *One Hundred Years, One Hundred Voices: The Millworkers of Girangaon: An Oral History*. Calcutta: Seagull Books.

Anjaria, Jonathan Shapiro. 2006. 'Street Hawkers and Public Space in Mumbai'. *Economic and Political Weekly* 41 (21): 2140–46.

Bhattacharya, Sabyasachi. 1981. 'Capital and Labour in Bombay City, 1928–29'. *Economic and Political Weekly* 16 (42–3): 36–44.

Bhowmik, Sharit K. 1998. 'The Labour Movement in India: Present Problems and Future Perspectives'. In *Towards People-Centered Development (Part II)*, edited by M. Desai, A. Monterio, and L. Narayan, 147–66. Mumbai: Tata Institute of Social Sciences.

Bhowmik, Sharit K. 2001. Hawkers and the Urban Informal Sector: A Study of Street Vending in Seven Cities. National Alliance of Street Vendors in India (NASVI). Online at http://www.nasvinet.org/userfiles/file/A%20study%20of%20street%20vending%20in%20seven%20cities.pdf (accessed 4 April 2011).

Breman, Jan. 2004. *The Making and Unmaking of an Industrial Working Class: Sliding Down to the Bottom of the Labour Hierarchy in Ahmedabad, India*. New Delhi: Oxford University Press.

Chandavarkar, Rajnarayan. 1994. *The Origins of Industrial Capitalism in India: Business Strategies and the Working Classes in Bombay, 1900–1940*. Cambridge: Cambridge University Press.

______. 1998. *Imperial Power and Popular Politics: Class, Resistance and the State in India, c.1850–1950*. Cambridge: Cambridge University Press.

______. 2009. *History, Culture and the Indian City: Essays*. Cambridge: Cambridge University Press.

Cholia, Rasiklal Popatlal. 1941. *Dock Labourers in Bombay*. London, New York and Calcutta: Longmans, Green and Co. Ltd.

D'Monte, Darryl. 2002. *Ripping the Fabric: The Decline of Mumbai and its Mills*. New Delhi: Oxford University Press.

Ghorpade, Kedar. 2005. 'Mumbai: Economic Restructuring by Default'. In *Public Problems – Private Solutions? Globalizing Cities in the South*, edited by K. Segbers, S. Raiser and K. Volkmann, 35–50. Aldershot: Ashgate.

Gokhale, R. G. 1957. *The Bombay Cotton Mill Worker*. Bombay: The Mill-owners' Association.

Gupta, Dipankar. 1982. *Nativism in a Metropolis: The Shiv Sena in Bombay*. New Delhi: Manohar.

Hansen, Thomas Blom. 2001. *Wages of Violence: Naming and Identity in Postcolonial Bombay*. Princeton: Princeton University Press.

Harriss-White, Barbara. 2003. *India Working: Essays on Society and Economy*. Cambridge: Cambridge University Press.

Kanga, Jamsheed. 2006. 'Private vs. Public: The Legal Battle'. In *Mills for Sale: The Way Ahead*, edited by D. D'Monte. Mumbai: Marg Publications.

Kidambi, Prashant. 2007. *The Making of an Indian Metropolis: Colonial Governance and Public Culture in Bombay, 1890–1920*. Aldershot: Ashgate.

Katzenstein, Mary F. 1973. 'Origins of Nativism: The Emergence of Shiv Sena in Bombay'. *Asian Survey* 13 (4): 386–99.

Krishnan, Shekhar. 2000. 'Murder of the Mills: A Case Study of Phoenix Mills'. Lokshahi Hakk Sanghatana and Girangaon Bachao Andolan Report.

Kulkarni, Suhas, ed. 2004 (2001). *Ardhi Mumbai*. 2nd ed. Mumbai: Majestic Prakashan.

Mhaskar, Sumeet. 2012. 'The Unmaking of the Worker-Self in Post-Industrial Mumbai: A Study of Ex-millworkers Responses to the Closure of Textile Mills in Girangaon'. Unpublished D.Phil thesis, University of Oxford.

Morris, Morris David. 1965. *The Emergence of an Industrial Labor Force in India: A Study of the Bombay Cotton Mills, 1854–1947*. Berkeley: University of California Press.

Municipal Corporation of Greater Mumbai. 2005. Mumbai City Development Plan 2005–2025. Available at http://www.mcgm.gov.in (accessed 21 March 2007).

Newman, Richard. 1981. *Workers and Unions in Bombay, 1918–1929: A Study of Organisation in the Cotton Mills*. Canberra: Australian National University.

Panini, M. N. 1996. 'The Political Economy of Caste'. In *Caste: Its Twentieth Centruy Avatar*, edited by M. N. Srinivas, 28–68. New Delhi: Viking.

Patel, B. B. 1988. *Workers of Closed Textile Mills: Patterns and Problems of their Absorption in a Metropolitan Labour Market*. New Delhi: Oxford & IBH.

Prakash, Gyan. 2010. *Mumbai Fables*. Princeton: Princeton University Press.

Prime Minister's High Level Committee. 2006. 'Social, Economic and Educational Status of the Muslim Community of India – A Report'. New Delhi: Government of India.

Robinson, Francis. 1974. *Separatism among Indian Muslims: The Politics of the United Provinces' Muslims, 1860–1923*. London: Cambridge University Press.

Roy, Tirthankar. 1998. 'Development or Distortion? "Powerlooms" in India, 1950–1997'. *Economic and Political Weekly* 33 (16): 897–911.

Sen, Amartya. 2000. 'Social Exclusion: Concept, Application, and Scrutiny'. Social Development Papers No. 1. Manila: Asian Development Bank.

Singh, J. N. 2006. 'Handbook on Powerloom'. Mumbai: Ministry of Textiles, Office of the Textile Commissioner.

Srinivas, M. N. 1969. 'The Caste System in India'. In *Social Inequality*, edited by A. Béteille, 265–72. Penguin Books.

Thorat, Sukhadeo and Katherine S. Newman, eds. 2010a. *Blocked by Caste: Economic Discrimination in Modern India*. New Delhi: Oxford University Press.

Thorat, Sukhadeo and Katherine S. Newman. 2010b. 'Introduction: Economic Discrimination, Concept, Consequences, and Remedies'. In *Blocked by Caste: Economic Discrimination in Modern India*, edited by Sukhadeo Thorat and Katherine S. Newman, 1–34. New Delhi: Oxford University Press.

Varerkar, Bhargavarama Vitthala. (1933) 1972. *Dhavata Dhota*. Mumbai: Abhinav Prakashan.

Wankhede, Harish. 2010. 'Secularism and Social Justice: Religious Minorities and Pursuit of Equality'. Unpublished PhD thesis, Jawaharlal Nehru University.

Weinstein, Liza. 2008. 'Mumbai's Development Mafias: Globalization, Organized Crime and Land Development'. *International Journal of Urban and Regional Research* 32 (1): 22–39.

Wersch, Hubert W. M. van. 1992. *Bombay Textile Strike, 1982–83*. Bombay: Oxford University Press.

Part III

RESOURCES AND DEVELOPMENT

Chapter 10

DAMS, DEVELOPMENT AND THE EXCLUSION OF INDIGENOUS GROUPS: A CASE FROM ODISHA[1]

Deepak Kumar Behera

Mega-dam building in India in the post-independence era became a major symbol of modernization. Even today, the mega-dam continues to be seen as a symbol of progress, of man's supremacy over nature, of prosperity and of pride. However, due to construction of dams, many indigenous communities are displaced involuntarily and compensated marginally. It severely damages the rich sociocultural fabric of the marginalized people. In this process, the indigenous people suffer from economic and social marginalization in many important areas of community life. The rehabilitation and resettlement policies have often further marginalized the already marginalized people from life's opportunities. This has deprived this segment of the population from the rights and privileges enjoyed by the dominant sections of society. Countless studies and reports have documented that the interests of 'development oustees' were rarely taken into consideration when mega projects were built (Oliver-Smith 1991; Thukral 1992 and 1996; Parasuraman 1993 and 1999; Scudder 1996; Colson 1999; WCD 2000). Indigenous people seldom understand the long-term implications of development projects, and hence fail in their efforts to devise measures to counter them.

Recognizing this problem, World Bank sociologist Michael Cernea developed the highly influential Impoverishment Risks and Reconstruction (IRR) model (see Cernea 1994, 1997, 1998, 1999, 2000) now widely used in resettlement research (for example, Mathur and Marsden 1998). This model has been key in showing how displacement goes hand in hand with physical, social and economic exclusion. Marginalization of the already marginalized results in a broad range of impoverishment risks, namely, landlessness, joblessness, homelessness, marginalization, increased morbidity, food insecurity, loss of access to common property and social disarticulation (Cernea 1997). Resettlement of displaced people is thus a process that is acknowledged as entailing several risks. These risks render resettlement inherently problematic and, indeed, impoverishment and disempowerment have been the rule rather than the exception with respect to resettled people around the world. One of the IRR's aims is to help operationalize a just planning process around resettlement (Cernea 1997 and 1999).

Figure 10.1. Impact of Dams, from International River Network and Friends of the Earth. 2003.

Source: *Dammed Rivers, Damned Lives: What the Water Establishment Doesn't Want You To Know*. Berkeley: INR and FoE.

The Concept of 'Social Exclusion' and 'Marginalization'

The two terms that will be used frequently in this chapter are 'Social Exclusion' and 'Marginalization'. In fact, these two concepts are complementary and supplementary to each other. Finding a distinction between these overlapping concepts is not an easy task.

By 'social exclusion' we mean a multidimensional process of progressive social rupture, detaching groups and individuals from social relations and institutions and preventing them from full participation in the normal, normatively prescribed activities of the society in which they live. It refers to processes in which individuals and entire communities of people are systematically blocked from rights, opportunities and resources. Social exclusion may be defined as a 'rupture of social bonds'. Social exclusion is used in this chapter to characterize different forms of social disadvantage. The outcome of multiple deprivations prevents individuals or groups from participating fully in the economic, social, and political life of the society in which they live.

By 'marginalization' we mean the social process of becoming or being made marginal or pushed to the margins of society. Marginalization of tribal communities is a product of colonization in the past. Tribal communities lost their land, were forced into destitute areas, lost their sources of income and were excluded from the labour market. Additionally, many tribal communities lost their culture and values through forced assimilation and they lost their rights in society. Today, various communities continue to be marginalized from society due to the development of practices, policies and programmes that meet the needs of multinational companies and the nation and not the needs of the marginalized groups themselves. Another example of marginalization at the community level is the marginalization of women. Women were excluded from the labour force and their work in the home was not valued.

Material deprivation is the most common result of marginalization found when examining how unfairly material resources (such as food and shelter) are dispersed in society. Along with material deprivation, marginalized individuals are also excluded from services, programmes and policies.

Globalization, immigration, social welfare and government policies are broader social processes that have the potential to contribute negatively to a person's access to resources and services. Any of these processes may result in marginalization of individuals and groups. Globalization has decreased the role of the state through an increase in support from various corporate sectors. This process has resulted in gross inequalities, injustices and marginalization of various vulnerable groups. Globalization and structural forces aggravate poverty and continue to push individuals to the margins of society, while governments and large corporations do not address the issues. Insecurity and fear of an unknown future and instability can result in displacement, exclusion and forced assimilation into the dominant group. The provision of so-called 'welfare' itself also produces new injustice by depriving those dependent on it of rights and freedoms that others have. Marginalization is unjust because it blocks the opportunity to exercise capacities in socially defined and recognized ways. Thus, social policy and welfare provisions reflect the dominant notions in society by constructing and reinforcing categories of people and their needs. It ignores the unique subjective human essence, further continuing the cycle of dominance (Wilson and Beresford 2000).

Exclusion in Relation to Place

The local area is a key influence on indigenous people's experiences. Indigenous people's opportunities and frames of reference are highly localized. All their gods and goddesses live close to their surroundings. They heavily depend upon their local social networks for various economic and socio-religious activities. The nearby forest provides them with fuel, food and fodder. Their future progress is largely dependent on their physical proximity to the neighbourhood. Friends and leisure activities are also highly localized. Indigenous people often face problems and stigmas as a consequence of being negatively labelled by other ethnic groups. Nevertheless, they remain positive about living in their neighbourhood, and most wish to carry on living there in the future.

Based on my research, this can be understood in terms of the value they place upon their local networks and knowledge. They feel connected to the place and feel that if they move out to another place, they will lose the local networks they learned to rely upon for socializing and support. Thus, the subjective experiences of indigenous people growing up in a particular place, embracing the local knowledge system and navigating local networks are clearly examples of 'social inclusion'. So, when they are forcefully uprooted from their ancestral land due any mega-development project, they feel 'socially excluded' and start experiencing the process of marginalization.

Objectives

An attempt has been made in this chapter to present the process of marginalization and social exclusion experienced by the indigenous people of a remote area in Odisha as a result of the construct of Upper Indravati Hydroelectric Project (UIHEP). The three key questions that the chapter primarily addresses are: (1) What experiences and processes generated social exclusion or promoted resilience among the project affected indigenous people of UIHEP? (2) What are the impacts of social exclusion, resulting from the displacement, on the already marginalized indigenous people? and (3) What is the relationship between being geographically excluded and being a marginalized group in the context of this study?

The chapter also deals with the impact of a mega-dam project on the long-standing cultural adaptations of the indigenous people. It critically examines the resettlement and rehabilitation policies of the state and central governments from a cultural perspective. The paper analyses various changes that have occurred in the traditional adaptation processes of the indigenous people due to their exposure to external forces. Some of the other questions that I address in the chapter are: How has the UIHEP impacted the socially marginalized indigenous people more specifically in terms of loss of Common Property Resources (CPRs) such as forests or water? What kinds of customary rights are they deprived of when displaced by the UIHEP? What are the changes in their sources of livelihood in the post-displacement era? How has the UIHEP affected the traditional values, culture, kinship network and other social support systems? What are the relative costs and benefits that accrue to different sections of society (the project beneficiaries vis-à-vis the indigenous people)? How have the indigenous communities coped with the changing situation in the post-displacement era? Answers to these questions provide a better understanding of the existing resettlement and rehabilitation policies of the state and central governments from a cultural perspective.

Upper Indravati Hydroelectric Project

The plan to construct a multipurpose hydroelectric project on the river Indravati in Odhisa was conceived in the year 1959 and in the same year, investigation of its feasibility commenced. However, its approval by the Union Planning Commission was delayed until 1977 because of problems concerning the equitable distribution of water resources. Construction began only after obtaining financial assistance from the World Bank in 1985. According to official sources, about 17 thousand people from 97 villages – 44 villages from undivided Koraput and 53 from Kalahandi districts of Odisha – were affected by the construction of the dam (RRU 1997, 3). Yet the Krushak Mahasangha and the Indravati Gana Sangharsha – two local NGOs (Non-Governmental Agencies) – put the figure at 30 thousand. Evacuation started in 1989 and continued till 1993 and was carried out in four phases.

The long-drawn-out process of displacement of indigenous people due to the construction of the UIHEP exacerbated the process of social exclusion. Various impoverishment risks, as analysed by Cernea (1997), are clearly visible in the case of the project-affected people of UIHEP. A majority of the indigenous people are now socially and economically excluded and experiencing situation of landlessness, joblessness, homelessness, marginalization, food insecurity, increased morbidity and mortality, loss of access to common property and social disarticulation. Those who moved out from their ancestral land and settled elsewhere remained outside their social network in the traditional village. As they bought land at distant places by using part of the compensation received in the form of cash, they could not cultivate the land due to lack of infrastructure in hilly regions.

Methodology

The study conducted during 2005 (funded by Winrock International, India) covered 12 villages/resettlement clusters of undivided Guturkhal Gram Panchayat of Thuamul-Rampur Block in Kalahandi district. The villages/resettlement clusters have been classified into five categories:

- Independent resettlement clusters (Purnapadar, Bagbeda, Luthkudi and Dhepoguda and Gutrukhal)
- Resettlement clusters as part of traditional villages (Talnagi and Hatisalmurka)
- Traditional village (Bahadaghat).
- Submerged villages (Badnagi, Dommurka and Guturkhal)
- Partially submerged village (Sukuli)

The five different settings provided us a comprehensive frame for the impact assessment. They were chosen to examine the varying impact of the mega-dam project on the indigenous people of the area. In the first category, only oustees were rehabilitated in newly constructed settlements in the region. In the second category, displaced people were rehabilitated in resettlement clusters constructed close to some traditional villages. Some families from a traditional village not affected by the mega-dam project were included in the sample for comparison. Some households from three submerged villages and a partially submerged village were also included for varying impact assessment.

The sample households were from various ethnic groups, namely, Jhadia, Kondh, Dom, Luhura, Paik, Sundhi and Gouda. The study covered 197 resettled households from five independent resettlement clusters as well as two resettlement clusters that are part of two different traditional villages. It also covered 104 households from a traditional village and two other villages that are inhabited by some oustees of the submerged villages. All the heads-of-households (HOHs) were taken as the sample respondents for the study. Of the seven sample resettlement clusters, five were independent and isolated clusters, whereas the remaining two were part of two different traditional villages. The pre-displacement scenario of three submerged villages was reconstructed by collecting information from the living memory of the displaced indigenous people of the resettlement clusters. Though Sukuli was included as one of our sample village, data relating to only the protest movement was gathered from this village to supplement our analysis. Data was collected through observation, case study, focus group discussion (FGD) and informal interview methods. Secondary data, especially of the Rehabilitation and Resettlement Unit, Khatiguda, was used for the analysis. The major aim of this study was to assess the impact of the mega-dam project on the indigenous people from a cultural perspective, focusing on the adverse consequences of the project in terms of social exclusion and marginalization of the indigenous people.

Indigenous Communities

The indigenous communities studied were vulnerable to being disadvantaged in the development process, maintain close attachment to ancestral territories and to natural resources in these areas, and use an indigenous language, often different from the state/national language. The study examines communities where customary social and political institutions continue. People in such communities rely primarily on subsistence-oriented production. They worship the mountains, forests and the undergrowth beneath the forest canopy as gods and goddesses and hold them in high esteem. The mountains have sustained them both materially and spiritually for centuries. They worship forests, hills and water with the belief that these aspects of nature are controlled by the presiding gods and goddess, and that unless they satisfy these spirits, the spirits will cause misfortune. The indigenous people believe that the village deity and other demigods protect them; hence, they feel more confident and secure in their ancestral land. They are hardworking people, subsisting on a simple technology. They consider themselves as the original settlers and the first users of a specific territory and resources. They perpetuate their cultural distinctiveness, which includes aspects of social organization, religion and spiritual values, modes of production, laws and institutions. The term indigenous community includes both scheduled tribes (ST) and nonscheduled tribes (non-ST) (locally known as *Desia* and *Parja*, respectively).

The indigenous people living in the jungle traditionally adapted themselves to live in harmony with their immediate environment without damaging it. They live close to nature and depend upon forest resources for their basic survival. They ensure the reproduction of the jungle through a symbiotic relationship. These adaptations have survival value and protect the forest communities from extinction (Gadgil and Guha 1995; Arnold and Guha 1995).

However, the mega-dam project has adversely influenced such arrangements. The once meaningful practices now fail to bring the desired results in the changing conditions. Many mega-development projects among indigenous populations are mostly designed without taking the interest of the indigenous population into account and are thus unsustainable. They are unsustainable because they are not culture-friendly and eco-friendly; they do not use traditional channels, resources and knowledge for development, and they do not meet the requirements of the present generation without depriving the future generation of their resource base.

The present study is confined to the indigenous people living in a mountain pass that forms part of the Eastern Ghats. Scattered in this *dongerla* (forested) region are numerous small hamlets of the indigenous people. The indigenous communities living in this region consider themselves as Parja – the ruled or the commoners – and also identify themselves as Desia – the indigenous. While the word Parja has a political meaning, Desia connotes the people living within the territory. These indigenous people can hardly conceive of living in any territory outside their social boundary. Though interdependent in many walks of life, each group has its own distinct socio-cultural system. Inter-ethnic communication in this region is carried out within a common lingua franca known as *desia bhasa*. The highlanders are less exposed to the outside world than their brethren in the plains.

Their economy has multiple loci, centring on cultivation by slash-and-burn, collection of forest produce, hunting wild game, and wage earning as agricultural labourers. The Desia are aware that the natural resources have survival value and that their depletion by improper utilization may prove fatal to the community. Management of these resources, such as forest, land and water needs collective action and there is no ambiguity whatsoever among the Desia regarding resource management through cultural practices. A traditional village in the region has various functionaries.[2]

The traditional adaptation of the indigenous people of this area is shifting cultivation, which demands pooling of work at the time of clearing and burning the forest. Conversely, during the three lean months of the year, there is a need to redistribute the results of the dispersed productive activities that are possible (fishing, gathering of forest products) in order to ensure survival for all. This production cycle was regulated by the ritual year, which helped to ensure that resources were not used prematurely and were thus maximally distributed. Kinship networks ensured the necessary co-operation and flexibility of personnel. The impact of the dam has been to destroy or separate common territory, making cooperation difficult, as also to separate kin groups from each other, disturbing patterns of marriage and co-operation among kin.

The Project and Its Context

It was only in the 1990s that social impact of the dams brought ecological and economic arguments to the fore as marginalized and displaced communities gained a voice in the political arena. Even today, the livelihood of the displaced people has not been restored; in fact, the vast majority have become impoverished (Mohapatra 1990). The millions of people forcibly dislocated from their lands are usually from among the poorest and most vulnerable sections of the population. Upon dislocation, these communities are pushed into further poverty. This in itself constitutes grave violations of human rights.

Most mega-dam projects in Odisha are located inland in the hills, basically inhabited by ethnic communities belonging to ST, Scheduled Castes (SC) and Other Backward Classes (OBC) (Swain and Panigrahi 1999, 164–5). Needless to say, big dams and irrigation projects are the most important cause of displacement. It has been calculated that during the last forty years about 56,377 families comprising a population of some 270 thousand have been displaced due to irrigation projects in Odisha. In other words, on an average 5 thousand persons have been displaced per year (Daula 1993, 25). The case of the Hirakud dam may be cited as an example. It has affected 249 villages, 22,144 families, 18,432 houses and 112,039 acres of cultivated land submerged by the Hirakud reservoir (Baboo 1992, 31).

In spite of fanciful claims of welfare for the indigenous people as a goal in the planning era, the indigenous people remain victims of exploitation by the so-called civilized people from the plain areas. Land alienation, de-peasantization and indebtedness continue unabated (Patnaik 1972; Pathy 1982; Fürer-Haimendorf 1982; Mohanty 1997; Agnihotri 1996). Most of the mega-dams, mines, wild life sanctuaries and heavy industries were set up in remote areas, displacing indigenous people on a massive scale (Areeparampil 1996; Fernandes 1991, 1997; Mohapatra 1990; Mishra 1996). Among them, the cumulative effect of these experiences has gradually forged animosity and hatred towards the people of the plain areas. They consider the larger society as exploitative and oppressive, as a category to be opposed and fought. Thus the planning and execution of the mega-dam projects could never become a standard of evaluation, emulation and aspiration (Xaxa 2001, 2770).

In this context developmental measures planned and implemented under the tutelage of representatives of the larger society are not easily accepted or appreciated by the indigenous people (Mohanty 2003, 92). To quote Fürer-Haimendorf (1982, 128):

> As long as they operate within their familiar atmosphere tribals evince as much perspicacity, skill and even true wisdom as any other population, but as soon as they are faced by social attitude rooted in a different system they become unsure and often behave in a manner detrimental to their own interests.

The indigenous people remained victims of exploitation by outsiders, as indigenous people are less organized. The outsiders (locally known as *dikus*) use different means for their exploitation (e.g. money lenders and distillers). Forests, the mainstay of the indigenous economy, were reserved in the interest of the nation, with indigenous people at the mercy of officials from the plains. Forest resources were taken away from the remote areas for the development of the more advanced communities (Vyasulu 1985; Mohanty 1997).

Cernea examined the empirical findings of many field monographs and concluded that the common factor underlying the consequences of displacement was the *onset of impoverishment.* This is caused through production systems being dismantled, established communities being disorganized – scattering kinship groups and family systems – and the informal networks providing mutual help are rendered non-functional. Forced displacement can start a vortex of impoverishment that extends beyond immediate visible effects. The damage so caused deepens with time and can cast whole communities into a downward spiral of despair that even the most resilient of communities find difficult to overcome.

Participation of affected people in the planning and implementation process of dam projects is practically nonexistent. Displacement has essentially occurred through official coercion. The denial of development opportunities, for years, has characterized the process of resettlement.

Mode of Production, Resource Collection and Utilization

Sustainable practices are important for tribal people since it was traditionally the only guarantee for their survival (Behera and Erasmus 1999, 28). The value of indigenous knowledge is increasingly recognized, especially in the context of management of resources. Local communities have a number of sociocultural practices for resource management, which contribute significantly toward long-term sustainability of resources. The Desia produce for subsistence, and surplus or hoarding do not make any sense to them. Their calendar year starts with Poos (mid-December to mid-January) to end with Pond (mid-November to mid-December).[3] Their economy centres round *khadi* (food), and they organize themselves to be assured of it all round the year. Their economy is seasonal and they pursue different kinds of economic activities in accordance with the availability of natural resources.

Most of the Desia are landless and those having land are marginal landholders. Many of them possess land without right of record (customary rights). They practice shifting cultivation on the slope of the hills, and the amount of land used for crop production barely exceeds two acres per household. Though they are not nomadic by nature, those living in the *dongerla* region and practicing shifting cultivation change the site of settlement along with their clearings. These movements are restricted to preselected sites, following a cyclic order. Their mode of cultivation is primarily a multiple cropping pattern. They grow a variety of crops in the same field and at the same time, ranging from different minor millets to coarse cereals and pulses; rice is also grown in the *dongar* as well as in the plain. On average, the land requirement for the indigenous peoples' shifting cultivation is much less than that of peasants from the plain practicing settled cultivation.

Cultivation activities start from the month of Landi (mid-May to mid-June). Having selected a patch of land the indigenous peoples slash the growth and undergrowth and leave the plants exposed to the sun for drying. Once the felled trees and shrubs are ready to be fired, the indigenous peoples go out with their drums to the site and shout at the peak of their voice. By doing so, they try to drive away all living creatures from the land. This they do for three consecutive days before the trees and shrubs are finally put to fire. This procedure speaks for the concern of the indigenous peoples for all living beings, may they be the smallest creatures like insects and worms. During the month of Ashad (mid-June to mid-July), both men and women furrow the land with the help of an iron instrument locally known as *kodki*. Then different varieties of selected seeds from the previous year's harvest are blended and broadcast on the fields. They prefer this mixed type of cropping as it is more viable in hilly regions. In case of failure of one variety of crops, they fall back on other varieties.

Economic Activities and Associated Rituals

Most of the requirements of indigenous people are met by their own production, and their dependence on the market is minimal. The produce from the field is rarely sold in the market, but may be bartered when needs arise. Their main crops are *kuling* (paddy) and *dera* (bottle brush millet). These crops, as well as *kohoda* (a kind of minor millet), *arku* (minor millet), and *kating* (a kind of pulses), are mainly produced for home consumption. They have elaborate rituals concerning the cultivation of these crops, which are harvested and brought to the *katar* where they are threshed and after Katar puja (a ritual performed during harvesting and threshing) the crop is divided among the claimants and taken to their respective homes.

The months of Dussera, Diali and Pond are time of rejoicing. At this time, the homes of the indigenous people are full with *pachee* (harvest). Old debts are repaid and new investments are made in buying clothes, fowl or cattle.

The indigenous people experience a lean period during the months of Ashad, Saraban (mid-July to mid-August) and Bhodo (mid-August to mid-September). During these crucial months, they rely heavily on natural resources like forest, rivers, and ponds, for mere survival. Their needs are met partly by gathering from the forest, by fishing in rivers and ponds, and also by wage earning both within and outside the village. This is the time when they fall back upon their social networks to survive. Distribution during the lean season therefore emerges as a pragmatic adaptation, which has endured the ravages of time and sustained the indigenous people through the vagaries of life.

The indigenous people's resource utilization, then, is characterized by aggregation during part of the year and distribution and utilization at other times. The entire cycle from resource collection to utilization is guided and monitored by cultural sanctions and institutions. During the month of Chait (mid-March to mid-April) the indigenous people perform two rituals, namely, Chaitparbu and Pidlaiparb. Chaitparbu heralds the beginning of the hunting expedition. During Chaitparbu, all able-bodied men go hunting in the forest. When the kill is made, all members of the community share it equally. The practice of going to the forest for game is known as *bentaboola*. For eight days the male members go hunting and once they make a kill they return home. Not until the eighth day are other economic activities resumed. Thereafter, *bentaboola* ceases to be a regular activity and eventually stalls during the month of Landi.

It is forbidden to pluck mangoes before the performance of Pidlaiparbu ritual in Chait. If someone does so without performing the ritual it is believed to bring bad luck for the whole village. It is interesting to note that the indigenous people perform more than one ritual for using different parts of the same product. For example, they can eat only the pulp of the mango by performing the Pildaiparbu; another ritual known as Takuhanas must be performed if the mango kernel is to be eaten. It is dried and stored for use during the lean period, when a kind of gruel is made from mango kernel. Both the Pilaiparbu and Takuhanas rituals are performed at a fixed time of the year and there can be no deviation whatsoever. The Takuhanas ritual is performed in the month of Ashad, at the beginning of the lean period. Several other rituals are performed during the collection of other forest produces like roots, tubers, leaves, honey, resin, etc. The mode of collection of these resources shows their efforts at managing them.

A careful analysis of various rituals and their timing reveals that these cultural practices have been devised by the indigenous people to space the utilization of resources in accordance with the need of the people, minimizing risk and uncertainty. These mechanisms act as a cultural safety-catch and regulate the over-exploitation or over-utilization of the resources. Viegas and Menon are right in stressing that 'the tribals built cultural and religious myths, rituals and social control mechanisms which were geared to maintaining a balance between human and ecological needs' (1989, 59).

During the hunt, game is carefully selected. Pregnant animals are seldom hunted and the very young ones are released when trapped. All this shows an endeavour to space the available resources and restrain the users from over-exploiting them, saving them for when they are highly needed, and checking depletion of natural resources. Hence it can be argued that the economy of the indigenous people is embedded within the cultural matrix and each component of the economy is culturally ordained and patterned. The economy of the indigenous people is so designed that it not only provides livelihood in the present but also assures the basic needs of future generations.

The cultural practices of the indigenous people are, in fact, adaptive processes which maintain a balance between the population and nature as well as serve as social resources within their immediate environment. However, such arrangements have been seriously impacted by the mega-dam project under the aegis of development. As a result, the age-old adaptation fails and institutions once benign become deleterious. The resettlement process turned into a process of social exclusion and marginalization. As numerous commentators acknowledge, involuntary resettlement is a traumatic process, regardless of one's social or economic background. The World Bank, for example, has stated:

> When people are forcibly moved, production systems may be dismantled, long-established residential settlements are disorganized, and kinship groups are scattered. Many jobs and assets are lost. Informal social networks that are part of daily sustenance systems – providing mutual help in childcare, food security, revenue transfers, labour exchange and other basic sources of socio-economic support – collapse because of territorial dispersion. Health care tends to deteriorate. Links between producers and their consumers are often severed, and local labour markets are disrupted. Local organizations and formal and informal associations disappear because of the sudden departure of their members, often in different directions. Traditional authority and management systems can lose leaders. Symbolic markers, such as ancestral shrines and graves, are abandoned, breaking links with the past and with peoples' cultural identity. Not always visible or quantifiable, these processes are nonetheless real. The cumulative effect is that the social fabric and economy are torn apart. (World Bank 1994, iii–iv)

It is significant to note that the above statements made by the World Bank closely correspond to the ground realities in the sample area.

Impact of Forced Displacement

At the beginning of the project, the Resettlement and Rehabilitation Unit constructed two rehabilitation colonies, Sashahandi and Talejaring, to relocate the displaced. These sites, however, were found unsuitable by the evictees. As a result, they were given a free hand to relocate in their place of choice. Most of them preferred to settle near the shores of the reservoir, with minimal displacement from their ancestral land and social network. The majority of them are tribals, who lived in the fertile Indravati river valley. Among the various indigenous peoples, the tribal populations are the largest group seriously affected by the project. They felt the impact of the dam from the very conception of its construction.

For all indigenous people, access to land is fundamental, not only in an economic sense. The importance of land is usually reflected in almost all parts of indigenous culture. Their religion is commonly related both to land and kinship system. If sudden and extensive changes occur, they have consequences for the entire culture. Loss of land and of the traditional resource base, then, is not merely economic. Displacement as a consequence of the Indravati project has led to physical exclusion from a geographic territory but also to economic and social exclusion from a set of functioning social networks. The consequences of displacement also include desecration of ancestral sacred zones, scattering of kinship groups and families, with the disorganization of informal social networks. This happens to those oustees who had no other option than settling down in remote resettlement clusters.

The project has altered land use patterns that traditionally supported farming, grazing and fishing. Thus indigenous populations have lost substantial parts of their traditional income base, and were marginalized when they had to move from fertile valley-bottom lands uphill to inferior soils. Marginalization also occurred through the loss of other sources of income. Economic marginalization was accompanied by social and psychological marginalization.

Designers and planners of mega-projects, such as dam building, rarely recognize the customary rights of indigenous and tribal people and women, including their access to common property resources. These rights are often enshrined in informal arrangements recognized by customary law that is rooted in local understandings of property regimes. In particular, women largely have rights and control over resources in customary arrangements. These are often corroded in newly created formal resource use agreements that give rights to males and also ignore local dynamics (Mehta 2002). This manifests itself in official categories such as the 'landless' for those who lack official titles, despite the fact that they may control and cultivate vast tracts of forest and so-called 'waste' land (for extensive documentation of this in the Indian context (see Morse and Berger 1992).

The following quote of Bennett, Butt-Colson and Wavell 1978 in their analysis of the Akawaio Indians of Guyana gives us good idea about the dependence of the indigenous people on land:

> This land is where we belong – it is God's gift to us and has made us who we are. This land is where we are at home, we know its ways: and the things that happened here are known and remembered, so that the stories the old people told are still alive here. This land is needed for those who come after - we are becoming more and more than before, and we must start new settlements, with new farms around them. If we have to move, it is likely that there will be other people there and we shall not be free to spread out as we need to: and the land will not be enough for our people, so that we will grow poor. This land is the place where we know where to find all that it provides for us – food from hunting and fishing, and farms, buildings and tool materials, medicines. Also the spirits around us know us and are friendly and helpful. This land keeps us together within its mountains – we come to understand that we are not just a few people or separate villages, but one people belonging to a homeland. If we had to move, we would be lost to those that remain in the other villages. This would be a sadness to us all, like the sadness of death. Those who

> moved would be strangers to the people and spirits and places where they are made to go. (Bennett, Butt-Colson and S. Wavell 1978, 6)

People still feel that their land and other property belong to gods and goddesses who protect their property. No one is above them; they are supreme. For example, asked by the investigators from a Catholic Management Institute, 'what does the dam construction on the Indravati mean to you?' villagers from the project area answered:

> We are people in the woods. We need the woods because we manage our livelihood from them. To our belief, the land belongs to Gods, not to the Government. If it belongs to the Gods, how can the Government take it away from us? We shall neither abandon this land nor our houses. If the wood disappears under water, the people will go down too. (XIM 1994)

The institute report also reveals that the baseline survey failed to determine the exact number of people displaced, and there was no meaningful participation of the affected people in the planning, implementation and monitoring of the project. The indigenous people did not receive complete and authentic information on the project, on the extent of displacement, or on the rehabilitation and resettlement (R&R) provisions. The delay between the decision to build the dam and its actual construction forced the indigenous people to live for decades starved of development and welfare investments. The government did not want to spend money for the development in a region that was going to be submerged. The affected people experienced a series of problems related to infrastructure, occupation, and social support mechanisms in the resettlement sites. The submergence of vast areas land brought a major setback to the economy of the indigenous people, yet they did not receive water or electricity services or any social or economic benefits. Large inequalities were found in the compensation packages given by the project authorities to the evacuees, leading to marginalization of some already weak sections of the population, like women, children and widows (XIM 1994).

UIHEP undoubtedly provided some wage-earning opportunities to the indigenous people as the dam was constructed. However, at the same time, the dam project displaced local people from their homes and traditional livelihood. While employment generated from dam building is transient or temporary in nature, the deprivation of indigenous people from their sources of livelihood is permanent.

UIHEP deprived and displaced people. The inundation of land for the reservoir submerged communities, altered the riverine ecosystems (upstream and downstream) and eliminated their traditional livelihoods. The resettlement policies of UIHEP predominantly focused on the process of physical relocation rather than restoring the livelihoods of displaced indigenous people. The absence of an economic and social development dimension of resettlement policies such as livelihood opportunities, forced many project-affected indigenous people to abandon resettlement sites and migrate.

Not all affected indigenous people of UIHEP were adequately compensated. For example, there were those who were excluded due to technicalities (e.g. by the definition or the categorization of people to be affected by dams). It was at the time of the dam design of UIHEP that many people were not considered as affected people. They include: indigenous communities situated downstream, those without land or legal title, indigenous people and those affected by project infrastructure.

Exclusionary Processes

A time period of 26 years elapsed between the plan to construct this multipurpose hydroelectric dam in 1959 and the beginning of the construction work in 1985. The government did not invest any resources for infrastructure development during that long transit period. Knowing the fact that the area was going to be submerged, the government declared it a condemned area. Thus, the indigenous people were excluded from receiving even the minimal infrastructure development resources during that period. However, the engagement of the people in the construction work provided them some opportunities for wage earning. The state probably included the indigenous people as unskilled labourers with a distant vision of excluding them from sharing the benefits of the mega-dam project. The indigenous people working in the construction site had no idea that one day their Jangal and Jamin would be submerged. Essentially, they were digging their own grave by receiving wages from the project officials. The entry of people from the plains areas (as project officials) created a cultural genocide in the region by disrupting the social network. The submergence of the *dongars* deprived people from Jangal and Jamin of key economic and cultural aspects of life. For example, the majority of the medicinal plants were submerged, the common property resources were shattered, and women did not receive any compensation, as such compensation was given only to the head of the households, who were, in most cases, men. With the submergence of the forest, the indigenous knowledge system slowly withered away. The huge lake that formed between the hills disrupted their marriage ties. People stopped establishing marital relations with villages that were separated by the large lake. People lavishly spent the money they received , thinking that the salaries would function like a *pachi* (annual harvest). They never realized that it was a one-time compensation. Thus the process of pauperization began. Many of the oustees have now turned into environmental refugees and thereby have migrated to nearby urban centres in search of employment. However, the protest movements which I will describe shortly brought a sense of solidarity among the socially excluded communities. Those movements could not continue for a long time, as the project officials created division among the protesters to diffuse the movements. In the absence of effective leadership and resources, the movements lost their momentum after achieving some initial success.

The derogatory label of *budi anchal ra lok* (people from the submerged region) excluded them from active social participation in the new resettlements. They remained socially excluded. The early settlers of the village looked upon them with contempt and did not include them in their social network.

Disruption of Social Network

Most of the Desia evictees preferred to stay as close as possible to their ancestral lands and social networks because they did not like to start life afresh in a new environment about which they felt uncertain. Baboo (1991, 288–303) made a similar observation in his study on the evictees of the Hirakud dam project. He noted that people did not like to be cut off from their kinship, caste and village networks, especially when they were not the direct beneficiaries of the irrigation scheme.

But the indigenous people's idea of settling down close to their native villages and using the social networks did not work when the project officials came up with an innovative idea for their resettlement. They made it mandatory for the evictees to utilize at least 50 per cent of the cash compensation to buy land. This policy led to forced buying of land, which generated individual landholdings and gave property rights to the new landholders. The individual property right created a new individual 'self' which encouraged more selfish motives. The solidarity within the family and kin group was adversely influenced by this, and cooperation and collective action diminished, giving rise to animosity and mutual bickering. Generally, the indigenous people do not divide their land among the claimants. Most often, they cultivate the field jointly and share the produce equally. This arrangement has proved economically more sustainable than individual holdings and it also augments intra-familial cooperation. Labour is pooled from within the family, or exchanged with other members of the village without hiring from outside. Whenever labour is hired from within the village, all those who work are equally paid in kind, irrespective of age or sex.

All the nonsubmerged land available in the area was highly priced by the proprietors. Therefore, they bought new patches of land in different villages, far away from the place of resettlement, in order to qualify for the other half of the compensation money. Initially, they could manage economically, as the water in the reservoir was not impounded immediately, and the condemned land was still available for cultivation. They continued to cultivate their old lands for almost five years and did not concern themselves with the newly bought land. The new lands became a point of concern for them only after the impoundment of the reservoir and inundation of their *jhola* land. The *jhola* lands were the most fertile in the region and were suitable for paddy cultivation. Once the *jhola* lands were lost to the reservoir, the Desia were left with a little *dongar* land on the hills to cultivate minor millets by the slash and burn method locally known as *podu*. Only then did they start to take an interest in the new lands they had purchased in different villages. Since the people of one village had bought land in different places, far from the place of resettlement, they found it difficult to pool labour from the same village for cultivation. A larger unit would have been economically more viable than a nuclear domestic group, but exchange of labour among them became a thing of the past, as it could not be applied where they had bought their new land.

It is not argued here that the kinship ties have ceased to exist. The relationships still exist at the normative and ideal levels, but they have lost much of their meaning and purpose in the new resettlements. As the coming example will show, both the inter-village and intra-village relationships have undergone drastic change after displacement. Hiring in labour has increased the cost of production. As a result, some of the indigenous people have leased out their land in *adhi* ('half') to the landlords from whom they bought it, and now receive half of the produce as their share. A few have sold their land back to the same landlords. Unscrupulous landlords and local people have also encroached upon some of their lands, as the evictees are not there to look after them. These developments have adversely affected their economy, and led many of the male villagers to migrate for wage work to various urban centres, such as Nawrangpur and Bhawanipatna in the state and Raipur and Hyderabad outside Odisha, thus leaving many female-headed households behind.

The large reservoir created by the dam has alienated and disrupted the social networking of the Desia. Previously, they had a wider range of choices to find a spouse from their traditional affines, but now the barrier created by the reservoir has curtailed this practice. Traditionally, the young males of one village visit another village, where the girls welcome them. The girls and boys identify and assess the feasibility of marriage between them through *laga geet* (songs). All through the night they sing around a fire. They propose to each other by revealing the *mannahai*, their place of residence and ancestors. After impoundment of water, the communication with a good number of potential affines' villages was cut off, and the prospective grooms were left with fewer choices for selecting a spouse. The marriages are now governed by the access to resources in the form of forest and *dongar* land for sustenance in the affines' village. Today, uxorilocal residence has become very common among the Desia of the Indravati river valley, as the girls from traditional villages will not accept the reduced standards of living of the resettled groups. For example, a girl from Bhadaghat (a traditional village) would never marry a boy from a resettlement colony such as Purnapadar, Bagbeda, Luthkudi and Dhepoguda or Gutrukhal. There is a visibly reduced standard of living in the resettled colonies.

Resistance to the Project

A local leader from the district of Nawarangpur was instrumental in motivating the displaced persons of Nawrangpur to fight for their rights. The Budi Anchal Paraja Dabi Committee (BAPDC) is the protest committee of the project-affected people of the submerged area and was formed on his initiative, as was another such committee formed by the displaced persons of Kalahandi. The first meeting of the BAPDC was held in Kalahandi in 1977. Now, BAPDCs have been formed in all the affected areas – Kalahandi, Nawarangpur, Rayagada and Koraput.

At the time of displacement, many facts related to rehabilitation and compensation were not made public. The BAPDC played an important role in bringing to light facts which were deliberately suppressed by the project authorities. The movement also tried to make the evacuees aware of the long-term consequences of the project. The BAPDC organized a rally on 31 December 1997, attended by around 15 thousand people affected by the project. Their main slogan was 'do not keep quiet, disclose your identity while fighting for your rights'. Another major rally was organized in 1999 when a charter of demands was sent to the Governor of Odisha, followed by a hunger strike in 2001. But the demands have not been fulfilled, leading to considerable frustration. One assurance made by the project authorities was the inclusion of all sons more than 18 years old in the list of Project-Affected People. Though there was an advertisement inviting applications from all eligible sons, the officials have yet to take any action on the applications received.

The indigenous people have very little economic support to fall back upon if they begin an agitation; illiteracy is high and they do not have the confidence needed to deal with project officials and the state bureaucracy. Though some of the committee's demands have been fulfilled, project authorities sidelined many others.

In the initial phase, people participated enthusiastically in the committee's activities, but they slowly lost interest, finding it somewhat ineffective. The committee could not acquire the required momentum due to financial hardship, coordination problems and lack of effective leadership. As an alternative, some of the displaced people started fighting for their rights through a local lawyer.

Sukuli is a partially submerged village of Maligaon Gram Panchayat under the Thuamul Rampur Block. Here, the villagers, with support from some indigenous people, have launched a protest movement challenging some of the rehabilitation measures adopted by the project officials. In Sukuli, people have lost almost all their lands in the plain and are left with only a little *dongar* land. The reservoir, which surrounds their village on three sides, acts as a geographical barrier against collecting and selling firewood, a source of livelihood for evacuees of other settlement clusters. There are few wage-earning opportunities in the agricultural and nonagricultural sectors. The people of Sukuli made a representation to the Jana Samparka Sibira held in October 1996. A public relations camp was organized by government officials to register the complaints lodged by the people at the grassroots. While many government officials listened to their grievances, no significant action has addressed these issues so far.

Conclusion

The construction of the Upper Indravati Hydroelectric Project has had a deep impact on the social life of the indigenous people. It has devastated the social networking system – the lifeline of the community – and depleted the natural resources and the life-sustaining support system. It has eroded their values and their ethos – the guy wire of their social system – and created an atmosphere of uncertainty and fear among the people affected. The project's effort to rehabilitate the evicted population has in fact done more harm than good, as it was designed half-heartedly without any imagination or research.

Under the changing scenario, the economy of the Desia has undergone drastic changes. Their dependency on the forest has multiplied manifold. They now harvest forest produce, not only for their own consumption, but also for the daily market in the nearby town of Khatiguda. Many Desia are today selling firewood to officials and other outsiders in Khatiguda. It is a pity to see the constructive dependence changing into to an exploitative one. Since the *dongar* land is not adequate for their sustenance, the fallow period has diminished significantly from six to three years. The younger generation is no longer concerned about their totems, and some do not hesitate to kill them for their benefit.

The large reservoir provides an opportunity for fishing, but though the Desia used to fish in the Indravati River and small water bodies, their traditional technology is not suitable for fishing in large lakes. Moreover, this region has drawn many able fishermen from the Chakma refugee community (from Bangladesh). The Desia find themselves no match for these fishermen. While the Chakma have boats, the Desia fish from the banks with fishing hooks and small nets, and their catch is small compared to that of the Chakma. Still, they are trying to develop new adaptive strategies to survive. They now use many fishing hooks and poles at a time to make a better catch in a relatively short time. They install these fishing poles on the banks of the reservoir. Knitting of fishing nets has now become a popular pastime and a means of livelihood among the Desia, and young and old men are found engaged in this work.

UIHEP has disproportionately impacted indigenous people. Major impacts include: loss of land and livelihood, the undermining of the fabric of their societies, cultural loss, fragmentation of political institutions, breakdown of identity and human rights abuse. Desia women have been especially badly affected: some of the women are occupationally displaced. They are without any productive engagement in the new settlements, as they are away from their native resource base. Many of them now cover long distances to fetch food, firewood and fodder. With the reduction of their contribution to the household economy, their participation in the decision-making process and status within the family has deteriorated considerably. In sum, the majority of those affected are worse off than before.

Thus, this study shows that large dams continue to have serious, even devastating, effects on indigenous peoples. Specifically with respect to indigenous peoples, our policy for mega-projects should stipulate the need for:

- Informed consent by the affected people
- Their extensive participation in the design of the compensation and resettlement plan
- Full recognition of customary rights
- Fair compensation, including special measures to compensate for loss of cultural property (such as burial or sacred sites) and to minimize disruptions to existing patterns of socio-cultural organization
- Compensation with land for land lost where required
- Guarantees that indigenous communities are better off after removal. The status of indigenous communities should be much better in the resettlement colonies compared to their traditional village

It may be concluded here that the policymakers and planners should advocate for small projects as a substitute for mega-projects. It is also very important to make cost-benefit analyses of a project at the micro level instead of at the macro level. This will alleviate the process of social exclusion experienced by the indigenous people, who sacrifice much for the project but get almost nothing in return. The benefits of the mega-project are often enjoyed by people not affected by the project. Understanding the cultural infrastructure of the indigenous people is a very important precondition to any development project. A culture-friendly approach to development is more acceptable, as it uses traditional channels and resources to encourage the development of indigenous people. It further propagates indigenous knowledge as a way to contribute to a viable management of local resources with the active participation of the indigenous people.

Finally, we must direct attention to exclusion 'of whom and by whom' as well as exclusion 'from what' and 'how'. It is essential to determine the forces, processes, institutions and groups that cause indigenous people to be socially excluded. In fact, in this analysis, we see that the already marginalized people of the sample area became further excluded with adverse consequences. These people continue to be excluded from health care, education, gainful engagement, Common Property Resources (CPRs), social participation networks. They struggle to make a decent living within the systems and processes that are being managed by the state. The analysis presented here has suggested some steps towards developing policies that minimize the range of social exclusion and marginalization of indigenous people once the decision to build a mega-dam has been finalized.

Notes

1 I would like to extend my heartfelt thanks to Professor Christine Finnan, College of Charleston, USA for going through the draft copy of this paper and making necessary corrections.

2 A traditional village in this region has various functionaries such as the *dhangda majhi* (headman), the *jani* (priest and medicine man), the *disari* (astrologer), the *gunia* (shaman), the *gurmai* (lesser shaman) and the *barik* (messenger). The *barik* is often from the Dom community. He collects contributions for any festival or ritual from each household. The money is used to buy animals and other goods for sacrifice at the market. This is the *barik*'s duty, as he is adept at striking a good bargain.

3 Totem is an animal, plant or natural object serving among certain tribal or indigenous peoples as the emblem of a clan or family and sometimes revered as its founder, ancestor or guardian.

References

Agnihotri, Anita. 1996. 'The Orissa Resettlement and Rehabilitation of Project-Affected Persons Policy, 1994 – An Analysis of its Robustness with Reference to Impoverishment Risk Model'. In *Involuntary Displacement in Dam Projects*, edited by A. B. Ota and Anita Agnihotri, 19–42. New Delhi: Prachi Prakashan.

Areeparampil, Mathew. 1996. 'Displacement Due to Mining in Jharkhand'. *Economic and Political Weekly* 31 (24): 1524–8.

Arnold, David, and Ramachandra Guha. 1995. *Nature, Culture, Imperialism*. Delhi: Oxford University Press.

Baboo, Balgovind. 1992. *Technology and Social Transformation*. New Delhi: Concept Publishing Company.

_______. 1991. 'Big Dams and the Tribals: The Case of the Hirakud Dam Oustees in Orissa'. *Social Action* 41 (3): 288–303.

Behera, Deepak Kumar and Piet A. Erasmus. 1999. 'Environment, Tribal People and Development: Some Reflection from the Third World'. In *Contemporary Society: Tribal Studies Vol. 3: Social Concern*, edited by Deepak Kumar Behera and Georg Pfeffer, 21–35. New Delhi: Concept Publishing Company.

Bennett, G., A. Butt-Colson and S. Wavell. 1978. *The Damned: The Akawaio Indians of Guyana*. London: Survival International Document VI.

Cernea, Michael M. 2000. 'Risks, Safeguards, and Reconstruction: A Model for Population Displacement and Resettlement'. In *Risks and Reconstruction: Experiences of Resettlers and Refugees*, edited by Michael M. Cernea and C. McDowell, 11–55. Washington, DC: World Bank.

_______. 1999. *The Economics of Involuntary Resettlement: Questions and Challenges*.Washington, DC: World Bank.

______. 1998. 'Impoverishment or Social Justice? A Model for Planning Resettlement'. In *Development Projects and Impoverishment Risks*, edited by Mathur, Hari Mohan and David Marsden, 296–298. Delhi: Oxford University Press.

______. 1997. 'The Risks and Reconstruction Model for Resettling Displaced Populations'. *World Development* 25 (10): 1569–87.

______. 1994. *Bridging the Divide: Studying the Refugees and Development Oustees*. Washington, DC: World Bank, Environment Department.

Colson, Elizabeth 1999. 'Gendering Those Uprooted by "Development"'. In *Engendering Forced Migration: Theory and Practice*, edited by D. Indra, 23–39. Oxford: Berghahn.

Daula, A. K. 1993. *Environmental Impact of Large Reservoir Projects on Human Settlement.* New Delhi: Ashish.

Fernandes, Walter. 1997. 'Displacement of Tribals: Struggles and Implications for Resettlement'. In *Contemporary Society: Tribal Studies*, vol. 2, edited by Georg Pfeffer and Deepak Kumar Behera, 71–91. New Delhi: Concept Publishing Company.

______. 1991. 'Power and Powerlessness: Development Projects and Displacement of Tribals'. *Social Action* 41 (3): 243–70.

Fürer-Haimendorf, C. von. 1982. *The Tribes of India: Struggle for Survival.* New Delhi: Oxford University Press.

Gadgil, Madhav, and Ramachandra Guha. 1995. *Ecology and Equity: The Use and Abuse of Nature in Contemporary India.* London: Routledge.

International River Network (IRN) and Friends of the Earth (FoE). 2003. *Dammed Rivers, Damned Lives. What the Water Establishment Doesn't Want You To Know*, Berkeley: INR and FoE.

Lee, Richard B. 1988. 'Reflection on Primitive Communism'. In *Hunters and Gatherers: History, Evolution and Social Change*, edited by T. Ingold,, David Riches, and James Woodburn. Volume I, 252–8. Oxford: Berg.

Mathur, Hari Mohan and David Marsden, eds. 1998. *Development Projects and Impoverishment Risks.* Delhi: Oxford University Press.

Mehta, Lyla 2002. *Displaced by Development: Gender, Rights and Risks of Impoverishment.* Online: http://www.id21.org/society/Insights44art2.html (accessed 4 December 2002).

Mishra, Nita. 1996. 'Tribal Resistance in the Chhechhari Valley: A Report'. *Economic and Political Weekly* 31 (24): 1539–40.

Mohanty, B. B. 1997. 'State and Tribal Relationship in Orissa'. *Indian Anthropologist* 27 (1): 1–17.

______. 2003. 'Educational Progress of Scheduled Tribes: A Discursive Review'. *Man and Development*, XXV (2): 91–106.

______. 2001. 'Land Distribution among Scheduled Castes and Tribes'. *Economic and Political Weekly* 36 (40): 3857–67.

Mohapatra, L. K. 1990. 'Rehabilitation of Tribals Affected by Major Dams and Other Projects in Orissa'. In *A Report on the Workshop on Rehabilitation of Persons Displaced by Development Projects*, edited by A. P. Fernandes, 85–99. Myrada (Bangalore): Institute for Social and Economic Change.

Morse, B., and T. R. Berger. 1992. *Sardar Sarovar. Report of the Independent Team.* Ottawa: Resource Futures International Inc.

Oliver-Smith, Anthony. 1991. 'Involuntary Resettlement, Resistance and Political Empowerment'. *Journal of Refugee Studies* 4 (2): 132–49.

Parasuraman, S. 1999. *The Development Dilemma. Displacement in India.* Delhi: MacMillan Press and The Hague: ISS.

______. 1993. 'Impact of Displacement by Development Projects on Women in India'. Working Paper Series No. 159. The Hague: Institute of Social Studies.

Patel, Srikant, and Deepak Kumar Behera. 1999. 'Doomed by a Dam'. In *Contemporary Society: Tribal Studies Vol. 3: Social Concern*, edited by Deepak Kumar Behera and Georg Pfeffer, 85–100. New Delhi: Concept Publishing Company.

Pathy, Jaganath. 1982. 'Politics of Tribal Welfare: Some Reflections'. *The Eastern Anthropologist* 35 (4): 285–300.

Patnaik, N. 1972. *Tribes and their Development: A Study of Two Tribal Development Blocks in Orissa.* Hyderabad: National Institute of Tribal Development.

Patnaik, .S. M. 1996. *Displacement Rehabilitation and Social Change: The Case of the Paraja Highlanders.* New Delhi: Inter-India Publications.

Redfield, Robert 1955. *The Little Community: Viewpoints for the Study of a Human Whole.* Chicago: University of Chicago Press.

RRU (Resettlement and Rehabilitation Unit). 1997. Brochure on Resettlement and Rehabilitation Activities of UIP, Khatiguda.

Scudder, Thayer. 1997. *Social Impacts of Large Dams in Large Dams; Learning from the Past, Looking at the Future*, IUCN/WB, Gland.

_______. 1996. 'Development-Induced Impoverishment, Resistance and River-Basin Development'. In *Understanding Impoverishment, Providence*, edited by Christopher McDowell, 49–76. Oxford: Berghahn Books.

Stanley, N. F., and M. P. Alpers. 1975. *Man-Made Lakes and Human Health.* London: Academic Press.

Swain, M., and N. Panigrahi. 1999. 'Development, Displacement and Rehabilitation in Orissa.' *Man and Life* 25 (3–4): 163–75.

Thukral, E. 1992. *Big Dams, Displaced Peoples: Rivers of Sorrow, Rivers of Joy.* Delhi: Sage Publications.

_______. 1996. 'Development, Displacement and Rehabilitation: Locating Gender'. *Economic and Political Weekly* 31(24): 1500–1503.

Viegas, Philip and Geeta Menon. 1989. *The Impact of Environmental Degradation on People.* New Delhi: Indian Social Institute.

Vyasulu, Vinod. 1985. 'Under Developing Koraput'. *South Asian Anthropologist* 6 (1): 63–71.

WCD (World Commission on Dams). 2000. *Dams and Development: A New Framework for Decision Making.* London and Sterling, VA: Earthscan Publications Ltd.

Wilson Anne and Peter Beresford P. 2000. '"Anti-oppressive Practice": Emancipation or Appropriation?' *British Journal of Social Work* 30: 553–73.

World Bank. 1994. *Making Development Sustainable: The World Bank Group and the Environment, Fiscal 1994.* Washington, DC: World Bank.

Xaxa, Virginius. 2001. 'Protective Discrimination: Why Scheduled Tribes Lag Behind Scheduled Castes.' *Economic and Political Weekly* 36 (29): 2765–71.

XIM (Xaiver Insitute of Management). 1994. *Socio-economic Study of Displaced Persons Under Upper Indravati Project, Orissa.* Bhubanewar: CENDERET, Xaiver Insitute of Management.

Chapter 11

'SOLUTIONS EMERGE WHEN EVERYONE WORKS TOGETHER': EXPERIENCES OF SOCIAL INCLUSION IN WATERSHED MANAGEMENT COMMITTEES IN KARNATAKA[1]

Devanshu Chakravarti, Sarah Byrne and Jane Carter

Despite strong and highly progressive constitutional and legislative measures upholding equity, discrimination on the basis of caste, class and gender remains a reality for many of India's 1.4 billion citizens. Major disparities exist in poverty levels, mortality rates, educational attainments and access to resources between urban and rural areas, regions, social groups and between men and women. India today is a country of stark contrasts and striking inequalities. The starting point for this chapter is a reflection on experiences in social inclusion in the context of the Indo-Swiss Participative Watershed Development Project, a development project implemented in three districts in the South Indian state of Karnataka, with which two of the authors were closely affiliated. The chapter analyses the everyday functioning of new institutional spaces, in this case project-supported water management committees, for understanding the evolving dynamics between different individuals, social groups and localities while collaborating and competing in development initiatives. The authors are particularly interested in what happens to such spaces beyond the scope of the project intervention – whether they continue creating opportunities, building confidence and political capabilities for contesting exclusionary social practices and public resource distribution, or whether they are captured by resurgent patronage politics. Through the use of an extended case study method, based on interviews conducted with families in 2004, 2005 and 2010, as well as project data and observations, the authors seek to understand these temporal dynamics. The chapter is formulated specifically with reference to the challenge presented by Andrea Cornwall (2004):

> What is clear is that more attention needs to be paid to issues of difference, and the challenge of inclusion [...] The social and power relationships that exist within the

range of domains of association across which people move in the course of their everyday lives intimately affect their ability to enter and exercise voice in arenas for participation.

We proceed to provide an overview and definition of the related concepts of inequality and social inclusion. We then briefly review the existing literature on spaces for social inclusion within participatory development. This is followed by an ethnographic snapshot of participation, in the form of a case study of a revolving fund-based watershed development initiative and the spaces created for social inclusion. We conclude with a discussion on the tangible results sustaining in a post project scenario, more than five years after project closure.

Social Exclusion in India Today

Being a highly diverse country, there are many different groups in India that face social exclusion. Social exclusion describes a process by which certain people experience systematic discrimination on the basis of their ethnicity, religion, caste, gender, age, and so forth. Discrimination occurs in public institutions, such as through the legal system or education and health services, as well as in social institutions such as households and community groups. Unequal inclusion and exclusion between social groups refers to political and social, as well as economic, inequalities between people belonging to particular socially defined groups. The definitions of the groups can be more or less fluid over time, but the more 'fixed' they are defined, and the more historically they are rooted, the more challenging it is to address inequalities. In India, these groups include Dalits (also known as 'scheduled castes') and Adivasis (also known as 'scheduled tribes', or indigenous people), who together make up about a quarter of the population, as well as religious minorities such as Muslims (approximately 15 per cent of the population). Their exclusion is reflected in a lack of access (or unequal access) to political institutions, to public services (education, health care), to public places (police stations, government ration shops, post offices, schools, water facilities and village council offices), and to income-earning assets (in particular, land), among many others. Attempts by Dalits and Adivasis to secure their human rights and lawful entitlements have sometimes been met with resistance and even violence. There are a number of particularly infamous cases in which the representatives of the state have been implicated. Social exclusion has a gendered aspect as well. Across social groups, women face discrimination in many areas of life, although their status varies significantly according to their social and ethnic backgrounds. Disadvantage is amplified when identities overlap; thus, for example, Adivasi women are excluded, both as women and as Adivasis. Nevertheless, caution should be used in ascribing inclusion or exclusion to collective identities as a whole. When generalizing across collective identities, there is a danger of overlooking inequalities that exist between different individuals within the same group, often on economic grounds. In such cases, a more differentiated analysis is called for.

In addition to particular social groups being excluded from political, social or economic life, different regions, spaces or localities can also be seen as 'excluded'.

Regional inequalities, both between states and within states, or between urban and rural areas in India, are marked. India's economic growth has to a large extent been concentrated in a handful of cities, such as Delhi, Bangalore, Hyderabad, Chennai, and Mumbai, with many other areas lagging behind. The outcome of this multi-speed development has been labelled by the British Department for International Development (DFID) as the 'three faces of India': global India, developing India and poorest India (DFID 2008). Such inequality leads to migration from rural to urban areas. While in itself not necessarily a negative phenomenon, this migration carries with it the double risk of further decline in population in the rural areas and social tension in the urban areas. Although many rural people are migrating to cities, the majority of India's poor people still live in the vast rural parts of the country.

Spatial exclusion also refers to inequalities related to a particular locality, such as a neighbourhood. In rural areas, excluded places tend to be remote, with low agricultural or resource potential and poor access to services. Within urban areas, location-specific characteristics can lead to a concentration of environmental, economic and social disadvantage within a particular neighbourhood. For example, in the financial capital of Mumbai, while slum pockets cover a small percentage of the land, they are home to 60 per cent of the city's population. This land is in the heart of the city and is among the most valuable real estate in the world. But the residents do not have legal title to the land and are therefore considered to be illegally squatting. Slum dwellers live under a constant threat of slum demolition drives, a move that takes away the roofs over their heads. In addition to this chronic insecurity, the inhabitants deal regularly with issues such as paying 'protection money' to the local Mafia, lack of water, no sewage or solid waste facilities, lack of public transport, pollution and housing shortages. Spatial exclusion is also prevalent in rural India, where people from the same caste generally live in the same settlement or part of the village. The Dalit settlements are usually located on the outskirts of a village and have separate water facilities, as traditionally Dalits are not permitted to draw water from the water sources used by other castes. Despite legislation with punitive directives against the practice, in some places, even today, Dalits are forbidden entry to village temples.

Inclusion in/through Participatory Development Spaces?

In this chapter we look at the issue of inclusion and exclusion (both social and spatial) in the everyday functioning of a new institutional space, in this case a development project-supported water management committee. We take this example to illustrate and understand the evolving dynamics between different individuals, social groups and localities when they begin to collaborate and compete in development initiatives. Before proceeding to our specific case study material, we would like to briefly review the existing literature on this topic.

John Gaventa (2006) defines spaces as 'opportunities, moments and channels where citizens can act to potentially affect policies, discourses, decisions and relationships which affect their lives and interests.' In our particular case, we will mostly be examining the specific institutional spaces through which citizens can participate in decision making about watershed development. According to Gaventa (2003), participatory approaches generally have one, or a combination, of the following four purposes:(1) manipulation or co-optation: to support the status quo and to divert opposing voices, (2) legitimacy: to ensure wider ownership of and support for a given agenda, (3) efficiency: to make the projects more cost-effective, targeted and sustainable and (4) transformation: to change underlying social and power relations. To these four, a fifth could be added: de-politicization. Explored by James Ferguson in the seminal *The Anti-Politics Machine* (1990), and further developed by, among others, Tania Murray Li in *The Will to Improve* (2007), the de-politicizing potential (or effect, or intention) of development interventions has been a topic of much interest to development academics and practitioners alike. The debate about the different objectives and effects of the participation paradigm is carried out within the pages of two edited volumes: *Participation: the New Tyranny?* (Cooke and Kothari 2001) and *Participation: from Tyranny to Transformation?* (Hickey and Mohan 2004). While it is beyond the scope of our present endeavour to summarize this debate, this chapter has been developed in relation to it, particularly the call voiced by Andrea Cornwall (2004) for ethnographies of participation in practice, and the practical questions posed by Glyn Williams (2004), such as 'To what extent do participatory development programmes contribute to processes of political learning among the poor?'

In order to understand what happens in concrete cases, the concept of participatory spaces has been further developed by Ranjita Mohanty (2004a; 2004b) in several studies of participation in forest governance in Uttarkhand. The refinements she brings to the concept are key to how the concept will be applied in the particular case studied here. Mohanty starts from the assumption that power is central to the understanding of space and, thus, that institutional space is a contested terrain. On this basis, she makes two points that illuminate our understanding of the nature and dynamics of participation that takes place in these spaces. Firstly, Mohanty (2004b) points out that 'since institutions are the embodiment of power, the spaces created by them are political in nature. This makes spaces vulnerable to contestations and conflicts of various kinds…' Spaces are not neutral, and cannot be neutral, as far as politics is concerned. Thus, in analysing spaces we should always be aware of their political aspects, even if they are supposed to be nonpolitical or technical spaces. If a particular space is claimed to be 'apolitical' it is important to ask why (and indeed, whether) this is so. This point is reinforced by Vasudha Chhotray (2004 and 2007), who, writing on participatory watershed committees in Andhra Pradesh, shows how a discourse of depoliticization is in use to justify the creation of 'apolitical' watershed committees in contrast to 'political' Panchayats, ostensibly unsuitable for participatory development because they embody both political contestation and vested interests. This discourse, Chhotray writes, serves only to mask conflicts over resources and sets up the ground for depoliticization of another sort, by distancing watershed project spaces from pro-poor progressive politics. Our own case, explored in detail below, is similar in the sense that the watershed committees were explicitly established through project support as 'non political' institutions. However, it differs in the sense that this 'non political' space was explicitly used to build political capabilities to contest traditional socially and spatially exclusive practices. This dual political/apolitical nature is a significant feature.

Mohanty's (2004b) second argument is that

> Spaces are never created in a vacuum – they react upon already existing spaces, on spaces which are simultaneous and overlapping and on the wider social-economic-cultural setting in which they are embedded. This means that spaces remain transformatory – they are constantly being created, altered, defined and redefined, with positive promises and possibilities amidst manipulation, misuse and abuse.

This second argument is key to our analysis of the interplay between various institutional spaces interacting in the study locality: water management committees interact with self-help groups, local governance bodies (Panchayat and other), project management committees, and so on. As Mohanty points out, these spaces have to be considered in relation to both the other simultaneously existing spaces as well as the local context. This point is further reinforced by Andrea Cornwall (2004), who writes that

> No matter how equitable the intentions that inform the creation of an arena for participation might be, existing relationships cannot simply be left at its boundary; rather the traces of these relationships, and of previous experiences in other spaces, continue to exert an influence on what is said, and what is sayable within any given space.

Fighting Exclusion through Revolving Fund-Based Watershed Activities: The Case of Allapur

This section describes the pilot case of a revolving fund-based watershed intervention in the village of Allapur in Karnataka, supported under the Indo-Swiss Participative Watershed Development Karnataka (ISPWDK) with facilitation by the partner Non-Governmental Agency (NGO), MYRADA (Mysore Resettlement and Development Agency).[2] In 1995, when ISPWDK was initiated, Karnataka was one of the first states in the country in which watershed-based initiatives for developing rain-fed areas had been introduced. The project was conceptualized as a 'watershed plus' project, which meant that technical watershed improvement activities were complemented by activities supporting social inclusion and participatory governance. Indeed, the catch phrase of the project was 'People centred, people initiated and people driven'. ISPWDK was implemented until 2006, during which time the methods of project delivery through new participatory institutional spaces, such as village development societies and watershed management committees, evolved.

The hamlet of Allapur comprises 66 households, and lies not far from the larger village of Kodli, comprising over five hundred households. Both settlements lie in Chincholi *taluk*, Gulbarga district. Due to its remoteness and small size, Allapur community members had inadequate representation in the local governance institutions and hence, the hamlet was sidelined from government-funded development activities. Before the project intervention, the settlement of Allapur could be reached only by a poorly maintained dirt track that passed along a small valley, past a dam constructed during the 1990s, and then along the shores of the reservoir that this dam has created. A small stream had to be crossed in order to enter the hamlet. The road was potholed and prone to blockages by falling boulders or flooding during the monsoon rains. Allapur's inhabitants are of different faiths, with households of scheduled castes, scheduled tribes, other castes and Muslims making up the population. None have substantial assets, although among them, it is the Dalits and Lambanis (an Adivasi group) who are subject to particular marginalization. Most of the well-off families among the villagers moved away to nearby villages after the creation of the reservoir, which flooded the best agricultural land. A few of these wealthier households, however, continue to be influential by acting as local moneylenders and by leasing their land to sharecroppers in Allapur. It is largely on these lands that the poorest in Allapur work as agricultural labourers.

The inhabitants of Allapur have experienced discrimination in many ways, much of which can be traced to the unequal balance of power between this small settlement and the larger neighbouring village of Kodli. One manifestation of discrimination is the construction of the dam close to their hamlet. This was supported by powerful households in Kodli village who sought, and successfully obtained, funds for the dam from the District Panchayat. Construction took place over the period 1994–98. According to the residents of Allapur, they were neither consulted nor informed regarding the construction of the dam. The dam flooded their fields, but has created an important water supply for irrigating the downstream lands of Kodli village. Some compensation was paid to those who lost land, but there are many stories of money not reaching the right persons. There was also talk of resettlement, which initially raised hope among many villagers, although eventually nothing materialized. The prospect of resettlement only served to make people hesitant to invest in homes and land in Allapur.

Allapur falls under the Kodli Gram Panchayat (GP), and would normally have representation in this body, in the form of an elected member. Yet, it had none before the project period. Allapur and a Lambani hamlet comprise one ward in Kodli Gram Panchayat, so if a ward member is elected from the Lambani hamlet, Allapur remains unrepresented. Children from Allapur also attend school in Kodli after they have passed grade 5 (when they are about ten years old); this entails walking nearly 16 km to school and back on a daily basis. Similarly, Allapur residents have to seek whatever health care facilities they require from Kodli or beyond. In general, infrastructure before the project intervention was poor. Apart from the bad road, the drinking water supply was largely from open wells and of dubious quality. The solitary hand pump in the village used to break down regularly. Access to credit was restricted to arrangements with moneylenders charging high rates of interest. Although the government supported the Self Help Group (SHG) programme, Stree Shakti, which was operational in the village, it was functioning poorly.

Why Was the Intervention Planned?

ISPWDK began phase II project operations in Kodli village in 2000 by supporting the establishment of a Village Development Society (VDS) (ISPDWK 2005). Legally registered under the Societies Registration Act (1960), the VDS was promoted as a gender-balanced, equity-focused, village-level institution. One woman and one man from each household in the village became a member of the general body, and the governing council was required to have a minimum of one-third women, and have proportional representation of different caste groups. This structure was adopted to create space for women and members of marginalized social groups to have a voice in village development activities. Although a project-funded institution, the VDS was established with a vision of continuing beyond the project time frame, and with sufficient self-perpetuating financial resources to address the overall development needs of the village and not just the project requirements. The VDS operates in a complementary manner to the Gram Panchayat (which covers a larger territorial area), working with it on the implementation, planning and monitoring of development programmes and schemes. The Kodli VDS continues to function successfully, even after the project closure in 2006.

One of the results of the space created for members of marginalized groups to have a greater voice in the affairs of Kodli was that residents having family ties with households in Allapur shared their difficulties in the ISPWDK project meetings. While the facilitating NGO, MYRADA, was aware of these difficulties, it was bound by project-planning decisions to focus project interventions in Kodli. However, with the suggestion coming from Kodli VDS that something should be done in Allapur through project funding, this decision was revisited and the idea of a revolving fund-based watershed scheme was mooted for Allapur. MYRADA had pioneered the experience of supporting revolving fund-based (rather than grant-based) watershed interventions in their projects in Kolar, Chamrajnagar and Dharampuri Districts of South Karnataka. The modalities of this approach vary, but essentially farmers are provided credit at favourable interest rates to develop their land and livelihoods. Farmers pay back the loan in full to a village institution and the money is placed in a village development fund that can then be used for funding further loan-based investment. The model differs from the grant-based watershed approaches, under which the full cost of watershed development is paid by the project, and farmers contribute an additional sum (normally 25 per cent for farm land) toward a community contribution fund, which is also intended for future village development activities.

The proposal to take up Allapur as a loan-based watershed intervention was placed before the ISPWDK Programme Steering Committee (PSC) at its third meeting, in October 2003. VDS members from Kodli attended this meeting to present the proposal in person. The proposal was accepted with a funding of up to INR 20 thousand (drawn from a project contingency fund). Over the project period till 2006, the total financial support extended to the revolving fund watershed concept was INR 1.4 million.

What Was Innovative?

There is a widely held view that resource-poor farmers are too risk averse to invest in land development; and that they require a grant for such investment. If a loan-based watershed scheme was shown to be effective, it could have far greater potential for wide-scale replication than a grant-based scheme. Furthermore, if the people of Allapur, who are particularly disadvantaged, could manage to repay loans, there are good chances that villagers elsewhere could also repay loans for land development. Currently, under its priority-sector lending in rural areas, the government provides loans to individual farmers, farmers' cooperatives and self-help groups (SHGs) for farm-based and non-farm-based livelihood activities, but not for land development. Land development is covered under grant-based programmes.

Looking beyond the issue of loans versus grants, the intervention was innovative in taking advantage of changing social attitudes in a dominant village (Kodli) to promote empowering social processes in a hamlet that had had few previous development opportunities. Indeed, it was through the newly gained political influence of people in Kodli that such an intervention came about. It is this aspect of the intervention that is discussed and analysed here.

The Process Adopted

As in all ISPWDK interventions, considerable investment in capacity building was made when MYRADA first began to operate in Allapur in late 2003. Work began with many meetings and small group discussions to gain information about the hamlet and explain the nature of the watershed interventions. Tools used in this process included a variety of participatory mapping and ranking exercises. It was decided to establish a Watershed Management Committee (WMC) in Allapur, instead of a VDS, as the focus was more on the 'revolving fund' watershed concept rather than the village development concept of the VDS. In practice, there is little difference between the two bodies; like a VDS, the membership of the WMC is based on one male and one female member from every household in the village. Meetings are held regularly, and a representative from every household is expected to attend the meeting. Office bearers are rotated, as in the VDS. Like other VDSs, the WMC in Allapur was also registered and has a legal status as a society with written bylaws similar to that of the VDS.

A wealthy former resident of the village, working in a nearby town and who rarely returned to his ancestral home, donated the use of his house for the WMC's use as an office. Formalities such as the registration of the WMC, and the opening of bank accounts, were rapidly achieved, and loans were made available in early 2004. At the same time, the formation of SHGs was encouraged. SHGs have played an important role in the empowerment of women in the ISPWDK project area, not only through opportunities for savings and credit, but also as a forum for women to come together and share their livelihood, household and gender specific issues in their own separate space and to deliberate on approaches and strategies to address those issues. The SHGs are formed at the hamlet level, comprising women from nearby households. Women who demonstrate leadership qualities in SHGs are usually elected to the WMC by the community. In Allapur, the SHGs and WMC had a strong institutional relationship. Apart from the loans for the livelihood-/income-generation activities that were given only to the women members, most of the loans given to individual farmers for land development were later routed through SHGs, as they had effective systems for accounting and monitoring repayments.

For the community, the advent of the WMC meant that for the first time in their lives, residents had access to credit at reasonable rates. These rates varied from 12 to 15 per cent per annum and were cheaper compared to the prevailing rates of 36 per cent and above charged by local moneylenders. Initially, the loans were for livelihood support activities such as a goat raising or a petty shop, and had a fixed repayment schedule. The loans for the watershed structures were taken up by farmers after subsequent instalments of project support were released to the WMC. The loans for the watershed structures were repaid by farmers after six to nine months (differing from the fixed repayment schedule), in a single or two to three instalments after they had received payments for the harvest.

The community also gained a functioning village (hamlet) institution that met regularly and provided a forum for debate and community level discussions. All loan applications were discussed by the WMC in a village general assembly called the Village Gram Sabha. The Village Gram Sabhas decided, on a case-to-case basis, the amount of support to be extended to each applicant, the interest rate and the repayment schedule. The role of the WMC was to organize the Gram Sabha on a periodic basis, facilitate the discussions and follow up on the decisions.

Village Gram Sabhas were called by members of the WMC by providing door-to-door information to all households and by announcements made by a local drummer well before the stipulated date. Village Gram Sabhas provided a platform for the different factions in the village, aligned along caste, neighbourhood, occupation or political lines, to converge and discuss issues of community interest like village roads, infrastructure, physical access, access to credit, and so on, on a common platform.

Each village faction used the common village forums to further their own interests. Traditionally, these spaces were co-opted by the elites, as other communities would not dare to speak in front of them. Through project facilitation, the residents of Allapur arrived at a consensus on norms for the Gram Sabhas and focused on addressing social equity in its activities. The residents received numerous capacity-building inputs during the ISPWDK project period on subjects related to watershed treatments, leadership, organizational development, good governance, working with Panchayats, accounting and book management, loan repayment monitoring, norms of conducting Gram Sabhas, and so forth. Initially, the discussions within the Gram Sabha focused only on credit requirements for watershed development and livelihood needs. The availability of credit at low interest rates was greatly appreciated, and gradually the village Gram Sabhas also became a ground for debating social issues within the hamlet. As a result, many traditional attitudes of 'discrimination amongst the discriminated' were questioned.

What Happened?

In this section we outline some of the outcomes of project implementation, both in social and political/institutional terms. What the intervention has meant in social terms is illustrated by two representative examples of households selected from among the particularly poor and marginalized. The people concerned were first interviewed in February 2004, and again in October 2005 and in December 2010.

Hakkim Sab Mainoordin

In February 2004, Hakkim Sab was living in Allapur with his wife Rehana Begum, three children and his two brothers (one of whom is also married and has three children). His brothers were rarely resident in the village, having migrated to Bijapur and Mumbai. Hakkim Sab's family was somewhat exceptional in having official status as a Below Poverty Line (BPL) household. The household was surviving on what they could earn through wage labour, as they had no cultivatable land (a four-acre plot in their name was too barren to cultivate) or animals. No one in the family was a member of any SHG (although the government Stree Shakti scheme operated in Allapur, it had limited membership). When asked about what he would do if he had access to credit, Hakkim Sab shared that he would like to raise goats.

When interviewed in 2005, the family was still poor, but their prospects had improved. Hakkim Sab's two brothers had returned to the village on learning of the work being provided under the project, and the family had decided to invest in improving their previously uncultivated land. Rather than investing in goats, they had decided to take a loan of INR 12,000 from the WMC for land improvement, and had gradually paid it back. With the opportunities for wage labour through the watershed activities, Hakkim Sab and Rehana managed to earn nearly INR 10,000 over seven or eight months. Their land yielded its first crop in many years, although they had a major setback when the sesame crop, worth nearly INR 4,000, was stolen. The family also took responsibility for rearing the cow of a richer farmer; this provided milk for the children, and manure for the field. It was taken on a common local arrangement, whereby the carer keeps the first calf, and the second, once reared, is given back to the owner. Meanwhile, both Rehana and Hakkim Sab's mother Sherifabi had become members of a (project-supported) SHG. The family was still dependent on earnings through wage labour. They had to work hard, but, Sherifabi pointed out, they could sleep soundly at night, after a full meal. They had enough food for all and fewer worries; they could even dream of renovating and expanding their small house through credit at an affordable rate of interest, which was previously impossible. Furthermore, they were playing a more active role in the village; Sherifabi had become the treasurer of the WMC.

In December 2010, Hakim Sab was pleased to say that that he had been cultivating his land regularly for the past three years. In the first year, he sold pigeon pea for INR 6,000 (10 quintals). In the second year, in addition to the pigeon pea, he was able to make INR 3,000 from black gram and also produced cereals for household consumption. In 2010 he had a bumper crop of pigeon pea and *sorghum*. As the family was cultivating the land regularly, his wife applied for a loan to purchase a pair of bullocks. She had earlier taken a loan of INR 10,000 from the SHG for house construction, which loan had been duly repaid. Hakim Sab's family were rearing goats as this provided a regular income for the family and from this they intended to fulfil family obligations like their daughter's marriage.

Rajanan Nagappa Haligen

In February 2004, this Dalit family numbered seven: Rajanan, his wife, and five children. The elder son was working for a richer farmer under a bonded labour system.

Although landless, the household owned three cows; for this reason and the young age of the children, they chose not to migrate, but survived through local wage labour. Rajanan said then that if they had access to credit, they would like to raise goats.

A year later in 2005, the family had had to face major difficulties and huge unforeseen expenditure. The marriage of the eldest daughter cost them INR 20,000 (INR 11,000 in dowry and the rest on the wedding festivities). Part of this sum was covered by a loan from the farmer to whom the son was bonded (to be paid back); part from Rajanan's sister. Then Rajanan fell sick and had an operation. Overall, his medical costs (at the government hospital in the district town of Gulbarga) amounted to some INR 10,000. His health was poor, and he was advised not to undertake hard labour. The money for the treatment was again paid by the richer farmer, in return for the son's bondage being extended by one year (one year's labour is calculated at INR 16,000 – the INR 6,000 remaining after the medical expenses were to be used towards the family's food needs over the year). However, the family was able to get a loan of INR 8,250 through the project (WMC) to buy six goats. Rajanan looked after these and saw them as part of the family's future income; he shared the dream of building a herd of 20 or so.

Meanwhile, Rajanan's wife was contributing substantially to the household's subsistence, labouring for wages whenever work was available. She was also happy to have secured a new source of income as a cook for the school; as Dalit, this would have been unimaginable even two years previously, but the matter was discussed and decided in the WMC. The job earned her INR 300 per month.

Five years on, in December 2010, the Haligen family was still dependent on agricultural labour for their livelihood. Goat rearing was still a regular source of income for them. However, Rajanan was allotted a house under Ashraya Scheme of the Gram Panchayat, and his wife's salary as a cook was INR 1,200. The elder son continued to work as a labourer for a richer farmer, but was getting INR 30,000 per year due to improved wage rates. The daughter was married and had joined her new family.

As may be seen from these examples, the access to credit provided by the loan-based watershed was crucial for building assets within households. Even the Haligen family, who might otherwise have been rendered near destitute by Rajanan's illness, were able to generate, through goat rearing, a source of livelihood that is compatible with his frail health. Members of both households also specifically mentioned not only that they eat and sleep better these days, but that they have greater confidence and play a more active role in the village.

The Water Management Committee

While the above representative examples show how access to credit through the participatory institution of the WMC made a big difference in the lives of poor and marginalized families, the story with respect to the WMC itself is more mixed. The WMC in Allapur stopped receiving project funding when ISPWDK ended in 2006, but continued to function by maintaining a small office with two full-time paid staff. The WMC is financially self-reliant and earns around INR 50,000 from interest payments, membership fees and other income. Apart from meeting the administrative expenses of the WMC, a part of the income is also used for community functions such as Independence Day celebrations.

The WMC conducts monthly meetings and organizes four Gram Sabhas per year, wherein details of the loan repayments and sanctions are discussed, along with other village-related development issues. The WMC also uses a portion of the interest income for building the capacities of its members. Recently, the costs of transport for members to attend an agricultural fair in another part of the state were paid by the WMC. The WMC also hires services of MYRADA for capacity building by paying for the staff time of the NGO.

All eight SHGs formed through project support were still operational in December 2010. The Gram Sabha played a crucial role in supporting the institutions in the village. For example, in 2009, the Gram Sabha deliberated on a conflict in one SHG, where one member, belonging to a wealthy upper-caste family, influenced the SHG to pay a commission and get subsidized loans from a local bank for income generating activities. As the fund to the SHG was not disbursed in full, the other SHG members could not get the benefit from this fund. This led to some acrimony among the members and adversely affected the functioning of the group. The Gram Sabha decided that the SHG had to repay the loan to the bank in full and advised the SHGs not to undertake any unethical practices in the future. The Gram Sabha also decided to expel the member from the SHG.

Through the Gram Sabhas, the WMC was able to recover loans from defaulting members belonging to the elite and influential class in the villages. In one exceptional case, however, the loan amount was written off, as it was recognized that the household was suffering from huge debts due to land-related litigation with other family members.

However, trends emerging in 2010 regarding the Gram Sabhas may jeopardize the gains made by the community. Due to improved institutional linkages with the Kodli Gram Panchayat, the Gram Sabha was actively deliberating on the identification of beneficiaries for government social security programmes. Most households, especially those from the Dalit and Lambani communities, wanted to benefit from these programmes. Due to this pressure, the Gram Sabhas that were earlier forums for community decision making were being reduced to a forum for public squabbles and fights among members. It seemed that the capacity-building inputs that helped in improving the public speaking skills of the marginalized community representatives was being used for furthering individual causes and cornering personal benefits rather than focusing on common issues.

A member from Allapur was elected to the Kodli Gram Panchayat for the last two Gram Panchayat elections. With direct representation, the access of the village to government resources improved. The community was also able to raise funds from the District Panchayat to repair a large portion of the only road connecting it to Kodli. Small vehicles easily ply on this road. A culvert was placed over the stream and a bridge constructed. This helped in addressing their spatial inequality to some extent. Having been exposed to different government programmes in the *taluka* and district, some Allapur residents were able to influence government officials to get subsidized agricultural inputs from different programmes or schemes. However, according to community members interviewed, the greater interaction with other Gram Panchayat members and with different officials also influenced the elected representative from Allapur in adopting unethical practices. There are allegations of corruption, although nothing could be substantiated.

Due to their experience of implementing watershed activities, community members from Allapur were also selected as members of the committee that monitors the works being implemented under the Mahatma Gandhi Rural Employment Guarantee Scheme (MGNREGS) of the Kodli Gram Panchayat in the last term of the Gram Panchayat. The MGNREGS is a government programme that guarantees manual labour to an adult applying for work in rural areas. However, during the current Panchayat term, with a change of the members and the Panchayat secretary, the community members from Allapur were dropped from the monitoring committee and a new committee was appointed which did not have any member from Allapur. This was done as the new body wanted to have greater control over the programme and hence, curtailed the scope of the monitoring committee's work. The current Gram Panchayat member from Allapur was in collusion with other members and it is alleged by local people that along with the others, he was taking commissions for providing work to the community.

What Can This Tell Us about Social Inclusion?

Dismantling of caste and class prejudices

Having seen the benefits of being organized around credit and land resource-related issues, the communities in Allapur started playing an active role in the local institutions to address larger developmental issues. 'Playing a more active role' in village institutions and in the institutions of local governance is a highly significant aspect of social inclusion, as these institutions have become 'spaces for change' (Cornwall and Coelho 2007). With this empowering effect in mind, there is also a norm to change 33 per cent of the WMC members every two years. Hence, over the past few years, the entire body has been changed. This means that those beyond 'the usual suspects' are or have been included in the institution. Additionally, the quota for 33 per cent women has been greatly exceeded; women now comprise 70 per cent of the Allapur WMC membership, drawn mainly from the SHGs. These changing social dynamics are evidenced by changing social attitudes towards Dalits in Allapur. Although Muslims, Lambanis, and Hindus of different castes coexist without evident friction, caste-based discrimination was a strong force in the hamlet until recently. It was only with the advent of the project – in particular the investment in capacity building and community organization, as well as awareness raising on issues of gender and equity – that such matters came into open discussion, and were questioned and debated in WMC meetings.

Prior to the WMC formation, during common village feasts and social functions, the members from the upper caste would not sit and dine with members from the Dalit community. The Dalit community would sit separately during these festivities. In December 2010 it was reported that all members, irrespective of caste considerations, sat and ate together during social functions and marriages. School meals, which were consumed by all schoolgoing children, were being prepared (as mentioned earlier) by a Dalit woman. A flour mill owned by a Dalit household started operating in the village. This was the source of much discussion. In fact, two other Dalit men first purchased the mill, using money that they got from a government scheme specifically for Dalits. However, they could not install it due to village opposition and lack of finances. The matter came to the WMC for discussion several times and finally, the WMC approved a loan for INR 20,000 (INR 15,000 of which was needed as a deposit to get an electrical connection). The mill started operations on Republic Day in early 2005. Patronized by some in the beginning, by 2010 resistance had worn down and people from all castes were using the mill.

Local ownership of social change

In Allapur, the discriminating barriers of caste have thus to some extent been overcome through the community's own initiatives. Earlier, in any village meeting, Dalit people were not allowed to sit at the general platform or to speak their views. Now, everyone sits together on the platform and listens to what the others have to say. The secretary of the WMC, Tipanna, is a Dalit, while a woman Dalit member, Shekamma, is the secretary for the watershed loan recovery account. This demonstrates how local institutions help in building community capacities to address issues of exclusion. Furthermore, the processes of social change have been largely driven by the community. Although the project has provided a forum for debate and facilitated discussion, beyond the need for equal representation of different groups, it did not overtly try to force social change. The process of subtle social change taking place over time has local ownership and is thus more sustainable. It is often argued that trying to identify and work exclusively with the poorest is a high-risk strategy, likely to be resisted by the more influential. In this case, working through an approach of full participation, the project has been able to reach the marginalized without alienating the more powerful.

The growth of individualism?

Despite the positive trends noted above, local institutions also face fresh challenges, as illustrated by the trends in Gram Sabha discussions noticed in 2010. With people becoming more knowledgeable about the potential benefits available, and with improved skills in negotiating their access to them, community members started focusing on their own interests or that of their household. With the awareness of entitlement has come a heightened sense of competition for limited resources. Possibly, this is more a reflection of the limitations of the government schemes available than a result of the empowering processes that have taken place. Where financial resources have been in the hands of the WMC, and allocations have been decided at the local level (in Allapur itself), there has been broad fairness and few complaints. It is when decisions are put in the hands of persons outside the immediate community – even if they are quite close, for instance, in Kodli – that problems seem to arise. Allapur appears to demonstrate that a high degree of subsidiarity is needed for real accountability.

The alleged corruption of the current GP member for Allapur is another apparent demonstration of individual interest triumphing over the collective good. However, this, too, should be placed in perspective. Members of marginalized communities who are elected to public office often find the experience highly challenging. In addition to potentially low self-esteem due to discriminatory practices, they often have poor education. Thus, they can quickly be made to feel inferior by more senior government officials and 'technically' skilled persons with whom they are expected to negotiate. If invited to join in corrupt practices, it may be particularly tempting to acquiesce, and difficult to refuse. In addition, there are the costs that they are expected to bear. For each day they travel to the district headquarters on official work, they not only sacrifice a day's earnings, but must also pay for their transport and other costs, for which there is generally no reimbursement. How can they afford this if they do not exploit the system in some way? The difficulties faced by the potentially well-intentioned but cash-strapped GP representative should not be underestimated, and may be far less a result of individual self-interest than simple self-preservation. Ultimately, highly corrupt individuals will probably not be reelected by a knowledgeable and sensitized electorate, but nevertheless, the overall system often militates towards abuse.

Fluctuating spatial power dynamics

It has already been noted that the relationship between (neglected) Allapur and (influential) Kodli was a clear example of spatial inequality. With the formation of the WMC and through project interventions, the capacities of community members in Allapur were built, and they could better present their case in front of the Kodli Gram Panchayat. The Gram Panchayat has limited funds compared to the demand for services in different schemes. Usually, the distribution is according to the elected members' constituency rather than the 'merits' of the case. Having gained an elected member in the Kodli Gram Panchayat, the cases of Allapur are better presented in the Gram Panchayat and despite complaints against the elected representative, more development funds now reach Allapur than they did before the project intervention. Under ISPWDK, capacities of community groups were also built in Kodli. In the election in 2005, most of the active VDS/WMC members of Kodli and other project villages were elected to the Gram Panchayat. They also introduced a fresh approach of going by equity and the merits of the case in deciding the developmental interventions. Both the change in the decision-making processes within Kodli Gram Panchayat, and having their own elected representative therein, brought a change to Allapur's formerly excluded position, such that it could access development funds from the GP on a more equitable basis.

In this way, the existing power balance was clearly renegotiated and continued to be contested even after the development project left. However, even here, there are fresh challenges for the leadership to address if the community interests are considered paramount. Rather than the distancing of watershed project spaces from pro-poor progressive politics, in this case the watershed project spaces were central to addressing inclusion in decision making and in access to development funding both within the villages of Allapur and Kodli and between them. In this sense, though explained as an 'apolitical' intervention by project staff, the new institutional space of the watershed management committee was indeed deeply political in its position towards social inclusion.

According to Andrea Cornwall (2004):

> There is much that activist researchers can do to generate new ethnographies of participation that help locate spaces for participation in the places in which they occur, framing their possibilities with reference to actual political, social, cultural and historical particularities rather than idealised models of democratic practice.

We trust that this ethnograpic snapshot has served to shed light on how spaces for participation can have a truly empowering impact on the lives of the poor and marginalized. In particular, we argue the case for a very high degree of subsidiarity. We suggest that the lowest political and administrative level of the Gram Panchayat is often too large to provide the degree of devolved decision making that is needed to challenge the prejudices of social exclusion. It is at village or hamlet level that such change needs to be initiated.

Notes

1 The development project from which the case study is drawn was funded by the Swiss Agency for Development and Cooperation, and managed by the Swiss foundation Intercooperation (by which two of the authors were employed on the project). We would like to acknowledge the particular support of colleagues from MYRADA, particularly Mr S. D. Kalyanshetti, in gathering data. The views expressed nevertheless remain those of the authors. Corresponding author: Sarah Byrne, sarah.byrne@geo.uzh.ch.

2 For more information about the project, please see Gnehm (2004) and ISPWDK (2005, 2006).

References

Baviskar, Amita. 2004. 'Between Micro-politics and Administrative Imperatives: Decentralisation and the Watershed Mission in Madhya Pradesh, India'. *European Journal of Development Research* 16 (1): 26–40.

Chhotray, Vasudha. 2004. 'The Negation of Politics in Participatory Development Projects, Kurnool, Andhra Pradesh'. *Development and Change* 35 (2): 327–52.

______. 2007. 'The "Anti-politics Machine" in India: Depoliticisation through Local Institution Building for Participatory Watershed Development'. *Journal of Development Studies* 43 (6): 1037–56.

Cooke, Bill and Uma Kothari, eds. 2001. *Participation: The New Tyranny?* London: Zed Books.

Cornwall, Andrea. 2004. 'Spaces for Transformation? Reflections on Issues of Power and Difference in Participation in Development'. In *Participation: From Tyranny to Transformation? Exploring New Approaches to Participation in Development*, edited by Samuel Hickey and Giles Mohan, 75–91. London: Zed Books.

Cornwall, Andrea and Vera S. Coelho. 2007. 'Introduction'. In *Spaces for Change? The Politics of Participation in New Democratic Arenas*, edited by Andrea Cornwall and Vera S. Coelho, 1–29. London: Zed Books.

DFID 2008. 'Three Faces of India: DFID India Country Plan 2008–2015'. London: Department for International Development.

Ferguson, James. 1990. *The Anti-Politics Machine: 'Development', Depoliticization and Bureaucratic Power in Lesotho.* Cambridge: Cambridge University Press.

Gaventa, John. 2003. 'When Participation Meets Governance and Citizenship'. Bern: Swiss Agency for Development and Cooperation & Institute of Development Studies Workshop on Participation and Governance.

Gaventa, John. 2006. 'Finding the Spaces for Change: A Power Analysis'. *IDS Bulletin* 37 (6): 23–33.

Gnehm, Felix. 2004. 'Challenges of Livelihood Interventions in the Maramuri Watershed'. PSMU Report 2004. Bangalore: ISPWDK Project Support & Management Unit.

Hickey, Samuel and Giles Mohan, eds. 2004. *Participation: From Tyranny to Transformation? Exploring New Approaches to Participation in Development.* London: Zed Books.

ISPWDK. 2005. 'Empowering the People: Experience with Village Development Societies in Promoting Local Governance'. Hyderabad: Intercooperation.

______. 2006. 'Integrating Gender in Watershed Development : Lessons of Experience from the Indo-Swiss Participative Watershed Development Project'. Hyderabad: Intercooperation.

Mohanty, Ranjita. 2004a. 'Institutional Dynamics and Participatory Spaces: The Making and Unmaking of Participation in Local Forest Management in India'. *IDS Bulletin* 35 (2): 26–32.

______. 2004b. 'Linkages, Conflicts and Dynamics: Institutional Spaces and Participation in Local Forest Management in Uttaranchal'. PRIA Study Report no. 3. Delhi: PRIA.

Murray Li, Tania. 2007. *The Will to Improve: Governmentality, Development, and the Practice of Politics.* Durham and London: Duke University Press.

Williams, Glyn. 2004. 'Towards a Repoliticization of Participatory Development: Political Capabilities and Spaces of Empowerment'. In *Participation: From Tyranny to Transformation? Exploring New Approaches to Participation in Development,* edited by Samuel Hickey and Giles Mohan, 92–109. London: Zed Books.

Chapter 12

THE DEATH OF SHANKAR: SOCIAL EXCLUSION AND TUBERCULOSIS IN A POOR NEIGHBOURHOOD IN BHUBANESWAR, ODISHA

Jens Seeberg

It was a simmering hot summer day and Rosalyn, my research assistant, and I were standing together with Shankar and a number of fellow 'Pradhans' (name of a Scheduled Tribe (ST)) in the middle of an archetypical village scene with the clay houses so typical of small villages in rural Odisha; and yet, we were in the middle of the state capital of Bhubaneswar in one of the resettlement colonies that had grown as rural–urban migration took off in the latter half of the twentieth century. We discussed Shankar's tuberculosis (TB) and his continuous inability to follow the new TB treatment that had recently been introduced in the capital. Because he did not turn up at the clinic to get his medicines according to the schedule, the doctor had stopped his treatment. Now he had a fever, but he insisted that it was caused by the rain. I offered to accompany him to see the doctor on the following day – just before I had to leave India for a longer stretch of time – to help ensure that he was put back on treatment, and the small crowd of concerned family and friends surrounding this public discussion strongly supported the idea. But Shankar did not. I said, 'It's your decision; it's your life, if you want me to help you, I'll go with you on Monday morning, but if you don't want it, I can't help you.' Shankar said, 'Why should I take medicine? I'm feeling fine, I'm not feeling bad. Why should I take medicine? I'd rather go to work.' After a sermon about the way the medicine works and the required long duration of treatment, he finally pretended to agree to return to the clinic, albeit on his own.

The next time I visited the *basti*, Shankar had died – 28 years old. He died from TB because he was excluded from treatment at a time when universal and free TB treatment had been introduced in his city. Shankar's death, therefore, was a statement about the failure of the urban DOTS programme in the capital. But it was also a story about *his* failure to follow this treatment, which many people with varying degrees of – and eventually very little – success tried to make accessible to him. He also died from alcoholism and malnutrition. Or maybe he died from apathy, or from being a 'Pradhan' in this particular setting, or a mix of all these factors. I shall explore the background of Shankar's death as it relates to the social dynamics of in- and exclusion in Beluam Basti, a poor urban neighbourhood in Bhubaneswar, the capital of Odisha in the eastern part of India.[1]

A Note on Methodology

This chapter is based on ethnographic fieldwork in Bhubaneswar that was carried out in the context of a larger research project on 'Health System Reform and Ethics: Private Practitioners in Poor Urban Neighbourhoods in India, Indonesia and Thailand'.[2] Whereas the overall project focused on health services and the role of the private health sector as a main provider for people living in poor neighbourhoods in cities in India and elsewhere, the present chapter uses parts of the empirical material to focus on social dynamics within one such poor neighbourhood. Health is an integrated part of any discussion of TB-related death, but it is analysed not as an area in itself, but as a bodily expression of social realities of caste and class divisions, absolute and relative poverty and dynamics of structural violence.

The study used ethnographic methods including in-depth interviewing with practitioners and patients as well as observation in clinics and home visits to patients. A *basti* in the inner city of Bhubaneswar was initially selected on the basis of location, size and preliminary focus group discussions with inhabitants. A health economics household survey was conducted in four repeated rounds with a random sample of 200 households, and 25 households were identified for follow-up through repeated in-depth interviewing over 18 months during 2004–2006, with some additional field visits being conducted during 2006–2008 by the author.[3] A team of one male and three female research assistants were involved in data collection, and data was subsequently coded and analysed by the author, using NVivo for qualitative analysis and SPSS for quantitative analysis.[4]

Access to Health Care Services in Bhubaneswar, Odisha

Odisha, with a total population of nearly 42 million according to the 2011 census (Census of India 2011), is located in the eastern part of India. Despite its rich natural resources, the state is one of the poorest in India. Twenty-two per cent of the population are classified as ST, and 16.2 per cent as scheduled castes (SC) (Government of Orissa 2004). While the literacy rate has gone up, 27 per cent of the population and 36 per cent of women were still illiterate according to the 2011 census. Despite the expected inaccuracy of literacy statistics, these figures reflect social disparities in both rural and urban Odisha (and India in general) that allow daily life for many to be dominated by abject poverty and lack of access to public facilities and to basic information, while living in a parallel society separated from the burgeoning urban middle class.

The rate of urbanization is slower in Odisha, compared to many other Indian states, if seen as a ratio between urban and rural populations. However, state-level statistics may conceal more than they tell, since urban growth in some cities is very fast, and Bhubaneswar is a case in point. After it became state capital at the time of independence, it has grown seventeenfold over 40 years, from 38,200 in 1961 to 657 thousand in 2001 (Census of India).[5] In comparison, the total population of India has increased 2.34 times during the same period.

Not surprisingly, it is difficult for a fast-growing city like Bhubaneswar to keep up with infrastructure development. This is also true for health infrastructure. The main reference point for government-funded health care delivery in Bhubaneswar is Capital Hospital with 570 beds. The hospital serves as the referral point for most other primary- and secondary-level service providers in the city and illustrates that the main government presence is at the tertiary health care level. With the launch of the Revised National Tuberculosis Control Programme (RNTCP) in the municipality in 2005, a number of microscopy centres were identified, but apart from such exceptions, first-line health care delivery has been in private hands for decades. Even so, private hospitals are also relatively few compared to urban centres in many other Indian states. There are a number of private hospitals as well as corporate sector hospitals in Bhubaneswar, some of which also accept poor patients for outpatient services. Yet, for the poor, the main importance of the private sector in Bhubaneswar is at secondary and primary care levels, with predominantly private-for-profit structures (Gupta 2002). Chemist shops exist in abundance and often function as de facto primary care units (Seeberg 2012). In addition, there are many private homeopathic and ayurvedic clinics. While the composition of the health care system may be far from ideal in terms of public–private balance, physical access to health services is not a big problem in central Bhubaneswar.

Beluam *Basti*

The word *basti* has its origin in the Sanskrit verb *bas* which means to 'settle down' and is a rather neutral term for a 'settlement' in Hindi-speaking states of India (Kundu 1999). In Odiya, however, the word is 'associated with a congested settlement with high density, facing a deficiency of infrastructure and basic amenities' and is clearly negative (ibid.). In other words, it translates well into 'slum'. Terminology matters. Slums are areas to be demolished and 'slum dwellers' are people to be relocated by city planners in response to local political agendas, and the threat of demolition had earlier been experienced by inhabitants in Beluam Basti.

Beluam Basti was a small neighbourhood with a total of 520 households and a little more than two thousand inhabitants in 2004. It was surrounded by busy roads and intersections in the heart of the town, but was segregated from these by physical boundaries formed by high walls on two sides and a road on one side. The houses in the *basti* were evenly placed along lanes and bylanes in an orderly manner and a few of the inner lanes were comparatively wider. The houses were small and consisted mostly of brick walls plastered with mud or cement. The floors were a mix of mud and concrete, and thatched roofs alternated with roofs made of asphalt sheets or asbestos sheets. There was supply of electricity to the *basti* and about fifty households had legal connections, whereas about three hundred households had either taken extensions from the legally connected ones or had set up independent illegal wiring, and streetlights were scattered. A number of water pumps supplied the *basti* with water and reflected power relations at a certain point in time by being strategically, but unevenly, located. Some households had been able to install private connections in addition to the community taps. Apart from one open drain at one side of the *basti* that benefitted about fifty households living in its vicinity, there was no provision for drainage or for disposal of solid or liquid waste from the households other than dumping areas created through consensus-based usage where waste water and heaps of garbage accumulated. The absence of latrines was nearly total, so people mostly defecated along the approach road and at the boundary wall, and the stench in the area was harsh during summer.

The *basti* was established around 1970 by a handful of migrants from different districts of Odisha and from the neighbouring state of Andhra Pradesh who had joined the general drive to come to Bhubaneswar, the new capital town of Odisha, looking for better economic opportunities. Initially, the *basti* had only 14 families, half of them from a 'tribal' area in Andhra Pradesh (including the Pradhan ST) and the rest from different parts of Odisha. The newcomers worked as manual labourers in construction sites and as rickshaw drivers. Around 1972, a well was dug by the original inhabitants to meet their requirements for water. When it dried up more than 30 years later, the original community from Andhra Pradesh, to which Shankar belonged, lost its primary source of drinking water.

With time, the *basti* grew in size as a local manifestation of the rapid growth of the city. In 1983 the number of households had reached 140. It was an unauthorized and therefore illegal settlement, and in that year, the Municipality ordered the inhabitants to vacate the area in favour of construction of a park. The *basti* was completely demolished, and the inhabitants had to find shelter elsewhere in the city. However, in what might be considered a manifestation of the 'capacity to aspire' (Appadurai 2004), about half of the families regrouped and started settling down in the area adjacent to the new park. At this time, a drain and water pumps were established. The pumps were unevenly distributed across the *basti* and inhabitants of Pradhan Sahi had to go outside the *basti* to collect water after their well dried up.

Two hundred households constituted the *basti* in 1990. Still an unauthorized habitation, the inhabitants feared future eviction and started efforts to have the settlement legalized through the approval of the municipality. A committee with 14 members was formed to work with the issue. After persistent efforts with the Municipal authorities, electricity connection was granted to the *basti* in 1997 and in the same year, it was granted official recognition as an 'authorized slum'.

Change in legal status made it a more attractive place to settle down and relatives and acquaintances of the initial inhabitants came in large numbers, resulting in a size of 500 households in 2000 and about 550 households in 2004. Of these, about 450 families were house owners, the remaining100 families living as tenants in rented houses. A total of 388 families had been given 'Below Poverty Line' (BPL) ration cards, which entitled them to food articles (mostly grains) at subsidized prices from designated shops.

The majority of wage-earning inhabitants were engaged as daily labourers at construction sites and as rickshaw or trolley pullers. Less than 10 per cent had small businesses of their own, such as outlets selling vegetables, pan shops, local fast food shops, laundry, or they worked as hawkers of different products. Around 15 per cent were engaged in different types of low-grade service jobs, mostly in the private sector.

There was an Anganwadi Centre (AWW) in the *basti* that provided standard child development services such as health checkups, immunization, and health education for expectant and lactating mothers. The centre was, in principle, operational every day in the morning, but the AWW worker stayed in another colony, and this affected her performance and reputation in the *basti*.

Most children were enrolled as students in nearby government schools and the boys played during the afternoon hours at the big playground belonging to the nearby police camp, while most girls had to help with household chores. Ad hoc youth clubs were formed on the occasion of festivals and certain *pujas* and cultural functions in the *basti*. Earlier, under the previous councillor, a woman's group had been organized and given vocational training, but this had ceased to exist.

The high level of un- and underemployment left boys to hang around in the lanes or gather in the small market place. Idle youth and elders also engaged in playing cards during the day and evening, sometimes involving *satta* (gambling). There were a few hideouts for smoking *ganja* or for consumption of liquor or other drugs. Consumption of cheap country liquor and *ginger* (a popular cheap ayurvedic medicine with a high content of alcohol) was common during the evening hours. Police raids to nab people who engaged in playing *satta*, or who were involved in stocking and peddling drugs or liquor, provided an excuse for extortion and established a profitable role for the local political leaders in the *basti* to act as mediators based on a system of debts and loyalties.

The 'Community Management Group' (CMG) formed the political leadership in the *basti*. It had fourteen members with an elected president and secretary. The president was a state employee who owned the only concrete house in the neighbourhood. The formal representative of the *basti* in the municipal corporation was the councillor of the ward in which the *basti* was located. Due to neglect of the development of the *basti*, the current ward councillor did not command the same level of respect as the earlier councillor, who had been instrumental in initiating the extension of electricity and piped water supply and constructing the drain. The general demand for better infrastructure in the *basti* as a whole had not been met, even if certain individual households thrived.

Social Divisions in the *Basti*

There is a general tendency in development policy documents and reports (and some social science literature) to talk about 'the poor' as a rather homogenous black-box kind of category, and for certain types of moral argument this level of abstraction may suffice. Appadurai, who otherwise builds his discussion of the capacity to aspire on engagement in 'a detailed ethnographic account of a pro-poor alliance of housing activities' in Mumbai (Appadurai 2004, 70), provides an example, as he does not hesitate to conceive of the poor as 'a social group, partly defined by official measures but also conscious of themselves as a group' (ibid., 65). Appadurai's focus is on globalization and the emergence of global pro-poor grassroots NGOs (Non-Governmental Organizations) who share the need for classification of target groups with government bureaucracy; but this terminology also reflects a more general tendency to not differentiate social groups within the black box of poverty. Partially deviating from this tendency in their analysis of health care dynamics in a number of neighbourhoods in Delhi, Das and Das (2006) compared neighbourhoods in terms of income indicators at household level as a backdrop for a discussion of health seeking and treatment practices, but they paid less attention to social disparities within the neighbourhoods. However, in order to understand the untimely death of Shankar, it is necessary to go a step further and explore social divisions within the *basti*. In spite of its small size and the high level of poverty in general, social disparities prevalent in the country were replicated in this small area of approximately 200 by 115 metres, separating the poor from the destitute.

The *basti* was divided into a number of clusters, called *sahi*. Most people were Hindus, but there was also a minority of Muslim households who had given name to Muslim sahi. In Kondh Sahi lived a few Kondh (ST) families. These families originated from different parts of Odisha and were generally not related. Other *sahis* were named according to geographic location and were inhabited by more mixed groups: *tala* (lower), *majhi* (middle) and *upara* (upper) *sahi*. The *sahi*, where the president and secretary of the CMG lived, was paved and characterized by comparatively spacious brick houses with latrines and drainage. Even if the Muslims in Muslim Sahi were generally poorer in terms of income and housing, it was another *sahi* that stood out as visibly poorer than the rest of the *basti*, namely Pradhan Sahi. A couple of blind alleys with poorly constructed houses constituted the immediate physical horizon for a group of Pradhans, the ST that had been living in the *basti* since the initial settlement. Electricity and water supply to Pradhan Sahi had been disconnected, which forced the community to go outside the *basti* to a roadside water tap for water since they were not allowed to use water sources in the other *sahis*. They survived as daily labourers and were considered to be untouchables by the other inhabitants of the *basti*. Some of the women had been able to get a job as a maid or house cleaner in the houses of richer people living in the vicinity of the *basti*. Alcohol drinking and street quarrels were considered to be more common in Pradhan Sahi, and other *basti* people generally stayed away.

Reported household income in a community characterized by underemployment and dependency on the informal economy is bound to be inaccurate and underreporting is expected. However, assuming that this is more or less the case for all households in our household survey, this problem does not constitute a serious obstacle for comparison between different groups of households. The data in all tables and in Figure 12.1 stem from our household survey. Table 12.1 below gives an indication of social differentiation across *sahis* in terms of stated monthly household income, using INR 3,000 as an analytical threshold.[6] Figures are average values over all four rounds of household surveys to adjust for seasonal variation. This also partially adjusts for underreporting, since data may become more accurate over time as trust accumulates between respondent and interviewer.[7]

Table 12.1. Household (HH) income groups by sahi.[8]

		Sahi							Total
		Pradhan	Kondh	Muslim	Upara	Majhi	Tala	Others	
INR ≥3000	Count	11	27	31	47	71	26	110	323
	%	14.7	41.5	43.7	40.9	43.3	35.6	52.4	41.8
INR <3000	Count	64	38	40	68	93	47	100	450
	%	85.3	58.5	56.3	59.1	56.7	64.4	47.6	58.2
Total	Count	75	65	71	115	164	73	210	773
	%	100.0	100.0	100.0	100.0	100.0	100.0	100.0	100.0

Table 12.2. Selected income indicators by sahi.

Basti area	N	Maximum Income (INR)	Mean Income (INR)	Std. Deviation	HH Size	Per Capita income (INR)	Ratio to Pradhan PCI
Pradhan	75	4800	2246	904.6	4.2	535	100
Majhi	164	9000	2904	1199.6	4.7	622	116
Others	210	8000	3108	1361.9	4.6	669	125
Kondh	65	8000	3143	1587.5	4.5	700	131
Upara	115	7000	3023	1222.2	4.2	714	133
Muslim	71	5000	2793	1091.0	3.9	721	135
Tala	73	5000	2697	974.1	3.7	729	136
Total	*773*	*9000*	*2904*	*1255.3*	*4.4*	*664*	*124*

Sahi labels are not as unambiguous as they seem. A majority of participating households in 'Muslim Sahi' are in fact Hindu, and a number of comparatively well-off households in Kondh Sahi do not belong to the Kondh ethnic minority, and this obviously blurs comparison. Importantly, however, the Pradhan Sahi is almost exclusively 'Pradhan'.

Table 12.2 provides a more detailed overview of the income differences across *sahis* in terms of maximum and mean monthly household income and per capita income.

The last column to the right takes per capita income in Pradhan Sahi as index 100 and shows the difference to others as a ratio, that is, inhabitants in Tala Sahi had an average monthly income per capita that was 36 per cent higher than inhabitants in Pradhan Sahi. Figure 12.1 shows the mean household surplus for unforeseen expenses when all known expenses had been deducted from the reported income.

Figure 12.1. Difference between HH income and expenditure by sahi (4th round of survey).

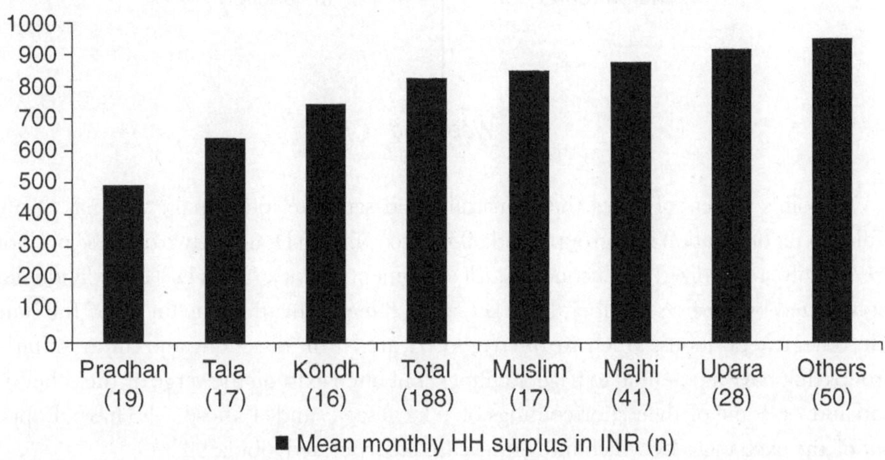

The average household surplus in the *basti* was 59.4 per cent higher than for the average Pradhan household. One concludes, then, that even if the entire *basti* was poor by economic standards, poverty was very unevenly distributed within this poor neighbourhood. But what is the connection between this unequal distribution of poverty and social and cultural dynamics within the *basti*?

Culture, Development and Social Exclusion

Mary Douglas, in her deconstruction of the concept of 'traditional culture' often used by economists to explain lack of 'rational' development, summarizes a century of anthropological debate when she defines 'social life as a system of exchanges between individuals and between groups', and culture as 'the series of local debates which thrash out the definition of a well-functioning person', that is, a social human being (Douglas 2004, 91). She proposes a universally applicable group-grid-based typology of culture that points to four cultural positions for groups and individuals in any society, and whose relative dominance will have direct implications for societal change. Figure 12.2 shows the culturally available positions that are highlighted in this analytical framework.

Figure 12.2. Map of measures of cultural coordination, based on Douglas (2004).

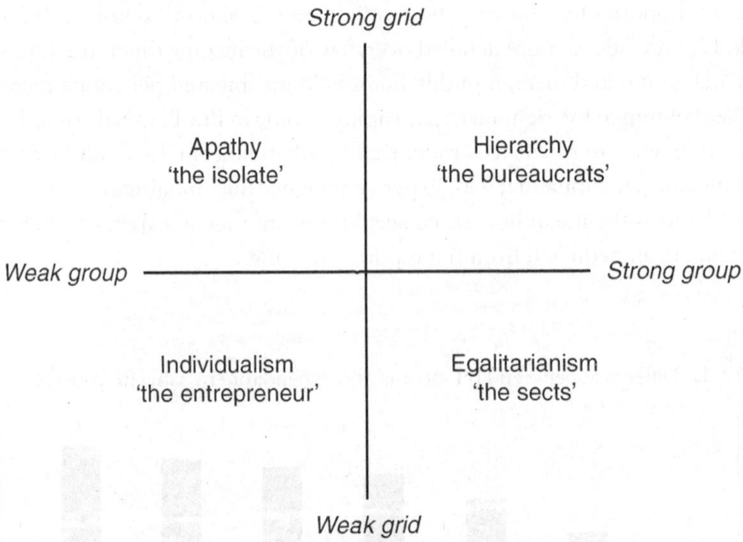

'Grid' points to sets of rules that constrain and separate individuals, whereas 'group' indicates incorporation into groups (ibid., 95). According to Douglas, two of these positions are readily recognized by economist development theory, namely, (1) individualism (epitomized by the free neoliberal market) and (2) hierarchy (the machinery of the state). The other two positions, which are often ignored, are: (3) the dissenting and communitarian groups that have a potential to trigger change, but often exist on the verge of the other two and address some of their shortcomings on a local scale, and (4) those 'who have dropped out of the exchanges by which individuals are incorporated' (ibid., 93).

Douglas' interest is somewhat different from mine; she is interested in pointing out why, in many cases, people are pushed into apathy in the face of grand development initiatives, to the bewilderment of economists and development planners. According to Douglas,

> Some circumstances can bring one of the four to dominate over the others. It might be the hierarchy, it might be the entrepreneurial individualist, it might be a god-fearing austere sect. The fatalist tendency is by its nature very unlikely to dominate the cultural scene. The indifference of the isolates can dissolve the tension and loyalties in the whole society, making it a non-functional apathetic society. (ibid., 107)

Accepting, for now, at face value the universality of this cultural theory, my interest is to explore the analytical capacity of the model to assist in our understanding of processes of social in- and exclusion – the latter primarily being linked to the position of apathy – and to see to what extent the social mechanisms involved in the dynamic exchanges between the positions bring us closer to understanding Shankar's death.

Social In/Exclusion of the *Pradhan* Community

Above, we saw household income figures that reflected patterns of exchange within the *basti*. Apart from illicit sale of 'ginger' that provided an excuse for people from other *sahis* to occasionally visit Shankar's neighbour Laxmi's house to buy a bottle, there was little exchange. Placed at the bottom of the *basti* hierarchy of groups, the Pradhans were effectively cut off from social and economical exchange with other *sahis*, except for the meagre income from selling alcoholic beverages that sustained their lowly image and rendered them vulnerable to police raids.

This marginal position was highlighted during a wedding in the *basti*. A marriage is an important occasion to demonstrate the social standing of the families involved; but on the occasion of Banamali's (Shankar's other neighbour) daughter's marriage, it was not possible to generate much money, and guests had to sit on the ground under a cloth held by bamboo poles to make up for a tent. The exchanges of money and gifts that usually take place before and after a wedding ceremony linking the wedded couple to the larger community had been kept inside the confines of Pradhan Sahi. Asked why, Shankar said about the other *sahis*:

> They hate us. We call it '*Pradhan Sahi*' but they call it '*Telenga*' *Sahi* […] They will say that Shankar is a drunkard so how can we go to attend his invitation. This way, they will ignore the invitation.

Telenga refers to people speaking Telugu, a predominant language of the state of Andhra Pradesh. Here, it was used by other groups in the *basti* as a derogatory term that emphasized otherness and lack of belonging.

Interestingly, in what seemed to be a deviation from the normal hierarchical pattern, the leaders of the CMG had recently become more friendly and approached the inhabitants of Pradhan Sahi to invite them to become followers of particular *babas* or *gurus*, offering a window to the sectarian group position in Douglas' model; Shankar had been persuaded by this and had paid the required INR 100.

> He tells me to become a follower of a particular *Baba* and I follow his instructions and become a disciple. Then, immediately he will say that, 'Shankar you must pay 100 rupees tomorrow for *Baba*'. So, I pay 100 rupees. Then he spends 50 rupees at home and the rest 50 rupees goes to *Baba*.

Occasionally, Pradhans were also invited to take part in *pujas*, but on the condition that they would both pay (to the CMG) to be involved and do the involved work – two roles that would normally be mutually exclusive. This mock involvement in social activities tended to further exploit and marginalize the Pradhan community, which in the process was reminded of the existence of social communitarianism without being granted real access.

The CMG was also handling the administrative processes necessary for obtaining the important BPL card that made it possible for the destitute to survive on government-subsidized food items. However, Shankar did not have a card.

> I have given my photos [for the card]; my name is on their lists [of eligible BPL card holders]. After this, a card is issued on my name. But they changed that card [...] Instead of Shankar Pradhan, he wrote his son's name. Then the card has been changed. These things are going on [...] 2–3 cards have been made but we haven't got our cards. We are also not running after them or enquiring about them. We thought that it will come on its own. Who will run behind it? But my mother is having [a card]. Mine hasn't been made. They have completed all the formalities, including taking 200 rupees from me; taken my photographs [...] these processes have been completed a long time back.

While the Pradhan community by far constituted the poorest group in the *basti*, the additional exploitation by a corrupt and self-appointed CMG and the denial of rights to poverty alleviation schemes like the BPL card nurtured the feeling of hopelessness that pushed the inhabitants of Pradhan Sahi into a position of apathy.

Health-Seeking Patterns in Beluam *Basti*

Generally, *basti* people would classify most ailments as (1) acute and minor (such as cough, fever, diarrhoea, minor injuries, pain), (2) acute and serious (high or continuous fever, violent diarrhoea, serious injuries, illness related to pregnancy, severe pain), (3) chronic and readily explicable (some cases of cancer, asthma, anaemia) and (4) chronic and extraordinary (any disease where magic is suspected to be involved, usually because of the nature of disease (like mental illness) or because it is incurable (other cases of cancer, asthma, anaemia)). In the four rounds of surveys, acute illness constituted 76–89 per cent of all reported illness episodes.

This somewhat fluid and implicit classification system would imply different treatment-seeking strategies that would seek to minimize direct and indirect costs at the risk of delay of diagnosis and correct treatment. For acute and minor ailments, the chemist would invariably serve as de facto primary health care institution. Frequently, a relative would go to the shop, describe the symptoms and, on the basis of the diagnosis made on the spot, be told what to buy. In some cases, this would be sufficient to give symptomatic relief until the illness disappeared, or there would not be any more money to spend; or, if the medicine did not work, the case would be pursued with the same or a different chemist, until the illness was reassessed as being more serious than initially assumed, at which point it was decided to consult a doctor.

In contrast to the poor in larger Indian cities such as Delhi and Mumbai where population pressure on hospital facilities is more massive, inhabitants of this *basti* could sometimes access corporate hospitals that were otherwise primarily serving the local police and employees of Odisha State Electricity Board. The corporate hospitals had a formal obligation to treat a certain percentage of poor patients outside the ranks of their primary clients. While the concept of hospital has been eased into the names of both institutions, some would consider this to be an exaggeration, given their very limited range of services and the absence of facilities for hospitalization; but people from the *basti* were readily accepted in the outpatient department (OPD) at both clinics. Since Police Hospital was quite close, it was frequently used and provided an in-kind service compensation for the regular police harassment inside the *basti*.

If a patient required hospitalization or more advanced procedures, or if he or she was in immediate risk of dying, the patient was almost always referred to 'Capital Hospital', the main government hospital in Bhubaneswar. In other cases, where chemists' and/or corporate hospital treatments had failed, a specialist was sought.

Das and Das (2006, 185–6) observed that in the low-income neighbourhoods they studied in Delhi, illness may be so common that it ceased to be extraordinary, but simply blended into the register of the normal, and that a given symptom (e.g. diarrhoea) could be considered either normal or an expression of illness only at certain points in time or only for certain age groups. This was also observed in Beluam Basti. On the basis of this framing and the perceived gravity relative to available resources, treatment was or was not pursued. Approximately one-third of all reported illness episodes were left untreated, without much variance across *sahis*. In fact, households in Pradhan Sahi reported a little less illness than non-Pradhans. All *sahis* had their share of both nonserious and serious illnesses. The most common complaints included cold and cough; fever; pain in muscles, joints, stomach, back or head; injuries and wounds; diarrhoea and vomiting; and infections of, for example, throat, ears, eyes, skin; swelling of limbs; high or low blood pressure (the latter associated with fatigue). Anaemia was not considered an illness, but head reeling was. The comparatively rarer cases of TB, cancer, brain malaria, diabetes and sexually transmitted diseases were evenly distributed across the *sahis*.

What was not evenly distributed was the capacity to seek medical help and buy the medicines that were rightly or wrongly perceived to be required. Table 12.3 compares the mean cost of all illness episodes per month per household with reported illness for Pradhan and other *sahis*, respectively.

Table 12.3. Capacity to spend on illness, by Pradhan and non-Pradhan sahis.

Mean cost (INR), all sick persons in HH, by Pradhan/non-Pradhan sahi					
Sahi	Mean INR	N	Std. Deviation	Min. INR	Max. INR
Pradhan	100.24	21	179.978	0	600
Non-pradhan	216.61	223	530.386	0	5000
Total	206.59	244	510.622	0	5000

Catastrophic health expenditure describes a situation where health expenditures threaten a household's financial capacity to maintain subsistence needs (Su and Flessa 2006). According to the World Health Organization (WHO), the definitional threshold for catastrophic health expenditure is at 50 per cent of a household's non-food expenditure, but other analysts have used a threshold of 5–20 per cent (ibid.). Catastrophic health expenditure is a common phenomenon in Beluam Basti, and it is common in Pradhan Sahi as well, despite the low budget that can be spent on health.

Table 12.4. Catastrophic illness at 20 and 50 per cent thresholds (health expenditure of noon-food expenditure).

		< 20	Catastrophic above 20%	Catastrophic above 50%	Total
Pradhan	Count	9	9	3	21
	%	43	43	14	100
Non-pradhan	Count	38	167	20	225
	%	17	74	9	100
Total	Count	47	176	23	246
	%	19	72	9	100

Table 12.4 points to an important conceptual paradox. Despite the small numbers, it is noteworthy that 43 per cent of Pradhan households stayed *below* the catastrophic 20 per cent threshold during data collection, whereas this was only the case for 17 per cent of the generally better-off population of the other *sahis*. The answer to the paradox may be quite simple. The level of poverty both in absolute and relational terms may prevent serious illness from giving rise to catastrophic expenditures, since there is little access to generating such additional funds. Therefore, the small Pradhan community had their own strategies for treatment, as explained by Shankar and his neighbour, Banamali:

SHANKAR: You apply kerosene. After coughing for a long time you will have pain in your throat. So, if you will apply kerosene at that place you will be relieved of that pain. [...] Whenever I have pain in my chest I apply it. [...] We always do that type of treatment. When a dog bites we don't give injections. […] The person bitten by a dog goes to another person's house and applies *haldi* [turmeric] at that place – the teeth of the dog must have gone through the skin – so, he applies *haldi* there and then he takes a pair of damaged slippers and hits at that place – how many times do you have to hit? Seven times?

BANAMALI: I think three times.

SHANKAR: He hits there three or seven times. He stays in their house for four days and the person hits him. All the poison comes out.

Irrespective of any potential beneficial effects of kerosene, turmeric and 'slipper slapping' in such instances, it is clear that expensive medicine is a last resort and that poverty implies delay of diagnosis and treatment. However, the suspicion of TB does fall in the category of serious illness requiring medical treatment, even in Pradhan Sahi. Above, I have described some of the social constraints and opportunities in Pradhan Sahi and highlighted the limited access to engage in social exchange across the perceived ethnic boundary constituted by the attributed tribal identity of Pradhans. I shall now turn to Shankar Pradhan's narrative and the mechanisms of social exclusion that I argue led to his early death.

Shankar's Trajectory

Shankar Pradhan was, in 2005, a young man at 26 who worked as a trolley puller on a daily basis and undertook any other odd job that he could find in order to help support his mother and two younger brothers. His father had died of TB shortly after the birth of his youngest brother. That was when Shankar first learned about the disease. This experience had made him disregard all warnings not to be near his mother when she was diagnosed with TB around a year and a half before we first met him. Shankar explained:

> [The doctor] told me to keep away from my mother. That day I felt afraid. I said, 'how can I do that, Sir? Can anyone forget his mother and go away from his mother?' I told him to write down the tablets and he prescribed also. At that time [free] government medicines were not available and I also didn't know about it. So, I bought all the tablets and gave them to my mother. […] I had given her medicines for as many days as I could. […] Still, many times I had not given her the tablets because the cost of one tablet was 11 rupees and another tablet was 13.

During her illness, Shankar took the main responsibility for supporting the family and taking care of his mother's treatment. Due to the financial constraints and expensive drugs, she was only treated intermittently. During our fieldwork, she was still coughing and despite her conviction that she was now suffering from asthma and did her best to find money to buy a cocktail of asthma medicine, antihistamine and antibiotics on the basis of the advice of a doctor at Capital Hospital, it was possible that she was still ill with TB; according to Shankar there was blood in her sputum.

Shankar had also started coughing and had been ill with fever for a month and a half. This was in October 2005. Shankar was lucky with the timing. Directly Observed Treatment – Short Course (DOTS) had just been introduced: a new standardized and free treatment promoted by WHO, defining the Revised National Tuberculosis (RNTCP) in India that was being implemented in Odisha and all over India, achieving nationwide coverage in March 2006.[9] This should guarantee free and easy access to the full duration of treatment for TB. However, the trajectory that Shankar had to follow to access treatment was intricately crooked and full of stumbling blocks. The story about his difficulties in trying to access free TB treatment evolved around three themes: poor treatment, alcohol and medicine, and work.

Poor Treatment

TB is predominantly a disease linked to poverty. Congested housing, unhygienic environments and exposure to a host of diseases that may allow latent TB to become active in generally immunocompromised individuals are associated with the epidemic. DOTS was designed to provide multiple drug treatment to poor patients over a period of six months. The DOTS strategy was highly complex and involved a wide range of processes at different levels that if not successfully managed could undermine the programme (Gericke, Kurowski, Ranson, and Mills 2005). Yet, even the long list of intervention points identified by Gericke and his coauthors does not include the relationship between the health system and the majority of poor patients. A multi-country study commissioned by WHO showed that senior hospital doctors across Asia (and certainly in India) tended to consider (perceived) poor patients on a par with minors and mentally incompetent patients in terms of (lack of) intellectual capacity; hence, the notion of patient autonomy often did not apply to perceived poor patients in everyday clinical practice (Addlakha and Seeberg 2000). The implication was that treatment of the poor risked being poor treatment. For Shankar, this was reflected in a dance with the health system managers as he strived to access free treatment. What follows is a brief summary of some of his steps back and forth between health care points, and a glimpse into communication challenges across social barriers.

SHANKAR: Sarathi Mamu [Shankar's uncle] knows a lot about the hospitals. He took 100 rupees from me and brought me to Capital Hospital. [...] They did the check up and the senior doctors examined me with their stethoscope. After examining the sputum they told me that I am suffering from TB. They said that I was in the preliminary stage of TB and I need not panic because of TB. When I heard that I was suffering from TB I became nervous. [...] The doctor said that TB is not at all a serious disease. It is equivalent to fever. The doctor told me that I will be given medicines. Then I was relieved. [...] After giving my signature, they accepted [me as patient] here [at ESI hospital].[10] Otherwise they were not doing my check-up here [at ESI hospital]. They used to turn me back. There is no provision for the poor people over there. [...] [When subsequently going to ESI to obtain the TB drugs], all those who are in service [i.e. entitled to treatment] were standing in a queue in that hospital and when I asked them which doctor was doing the check-up, they asked me whether I was having an ESI certificate. I said no. Then they asked me where I was employed and I said that I wasn't employed. When they asked me what work I do, I said that I pull a trolley. […] They said that a trolley puller can't do his check up here. […] Photo identity was needed, bank account was needed. […] I felt very bad and I also cried a bit. When I came out crying, two other lady doctors were standing outside. One of them called me, the one who does the sputum test in that hospital. She asked me why I was crying. Then I asked her 'is there no provision for the poor people in this hospital'? She said that there is one near the Panda Park. There is a hospital at Saheed Nagar. There, the medicines are available free of cost. Then I said that if it is Panda Park then why did the senior doctor send me here? […] After that they saw my card and told me to go to the Madam (doctor) with the card. Then I went to the Saheed Nagar hospital and showed it to the Madam. She told that it cannot be done today, even after seeing the letter. It was *Diwali* festival that day. She told me to go away instead of giving her tension as she was upset that day. So, I went away and I came again the next day. The next day they told me to go to another place.

Finally making it through the line, he is told to go somewhere else to get the medicine, due to the distribution of neighbourhoods among TB treatment points in the city. This, eventually, was too much for Shankar.

SHANKAR: Then I told them directly that I will go to Capital Hospital. They asked me, 'Why?' I said that I will ask the doctor over there why I am being asked whether I am doing any service or not. Why have they written this hospital? I am having my record in the ESI hospital and I would have gone there but they sent me to you and you are telling me that nothing can be done. I can't go here and there anymore. I said that I cannot go anywhere else so I am going to Capital Hospital again. On hearing this, the doctor said that I am talking too much. He told me many things [i.e. scolded] but I didn't tell him anything because I was in trouble. Then he told me to go to the lady who was doing the sputum test. But that lady was a nice person. […] She asked me 'what happened?' I told her that the doctor had sent me to her. She went and requested the doctor to give me medicines as I was very poor. Then they asked me to go [to the DOT Provider DP] and consume the medicines.[11] I went there with great difficulty to eat the medicines. I don't have a bicycle. My younger brother takes me on his cycle and drops me half-way. Now they have asked me to go to Unit 9 [area of the city] to take the rest of the medicines.

I have inserted this long extract to convey the level of desperation caused by the system – in spite of the help of friendly people – and the high level of motivation required for

Shankar to enter a treatment system designed to serve patients like him. Eventually, without necessary documentation and without a medical facility being responsible for the following week's medicine, he started medical treatment on a preliminary basis; from the very beginning he was considered a 'difficult' patient and he was constantly being shifted between different points of treatment and DPs. It was not possible in this process to establish a trusting relationship with any DP, and he was repeatedly blamed for the interruptions of treatment that to a large extent were caused by poor coordination within the health system.

Alcohol and Medicine

From the treatment system's point of view, Shankar is the paradigmatic 'defaulter' – a 'tribal', a poor and uneducated type of person known for alcohol consumption and a host of other non-Hindu non-virtues.[12] Shankar fitted the bill. As we have seen, selling alcohol in Pradhan Sahi allowed for minimal social and economical interaction with the rest of the *basti*, and alcohol consumption was a regular social activity in evenings. Shankar stated that he had been drinking alcohol since he was seven years old. Shankar's friends and neighbours asserted that medicine would have no effect unless Shankar would stop drinking. However, at the same time, in his increasingly poor state of health, alcohol consumption was a ticket to social inclusion: he had become part of a drinking group whose members used cheap liquor to reduce their pain. But even for Shankar, alcohol consumption was perceived to be incompatible with medicines. He tried to reduce or avoid alcohol intake on days when he took medicine, but the tablets were not easy for him to take. They were both too many (seven tablets three times per week) and too big for anybody to eat, he said. He only took five tablets and threw away the remaining two bigger ones (probably Pyrazinamide, a drug that stops the growth of Mycobacterium tuberculosis). From Shankar's perspective, these two tablets had a very bad taste and made him feel weak, and they were too big. If he took all tablets, his head started reeling, he had to vomit, he was unable to get back home from the hospital because he could not walk, his breath was bad, he got pain in his knees and his skin began to itch and develop a rash. He was not able to get sufficient food to counter these adverse effects. The family could hardly afford food since Shankar was too weak to work. Due to the drugs, his urine had turned red, but he had been informed that this was a common and harmless side effect. The doctors told Shankar that his vomiting was caused by some other condition that was not related to TB medicine. He did not believe this to be true, and somebody had told him that the medicine was not suitable for him. The adverse effects scared him, and he began to fear that the medicines could be as fatal as the disease.

Work

After around one-and-a half months of intermittent treatment, Shankar decided to go to Puri district to work. It was unbearable for him that the family had no food and he felt he was a burden within the household. During this period, treatment was stopped and his condition gradually deteriorated. He could not sleep at night due to his cough and after four weeks, he was sent home. When he returned to Unit 9 Hospital for treatment, he learned that he was no longer a patient there, nor was he registered at the Police Hospital where he was sent, and when he tried at Capital Hospital, the concerned doctor was absent. At ESI hospital, he was finally put on category II drugs for patients who have failed to follow the initial treatment regime. After some time, he was referred to Police Hospital and assigned to a DOT provider who suspected he was lying about living in the *basti*. Meanwhile, as he got a little better because of the treatment, he took up daily labour as a painter. This reintroduced the dilemma between treatment and work. On days when he took treatment, the combination of time spent on travel and waiting, and the impact of side effects, made it impossible for him to work. In turn, he could not afford food to counter the adverse effects, and when I met him for the last time, he had stopped treatment completely.

Ex- and Conclusion

Earlier, social exclusion was a deliberate part of TB treatment. Patients with an active infection were placed in isolation, and TB hospitals were built in socially secluded areas. While this is no longer the case, Mycobacterium tuberculosis may in itself be considered an agent of social exclusion. It acts most effectively in socially disadvantaged and marginalized groups where a range of factors associated with absolute (not relative) poverty provide it with a beneficial ecosystem. Furthermore, it acts to further social exclusion among those ill with TB, as their ability to engage in work slowly but surely withers away and as their surroundings resign and withdraw. Medical anthropologist and physician Paul Farmer has put forward a strong argument that the global epidemics of HIV/AIDS and TB must be seen as instances of global structural violence that allows millions of poor people to die as a direct consequence of unequal distribution of resources combined with an active lack of will to address problems that are solvable with existing technologies and resources (Farmer 2005). Addressing my initial question – Why did Shankar die? – one possible answer is to consider Shankar's death a result of structural violence. A mechanism – including a BPL card, had it not been stolen by the CMG – that would have served to equalize income levels effectively between the poor and the destitute *sahis* within the *basti* (not to speak of the Indian middle class or the super-rich upper class in the country) would have enabled Shankar to undergo treatment without having to work during the required initial two months of treatment. But the concept of structural violence does not easily distinguish between the middle class and those living in the neighbouring *sahi*. The concept of structural violence is politically strong but has to be based on circumstantial evidence, which (even if one believes in the conclusion) renders it analytically weak because circumstantial evidence is overwhelming. The framework of Douglas provides an analytical lens that in combination with the notion of structural violence, strengthens its operational range by differentiating the workings of bureaucracy and market that are often responsible for concrete cases of structural violence, as shown in Shankar's case.

According to Douglas (2004), hierarchies are inherently conservative and interested in maintaining the status quo, a description that fits much of political life in Beluam

Basti well. Hierarchy describes the combined practice of rule-based social inclusion (into caste or 'tribal' groups) and exclusion (from other than own group). However, a potentially fatal disease like TB represents a danger that cannot be addressed within the group and where the group may also be unable to ensure both access to and completion of treatment, which happened in Shankar's case. If Douglas' typology is perceived as positions that may be open to individuals to approach or enter, Shankar's drive towards treatment threw him into an individualistic position for which he was ill equipped. What could perhaps have saved him, or at least have increased his chances for survival, would have been a health care system positioned among the 'dissenting sects', where individuals would receive equal treatment. Such treatment is not generally available in India where class and caste hierarchies are merged with a medical hierarchy in ways that make it very difficult for the already socially excluded to become socially – and medically – included; but it is not unthinkable, since a large number of NGO-based TB treatment points have been introduced in areas where the state is unable to provide appropriate treatment. Not so in Beluam Basti. The constant conflict between access to medicines and opportunities to work, in the case of Shankar, is the most obvious symptom of this problem. At no point during the many contacts between patient and health care system could this issue be seriously discussed, despite the repeated efforts of the patient. Consequently, and eventually, his initial drive to enrol in treatment on the basis of the rules of hierarchy was replaced by a position in 'the culture of the isolates: whether they are pushouts or dropouts, they are generally apathetic, cynical about the motives of politicians, fatalist about the certain failure of actions intended to improve their situation' (Douglas 2004, 94). Irrespective of the strong moral tenor of Douglas' voice here, and if one replaces 'politicians' with 'health care providers', this is more or less where Shankar – accompanied by TB, alcohol and abject poverty – ended his life.

I have tried to differentiate between groups of inhabitants in a poor urban neighbourhood in the capital of one of the poorest states in India, with a view to disentangle or empirically 'deconstruct' the notion of poor. I have done so through a focus on the Pradhan Sahi of Beluam Basti and through the lens that the case of Shankar's death provided. In addition to compiling a range of factors that can be combined by the reader to understand the death of Shankar, I also suggest that the current political attention given to inclusive growth in India has to pay more attention to the local-level processes of social exclusion that effectively keep the destitute where they are. If poverty is defined as lack of access to enter the system of exchanges that make up society and therefore closely associated with conditions of apathy, a national programme on inclusive growth needs to focus on prevention of apathy by way of providing access not only to social change, but to social exchange for the socially excluded.

Notes

1 The name of the *basti* has been changed.
2 See www.hum.au.dk/hsre for details.
3 The data from these two studies will be presented elsewhere.
4 I am extremely grateful for the contributions of the local research team, and I wish to express my gratitude to Samir Diabagh, Sasmita Sahani, Amita Kanungo and Rosalina Baral for their

long-term work in the *basti*, and Ranjita Sahoo for assistance with transcription. Especially Samir, who spent considerable time in constantly following up with Shankar and helping him access the various TB treatment points in the capital. The questionnaire for quantitative data collection was developed in close collaboration with Prof. Supasit Pannarunothai, Naresuan University, Thailand, whose important contribution to the project is fully acknowledged.

5 I thank Dr Nilakantha Panigrahi, Nabakrushna Choudhury Centre for Development Studies in Odisha, for helping me obtain this information at a point in time when it was not yet readily available on the Internet.

6 The poverty line in India is contested. Using the World Bank definition of poverty line at USD 1 per day implies that 75 per cent of the population is poor, whereas the Government of India's BPL (Below Poverty Line) definition at INR 296 per month for urban and INR 276 per month for rural areas has been broadly criticized as unrealistically low. In the *basti*, with an average household size of 4.4 persons, the World Bank definition would imply a threshold at INR 5,886 per household per month, and the Government of India's definition is a threshold at INR 1,302 per household per month. INR 3,000 has been used as a meaningful compromise for an analysis that explores social disparity within a generally poor neighbourhood.

7 Income levels showed a rising trend over the four rounds of data collection. However, it is not possible to distinguish between seasonal variation and increased accuracy, which is why the accumulated data has been used in Table 12.1.

8 Not all households are placed in recognized 'sahi' areas and the large group of 'others' include these households. Households have been visited four times during a year. Hence, participating households constitute one-quarter of the numbers in the table. Since some households have moved out during this period, and some households have been unavailable for a particular round, the figures are not multiples of 4.

9 The author was working as a health systems research advisor to the Danida TB control project in Odisha in 2003–2005.

10 Employees' State Insurance Corporation; an insurance scheme for certain categories of employees, including medical benefits.

11 The DP keeps one medicine box for each patient assigned to him/her and oversees that the patient swallows the medicines three times per week during the initial so-called intensive treatment phase of two months' duration.

12 'Defaulter' is the official term used for a patient who fails to comply with the DOTS regime.

References

Addlakha, R., and Jens Seeberg. 2000. *Ethical Issues in Clinical Practice: A Qualitative Study in Six SEAR Countries*. New Delhi: World Health Organization.

Appadurai, Arjun. 2004. 'The Capacity to Aspire: Culture and the Terms of Recognition'. In *Culture and Public Action*, edited by V. Rao and M. Walton, 59–84. Stanford: Stanford Social Sciences.

Census of India. 2011. *Provisional Population Totals: Orissa Series 22*. Bhubaneswar: Office of Registrar General & Census Commissioner, India.

Das, V. and R. K. Das. 2006. 'Pharmaceuticals in Urban Ecologies'. In *Global Pharmaceuticals: Ethics, Markets, Practices*, edited by A. Petryna, A. Lakoff and A. Kleinman, 175–205. Durham and London: Duke University Press.

Douglas, Mary. 2004. 'Traditional Culture: Let's Hear No More About It'. In *Culture and Public Action*, edited by V. Rao and M. Walton, 85–114. Stanford: Stanford Social Sciences.

Farmer, P. 2005. *Pathologies of Power: Health, Human Rights, and the New War on the Poor (With a New Preface by the Author)*. Berkeley: University of California Press.

Gericke, C. A., C. Kurowski, M. K. Ranson and A. Mills. 2005. 'Intervention Complexity: A Conceptual Framework to Inform Priority-Setting in Health'. *Bulletin of the World Health Organization* 83: 285–93.

Government of India. 2008. 'Eleventh Five Year Plan (2007–2012): Social Sector'. Edited by Planning Commission, Government of India. New Delhi: Oxford University Press.

Government of Orissa. 2004. *Human Development Report 2004, Orissa*. Bhubaneswar: Government of Orissa.

Gupta, M. 2002. *State Health System, Orissa. Working Paper No. 89*. New Delhi: Indian Council For Research On International Economic Relations.

Kundu, A. 1999. 'Stigmatization of Urban Processes in India: An Analysis of Terminology with Special Reference to Slum Situations'. *Les Mots de la ville* 33–40.

Seeberg, Jens. 2012. 'Connecting Pills and People: An Ethnography of the Pharmaceutical Nexus in Odisha, India'. *Medical Anthropology Quarterly* 26 (2): 182–200.

Su, T., B. Kouyaté and S. Flessa. 2006. 'Catastrophic Household Expenditure for Health Care in a Low-Income Society: A Study from Nouna District, Burkina Faso'. *Bulletin of the World Health Organization* 84: 21–7.